AIRFIELDS
NORTH-EAST ENGLAND
IN THE
SECOND WORLD WAR

Martyn Chorlton

COUNTRYSIDE BOOKS

NEWBURY, BERKSHIRE

COUNTRYSIDE BOOKS
3 Catherine Road
Newbury, Berkshire

To view our complete range of books,
please visit us at
www.countrysidebooks.co.uk

ISBN 1 85306 529 3

EAN 978185306 931 4

Cover picture showing a trio of
79 Squadron Hawker Hurricane Mk.Is taking off
from RAF Acklington during the early stages of
the Battle of Britain is from an original
painting by Colin Doggett

Designed by Peter Davies, Nautilus Design
Produced through MRM Associates Ltd., Reading
Typeset by Techniset Typesetters, Merseyside
Printed by Woolnough Bookbinding Ltd., Irthlingborough

CONTENTS

AIRFIELDS OF NORTH-EAST ENGLAND IN
THE SECOND WORLD WAR

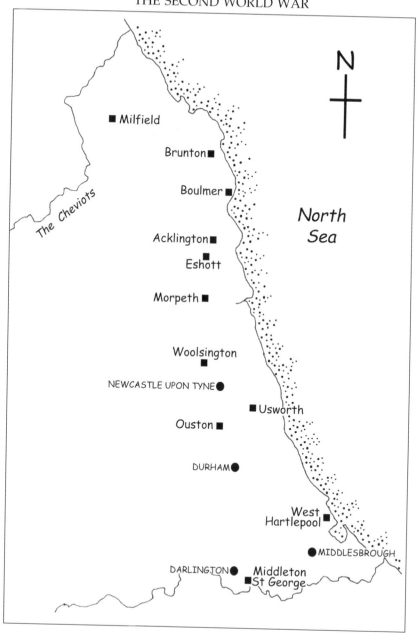

ACKNOWLEDGEMENTS

I would like to thank everyone who has provided me with information for the preparation of this book. From snippets taken from pilots' logbooks to the plethora of information available from the National Archives, all are of equal importance.

Individually, I would like to thank Brian Pears for access to his superb website, called the North East Diary 1939–45; Alan Evans, whose website on Milfield provided so much information; and Aldon P. Ferguson for providing me with additional photography and background information on several of the north-east airfields.

Thanks to Ann Dixon and the Newcastle Chronicle and Journal Ltd for help with photography in the Civilians at War chapter.

Finally, a special thank you to my wife for editorial work. Without her this book would have been impossible

Martyn Chorlton

I
SETTING
THE SCENE

The Early Years

The aerial exploits of a Mr Asgill of Blye Common, near Wooler in Northumberland first hit the headlines of the *Berwick Journal* in 1790, marking a very early connection with aviation and the North-East. Described as an air balloon, Asgill's creation was said to resemble a fish, and a very excited reporter described the incident as 'the finest exhibition in the world'.

Ballooning became more common throughout the 19th century, but it was not until the arrival of aviation pioneers such as American-born Samuel F Cody in the early 20th century that more imaginative flying machines began to appear. Cody came to the North-East in 1902 and actually made a stage appearance on 14th July at the Metropole Theatre in Gateshead. He stayed in the area for approximately six weeks while experimenting with one of his new kites on Town Moor in Newcastle.

The first aircraft builders to be established in the area were Messrs George and Jobling, whose main business was as motorcar agents and engineers. In 1909, an individual used the same premises in South Street, Newcastle to construct a Henry Farman biplane. This probably gave Arthur George the inspiration to design and build his own aircraft, which was simply named the 'G and J' and was ready to fly by March 1910. George was a keen aviator and the first pilot to hold an

One of the world's most colourful aviation pioneers, Samuel F Cody, visited the North-East in 1902.

official Pilot's Certificate in the North-East; he then went on to become one of the founder members of the Newcastle Aero Club.

Racecourses, in those early days of aviation, lent themselves perfectly to the operation of aircraft, and Gosforth, in particular, would become a significant location. Another pioneering aviator, Graham White, displayed his aircraft at the racecourse in August 1910. However, it was a well-established local business that saw the real potential in the site.

It was back in 1897 that the large engineering firm of Sir W. G. Armstrong, Whitworth and Co. Ltd was established in Newcastle. By 1912, the company, seeing the potential in the rapidly growing aviation industry, gave thought to the production of aircraft. The initial plan was to manufacture other companies' aircraft, such as Avro. However, this idea was rejected and focus was given to the production of aero engines instead. A contract was won to build engines for the All British Engine Co. Ltd but surprisingly the work had dried up before the start of the First World War.

In 1913, the company had been asked to tender for an Admiralty contract to build a single rigid airship and four non-rigid airships. The contract was won and that same year the company established an

8

Aerial Department, supervised by Capt. Fairbairn-Crawford and assisted by the established Dutch aircraft designer Frederick Koolhoven. The airship factory was established at Selby in North Yorkshire and a second attempt to enter the aircraft industry proper resulted in all potential new contracts and designs being built in Newcastle.

A tentative order by the War Office for a pair of Royal Aircraft Factory BE2as was received in late 1913. These were built to such a high standard that the War Office placed a second order for a more significant 25 aircraft, and, to cope with this, Armstrong Whitworth hired a disused skating rink at Gosforth. The completed aircraft were towed to and then flown from Town Moor in Newcastle, and eventually the company established more premises on the edge of the Moor.

By September 1914, Koolhoven had designed his first aircraft for the company, namely the Armstrong Whitworth FK.1. A flimsy underpowered design, the FK.1 was quickly abandoned, but Koolhoven followed with the more successful FK.3, orders for over 500 of which were received. Armstrong Whitworth's success resulted in the company having to sub-contract its own designs, and, with the arrival of the FK.8 in 1916, more success followed. A popular aircraft with service pilots, at least 1,652 FK.8s had been built when production ended in July 1918, many of them constructed at Gosforth.

The FK.3 was the second aircraft designed by Frederick Koolhoven for Armstrong Whitworth.

Other designs included an unusual triplane, nicknamed the 'aerial destroyer', and a pair of quadruplanes, designated the FK.9 and FK.10. None was successful but, despite the FK.10's poor performance, eight aircraft were still ordered by the War Office. Koolhoven left the company in 1917 to work for the British Aerial Transport Co. and Frank Murphy, the manager of the aeroplane department, became the chief designer at Gosforth.

The first of Murphy's designs was the FM.4 Armadillo, which made its maiden flight from Cramlington in April 1918. The aircraft was described as 'most unsatisfactory' by senior officials and only flew for about two months before it was unceremoniously disposed of. Murphy's second design, and the last to come from Gosforth, was a single-seat fighter called the Ara. Unfortunately, only three aircraft were ordered, of which just two flew. Despite these later failed designs, approximately 1,275 aircraft were built at Gosforth before the Aerial Department was closed.

In 1920, the Armstrong Whitworth Co. Ltd was formed after a merger with Siddeley Deasy, based at Parkside in Coventry, and Newcastle's own aircraft builders moved to the Midlands plant. Armstrong Whitworth went on to produce some excellent aircraft, which included the Siskin fighter, the Whitley bomber, and their last product, the Argosy transport. The company was then taken over by the Hawker Siddeley Group in the 1960s, which in turn was swallowed up by British Aerospace.

The First World War

The population of Hartlepool became victims of the conflict even before the main slaughter began in the trenches of northern France. On the morning of 16th December 1914, the German cruisers *Blucher*, *Seydlitz* and *Moltke* sailed undetected in a heavy mist and began to shell the town. The shelling was indiscriminate; at least 600 houses and several churches and hospitals were seriously damaged. Following 50 minutes of continuous shelling, the ships retreated after one of them was hit by a shore battery manned by the 18th Durham Light Infantry. The Hartlepool-based cruiser, HMS *Patrol* took on the three German ships but was damaged in the process, eventually limping back into port with four crew dead and several injured. The primary objective of the enemy ships was to lay mines and, as a result, more casualties resulted when three trawlers struck them and sank.

This brief action involving a foreign enemy attacking English soil was the first such occurrence since 1797, when the French landed at Fishguard in Pembrokeshire. The casualty figures were also the highest of any raid inflicted on the North-East during both world wars; 230 people were killed and another 500 were injured.

All other serious attacks on the North-East during the First World War came from above, namely in the shape of the Zeppelin. These were much feared by the civilian population, and at the beginning of the war defensive aircraft had great difficulty in gaining the necessary height to attack the giant airships.

The first attack by an enemy airship came on the evening of 14th April 1915. Zeppelin L9 was on its first raid; she crossed the coast near Blyth and steered north toward Cambois. It was here that L9 came under attack by rifle fire from the 1st Battalion Northern Cyclists but frustratingly for them it had little or no effect on the airship. Bombs were dropped at West Sleekburn, followed by fourteen more falling harmlessly in fields on a southerly course towards Wallsend. After dropping six incendiary bombs (IB), the airship headed back to Germany, completely unmolested.

Blyth was used as the crossing point again on the night of 15th/16th June. This time the Zeppelin was L10, and its main target was the strategically important Marine Engineering Works in Wallsend. This

By the end of 1916, Super-Zeppelins like this were becoming easy prey to the guns of the Royal Flying Corps.

was accurately bombed and was followed by an equally accurate attack on Palmer's Works in Jarrow. Seven High Explosive (HE) and five IBs were dropped, causing severe damage, and killing 17 workers and injuring 72 others. Bombs also fell on Pochin's Chemical Works and Cookson's Antimony Works, both in Willington. The L10 then headed out to sea, but not before dropping its remaining bomb load on Haxton Colliery and South Shields.

In April 1916, the amount of Zeppelin raids increased, with three in the space of a week. The first, by L11, was on 1st/2nd April: 21 bombs were dropped on Sunderland, killing 22 civilians and injuring over 120 others. The following night the attacks were further inland. L16 bombed Ponteland and Stamfordham, followed by Cramlington as the airship headed out to sea near Coquet Island. On this occasion little damage was caused. L16 returned on 5th/6th April and once again ventured further inland. Twenty-three bombs were dropped at Evenwood and Randolf Colliery, south-west of Bishop Auckland, demolishing 15 miners' cottages and damaging at least 70 others. Another colliery was bombed south-east of Bishop Auckland, killing one child and injuring a woman and two children.

The FE.2b was a typical example of a Home Defence aircraft during the First World War.

Armstrong Whitworth-built Airship R29 became the only British rigid airship to see action against the enemy during the First World War.

It was hoped that the formation of the Home Defence (HD) squadrons in 1916 would help fend off the ever-increasing Zeppelin attacks across the country. The main HD unit for the North-East was 36 Squadron, which was formed at the newly acquired airfield at Cramlington. The very north of the area was covered by 77 Squadron, that operated at least one flight from a landing at New Haggerston, south-east of Berwick-upon-Tweed. A variety of aircraft, ranging from the BE.2c and BE.2e through to the FE.2b, 2c and 2d, was used to equip 36 Squadron. The squadron was divided into three flights. Initially 'A' Flight operated from Hylton, 'B' Flight from Cramlington, and 'C' Flight from Ashington. This would change when the squadron moved to Seaton Carew later in the year. Several night landing grounds were also brought into use, in particular, Bishopton, Horsegate, and Spennymore – all in County Durham – and Alnwick, Cleadon, Currock Hill (still used for Gliding), and Longhorsley, in Northumberland.

Success finally came for 36 HD Squadron on the night of 27th/28th November 1916. Under the command of Kapitänleutnant Max Dietrich, the 'Super Zeppelin' L34 was on her first operational flight. After crossing the coast near Seaham, it was not long before the giant airship was caught in the beam of the Hutton Henry Searchlight at Castle

13

Eden, south of Peterlee. A few miles along the coast, Lt L V Pyott of 36 Squadron in a FE.2c took off from Seaton Carew. The giant airship was not difficult to spot; still trapped in the searchlight beam, the L34 had attempted to bomb the light, but, luckily for Pyott, had failed. Exactly what height the Zeppelin was flying at is unknown, but Pyott seemed to reach it without difficulty, attacking L34 in the mid-ships region seemingly without any effect. The Zeppelin flew on with Pyott following, unable to stop the airship dropping bombs on West Hartlepool before heading out to sea. Pyott continued to attack, firing over 70 rounds into the airship. Pyott's perseverance paid off: a small fire had broken out and within seconds the whole airship was on fire. L34 plunged into the sea off West Hartlepool, almost taking Pyott and his aircraft with it.

Seaton Carew was actually the site of two separate stations, one being the home of 36 Squadron, while the other was Seaplane Station. Also flying from the airfield was 495 Flight, operating the rare Blackburn Kangaroo, and from 1st May 1918 to the end of the First World War, the Flight flew more than 600 hours on anti-submarine patrols. The Flight took part in eleven attacks on enemy U-Boats, and one in particular, on 28th August 1918, brought about the destruction of UC 70. With Lt E F Waring at the controls in Kangaroo B9983, a single 500 lb bomb was dropped within 30ft of the enemy submarine. The U-boat was finished off by depth charges dropped by HMS *Ouse*.

Another success story which is worthy of mention occurred on 29th September 1918. The Armstrong Whitworth-built Airship R29 became the only British rigid airship to see action against the enemy. Whilst operating from East Fortune in East Lothian, the R29 spotted the German U-boat UB 115, commanded by Kapitänleutnant Renhold Thomsen, on the surface off Beacon Point near Newbiggin-by-the-Sea. The R29 dropped several bombs on the U-boat but could not confirm it as sunk. However HMS Ouse arrived on the scene and once again finished the submarine off with a brace of depth charges.

Between the Wars

The number of airfields in the North-East reached its peak by the end of the First World War. The cessation of hostilities in 1918 resulted in virtually every airfield and landing ground being closed, with only a limited number such as Town Moor and the Gosforth sites remaining open until 1919 and 1921 respectively.

The aviation market was also flooded with thousands of ex-military aircraft that had been converted for civilian use. The 1920s was a vibrant period throughout the country for aviation, giving many people the opportunity not only to joy ride but also to learn to fly. The period also spawned several new aero clubs; the oldest of them all, Newcastle Aero Club, was formed at the closed RFC airfield at Cramlington in July 1925. It is not known exactly what types of aircraft the club first operated but the general type of the day was the docile Avro 504K. The de Havilland DH.60 Moth would also have been a common site. Introduced in 1925, the first of the Moth series aircraft revolutionized the flying scene in the country throughout the 1920s and 30s.

The airfield could accommodate larger aircraft as well, with at least one visit by a Handley W.8 airliner belonging to Imperial Airways. A triple engine Westland Wessex light transport was also demonstrated on the airfield in 1930.

The creator of 'Biggles', William Earl Johns, who was no stranger to the area, has immortalized Cramlington in the book, *Biggles and the Black Peril*. Johns served with RAF at Marske, near Redcar, basing the early part of this story around the Newcastle and Durham area.

A Westland Wessex light transport was also demonstrated at Cramlington in 1930.

Introduced in 1925, the DH.60 Moth was the first of a series of de Havilland built aircraft that revolutionized the flying scene in the country throughout the 1920s and 1930s.

The club moved to Woolsington in 1935 after being asked for advice on how to build and run an airport by the Newcastle Corporation. The Aero Club managed the airport in its early years, whilst still offering flying training. The cost in 1936 was 35 shillings per hour and the entire course could be completed for £30. Even taking into account monetary changes and inflation, the average cost of a flying course today is between £4,000 and £5,000!

Despite the Aero Club leaving Cramlington, the airfield was still used by several local enthusiasts up to the beginning of the Second World War. A DH.60 Moth crashed on the airfield on 1st December 1939, two months after all civilian flying activities were supposed to have ceased!

The club has enjoyed several influential members over the years: Sir Alan Cobham was a member during the 1930s; Viscount Runciman of Doxford, who went on to become the Director General of British Overseas Airways Corporation (BOAC), was one of the pioneers at the club whilst at Cramlington; and the famous fighter pilot Air Vice Marshal 'Johnnie' Johnson was the club's vice-president until his death in 2001.

The Newcastle-upon-Tyne Aero Club still survives today and Woolsington is now known as Newcastle International Airport.

Sir Alan Cobham was one of many distinguished members of the Newcastle Aero Club during the 1930s.

It was twelve years before military aviation returned to the North-East, when another RFC landing ground location was expanded into a larger airfield. The formation of the Auxiliary Air Force (AAF) in 1924 signalled the beginning of the build up again of the rapidly depleted post First World War RAF. The old 36 Squadron landing ground at Hylton was expanded into a new airfield at Usworth, which was opened in March 1930. Its first occupant was the newly-formed 607 (County of Durham) Squadron AAF, flying the Westland Wapiti, which did not arrive until 1932. Usworth remained the only military airfield in the entire area until the beginning of 1938, when Acklington opened as an Armament Practice Camp.

Whilst Woolsington began to flourish, the quest for a regional airport of similar standing was taken on by the authorities of Hartlepool. The now redundant airfield at Seaton Carew, positioned a few miles down the coast, for some reason was not even considered. However, six new sites were surveyed around Hartlepool in 1931 and a piece of land near the village of Greatham was selected. The site was renamed West Hartlepool, but by the time the airfield was complete, RAF Reserve

Command took the site over in 1939, removing any chance of Hartlepool gaining its own airport.

The RAF expansion period began in 1934 and part of this plan was to increase the number of bomber airfields and squadrons available. As a result, a new site for an airfield was chosen at Middleton St George, between Darlington and Middlesbrough. However, by the time construction began, the Second World War had already started and the urgency to complete the airfield was increased significantly.

The Second World War

At the outbreak of war on 3rd September 1939, Usworth was the only RAF airfield in the entire North-East with operational squadrons, both bomber units, in residence. Acklington was still an Armament Practice Camp, and both Woolsington and West Hartlepool housed training units run by civilians.

The organization of Fighter Command was made up of several groups which controlled large sections of the country. The North-East and southern Scotland were under 13 Group control, whose headquarters were at Blakelaw Estate, Ponteland Road in Newcastle-on-Tyne. Under the command of Air Vice Marshal R E Saul DFC, it was predicted by senior staff that this particular area would receive far less attention than more southerly areas. This may have been the case but the area the group had to cover, with considerably less resources, was vast.

The command was also responsible for all information received by the Royal Observer Corps and the interpretation of messages from the many radar stations along the north-east coast. All searchlight units were under Fighter Command control and by the middle of 1940 all anti-aircraft batteries were the responsibility of the command as well.

The situation changed rapidly for Acklington, which was transferred to Fighter Command and would remain in this role for the entire war. Usworth's squadrons departed for France and the airfield was also transferred to Fighter Command, becoming the Sector Headquarters until the arrival of a new fighter station in 1941. Woolsington and West Hartlepool also came under the control of Fighter Command, their training activities now disbanded.

Leading up to the Battle of Britain, the defence of Tyneside and Teesside was in the hands of a few fighter squadrons based at four airfields, the majority of which were only resting from the fight in the south of the country. These four airfields were well spaced to protect the area and under good leadership were able to repel the massive attack by the Luftwaffe on 15th August 1940. Usworth was the main focus for the attack, the enemy obviously recognizing the fact that the area was depending on its fighter defences.

A purpose-built fighter station at Ouston opened in March 1941, became the new Sector Headquarters, and relegated Usworth to flying training. Eventually, even this role was transferred to a more suitable location. While Usworth faded from the scene, the fighter squadrons at Acklington and Ouston and detachments at West Hartlepool continued the role of convoy protection and the defence of the North-East on a regular basis until 1943. By this time, enemy air activity had subsided and all efforts were beginning to be directed to the forthcoming invasion of Europe.

One of the most common enemy bombers over the North-East was the Heinkel He 111, many of which were shot down on 15th August 1940.

19

A reorganization of Fighter Command in July 1943 resulted in 14 Group being disbanded and control was taken over by 13 Group. The group's area now covered not only the north of England but Scotland as well. This also meant that the headquarters had to relocate further north, and on 16th July 1943 it moved to Drummossie Hotel, near Inverness. Blakelaw became Ouston Sector Headquarters, followed by Catterick Sector Headquarters, until it was closed on 10th April 1946. Used by the government during the Cold War period, Blakelaw has been preserved and is open to the public today.

Fighter protection for the area was almost non-existent by June 1944 and during the actual invasion of Europe it was realized that the North-East had no cover whatsoever. Almost as an afterthought, a token group of Hawker Typhoons was sent to Acklington for a few days whilst the invasion took place.

From D-Day onwards, 13 Group's responsibilities dwindled as the war in Europe progressed steadily eastwards. Blakelaw went on to

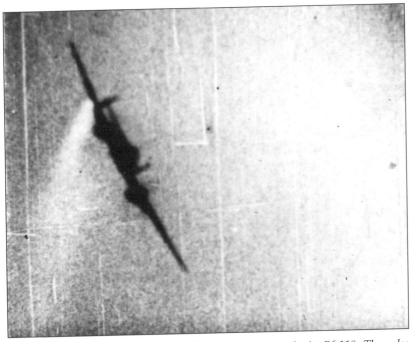

The Heinkel's escort on long-range raids was the Messerschmitt Bf 110. They also suffered heavy losses at the hands of the RAF on 15th August 1940.

20

become the North-Eastern Sector Headquarters, eventually disbanding with the entire group on 20th May 1946.

Flying Training

The continuous production of fully trained airmen was absolutely essential if the Allies were going to stand any chance of defeating the enemy. With the exception of Middleton St George, all the other airfields mentioned in this book had at least one dedicated training unit stationed at them during the Second World War. Even in Middleton's case it could be argued that the Conversion Flights of 76 and 78 Squadron were training units, although on many occasions these flights were expected to fly bombing raids with the rest of the squadron.

Back in 1935, a new training system was implemented to accommodate service pilots in the forthcoming RAF Volunteer Reserve. This was not officially formed until April 1937 and the scheme enabled men between the ages of 18 and 25 to enrol as airman pilots with the rank of sergeant. The units responsible were called Elementary and Reserve Flying Training Schools (E&RFTS) and the first to arrive in the North-East was 32 E&RFTS at West Hartlepool in April 1939. A second, 43 E&RFTS, arrived at Woolsington in June 1939 and was run by the already experienced Newcastle Aero Club, the leaders in the field of pilot training since its formation in 1925. Both schools were disbanded at the outbreak of war on 3rd September 1939.

The north of England, in general, lent itself perfectly to flying training, with its relatively clear skies uncluttered by the activities of operational squadrons. By the beginning of 1941, however, the area still lacked any new airfields to accommodate the plethora of Operational Training Units (OTU), which were being formed to train single seat fighter pilots. The Hurricanes of 55 OTU were the first large flying training unit to arrive; making Usworth its home from March 1941. The majority of OTUs were formed at airfields in the south of England, and, as this area became increasingly congested with front line squadrons, many training units took less busy locations further north. Usworth was certainly far from ideal for training. Its location was complicated not only by barrage balloons but also by industrial pollution. The average OTU had anything up to 100 aircraft on strength, and, without exception, to accomplish the rate of trained pilots required by the RAF,

These DH.60 Moths were purchased by the RAF in 1928 as primary trainers.

had to employ a second airfield, known as a satellite. In Usworth's case this was the more suitably located Ouston. By April 1942, Ouston became 55 OTU's new home, employing Woolsington as its own satellite airfield.

West Hartlepool became the satellite airfield for 6 OTU, operating the Lockheed Hudson from September 1941 at least to the summer of 1942. The American-built Hudsons, based at Thornaby, were a familiar sight in the Middlesbrough area until they moved to Silloth, in Cumbria, in March 1943.

The first new airfield to open in the North-East specifically for training was Morpeth, in March 1942. The airfield became the home for 4 Air Gunnery School (AGS) for its entire existence until it was disbanded in December 1944. Over 4,000 gunners were trained at Morpeth, the majority destined for Halifax and Lancaster squadrons.

By 1942, there was a high demand for airborne radar operators who were needed for the increasing number of new night-fighter squadrons. In June 1942, 62 OTU was formed at Usworth, mainly operating the Avro Anson, the majority of which were equipped with Airborne Interception (AI) radar. As with the fighter OTU, Usworth's location proved unsatisfactory for AI training and once again Ouston became the unit's new home in July 1943. 62 OTU's specialist training was in demand for the remainder of the war and it was eventually disbanded at Ouston in June 1945.

Milfield, the most northerly airfield covered in this book, opened in August 1942 and became the home of another large fighter OTU. Originally built for the use of a bomber OTU, its role changed before the airfield was completed, although all the additional buildings associated with a bomber unit were still constructed. Milfield's location was perfect for flying training, and Brunton, which opened around the same time, provided an equally useful satellite airfield. The main aircraft operated by 59 OTU was the Hurricane, although it was the intention for it to receive the Typhoon as well. Only limited numbers of Typhoons actually arrived before it was disbanded into the Fighter Leaders School (FLS) in January 1944. The FLS also absorbed another one of Milfield's units, namely 1 Specialized Low Attack Instructors' School, which needs no explanation of its role.

The concept of the FLS was formed from lessons learned during the RAF's withdrawal from northern France at the beginning of the war, highlighting the need for dedicated ground attack pilots and aircraft. Virtually all of the pilots trained at Milfield in ground attack techniques were employed during, and continually after, the invasion of Europe.

The Hawker Hurricane was a common sight throughout the war, many with student pilots at the controls.

Two other airfields were also specifically built for fighter OTUs, namely Eshott, which was opened in November 1942, and Boulmer, opened in March 1943, the last wartime airfield to open in the region. Eshott was the home of 57 OTU, a Spitfire unit that remained at the airfield until it was disbanded in June 1945. Boulmer was used as the satellite airfield for 57 OTU and also as a forward operating base for 4 AGS. Its location next to the coast saved valuable time and was convenient for the local gunnery ranges.

Other training units in the area included several gliding schools and the fledgling Durham University Air Squadron (UAS), established at Ouston in March 1944. The latter survives today in the guise of the Northumbrian Universities Air Squadron, now based at Leeming in North Yorkshire.

Bomber Command

The domain of Bomber Command during the Second World War is traditionally thought of as being located in Cambridgeshire, Lincolnshire and Yorkshire, but its most northerly airfield was located in County Durham. Middleton St George was the airfield in the North-

The Armstrong Whitworth Whitley, alongside the Vickers Wellington, was the mainstay of Bomber Command during the early months of the Second World War.

East that operated fully operational front-line squadrons from its opening to the end of the war.

Initially opened as part of the RAF's 4 Group, in January 1941, from January 1943 a re-organization meant that Middleton became part of 6 Royal Canadian Air Force (RCAF) Group. Leading up to this, the airfield housed Handley Page Halifaxes of 76 Squadron and Armstrong Whitworth Whitleys of 78 Squadron, the latter eventually converting to the Halifax as well. Both squadrons were involved in all of the important early operations carried out by Bomber Command, including the first of many attacks on the German battleship *Tirpitz*.

The first Canadian squadron arrived in October 1942, followed by 419 and 428 Squadrons in November 1942 and June 1943, respectively. The former was the only squadron within 6 Group to remain at one airfield. Both of these Halifax-equipped Canadian squadrons would remain at Middleton until the end of the war, both eventually re-equipping with the Canadian-built Lancaster Mk.X. Middleton's loss rate was very high. A contributory factor to this was its northerly location, which meant that its crews would have to fly further than the Lincolnshire-based aircraft, especially against targets in Germany,

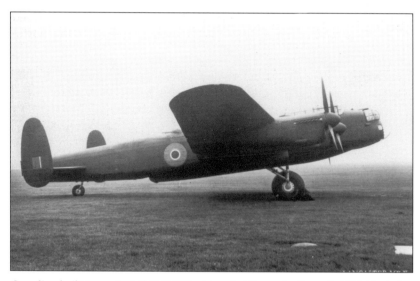

Canadian-built Lancaster Mk.X KB783 pictured at Boscombe Down in Wiltshire before being transferred to Middleton St George. KB783 served with both 419 and 428 Squadrons before returning to Canada in June 1945.

making them more vulnerable. The Canadian group as a whole would suffer high losses; all of its squadrons were first equipped with either the Wellington or the Halifax, both of which were relatively easy prey when operating with the Lancasters from the more southerly-based groups.

The Canadians' contribution to the Bomber Command campaign was very impressive. From 6 Group's formation, the RCAF flew 40,822 sorties and dropped a total of 126,122 tons of bombs and mines. In August 1944 alone, the group's Halifaxes and Lancasters dropped 13,274 tons of bombs on targets throughout France and Germany. This was more than the Luftwaffe dropped on London during the entire war!

The need for Canada's contribution to the war effort was also reflected in the fact that 6 Group, with the exception of non-RCAF aircrew's pay, was totally funded by the Canadian Government. The cost of maintaining the squadrons and the supply of ammunition and fuel was all gleaned from Canadian taxes. With the arrival of the Canadian-produced Lancaster Mk.X, even the cost of the actual aircraft was covered by local taxes.

The RCAF also contributed with their lives, and by the war's end, 6 Group had reported 814 aircraft missing, which equated to 9,919 aircrew killed. This was 17.8% of all Bomber Command aircrew lost.

On several occasions, when their home bases were weatherbound, the airfields of the North-East provided sanctuary for returning bomber crews. The unforgiving terrain, especially in the Cheviot Hills, could also be a final resting place. Many bombers, either on training sorties or returning from a raid crashed in the region. It was the seemingly never-ending task of recovering the wreckage that fell upon 83 Maintenance Unit, based at Woolsington.

Bombing and Gunnery Ranges

The combination of several training units and a long coastline resulted in several bombing and gunnery ranges being constructed throughout the North-East. With the opening of Acklington as 7 Armament Training School (ATS) in 1938, the first of several coastal ranges opened at Drurridge Bay. At the time, 7 ATS was equipped with the Boulton

Paul Overstrand and Fairey Seal, both obsolete but ideally suited to teach the basics of delivering ordnance to a ground target.

Although not covered in this book, owing to its location in North Yorkshire, Thornaby gained a pair of ranges with the arrival of 6 OTU in July 1941. Approximately 30 miles off Hartlepool, a large rectangular area of sea was used for bombing and gunnery training. Brightly-coloured buoys serving as a warning to local shipping edged the range. The second range used by the OTU was located at Seal Sands in the estuary of the Tees, not far from the airfield at West Hartlepool. Both ranges remained in use until 6 OTU's departure in March 1943.

Air-to-air firing also required a dedicated range area, with strict rules so the attacking aircraft did not spray the local population with live rounds. Several air-to-air ranges were allocated, mainly off the coast so that rounds and empty cases could fall harmlessly into the sea. Both trainee fighter pilots and aerial gunners made use of these ranges; their target was generally a banner towed by a Westland Lysander, which was replaced by the Miles Martinet as the war progressed.

The first unit in the area to actually have its own air-to-air range was 4 AGS, located off Amble, followed by a second off the coast near Boulmer. Being a dedicated gunnery school, the unit also had its own target-towing flight with the majority of other units in the area relying upon detachments of visiting flights.

The arrival of the FLS at Milfield resulted in at least three new ground attack ranges in the north of the area. Two ranges were constructed at Goswick Sands, both liberally covered in a host of inviting ground attack targets. This range also doubled for air-to-air firing and was strictly controlled by permanent staff on the ground. Another ground attack range was constructed between Yeavering Bell and Newton Tors, only minutes from Milfield. The resident Typhoons and Hurricanes could begin their attack run immediately after take off, a scenario that actually occurred when Allied aircraft began to operate in Normandy in June 1944. A third range was set up at Doddington Moor, once again very close to Milfield. The many tactical exercises that the FLS were involved in effectively made the whole of the North-East and southern Scotland one giant practice range.

2
ACKLINGTON

It is a common misconception that the Battle of Britain was fought and won over the skies of the south-east of England. Admittedly, the bulk of the fighting occurred in that region, but airfields further north, in particular in the North-East became, almost by accident, crucial to the overall victory.

Acklington would become the linchpin to the defence of the industrial might of Tyneside, its day and night fighter squadrons successfully achieving high kill rates throughout the war. Thirty four years of continuous service, which saw over 50 different units pass through its gates, elevated Acklington's role to one of the most important airfields in the area. It seems quite fitting therefore that it is the subject of the first chapter in this book.

Aviation on the site can be traced back to the First World War. It was then that 77 Squadron was formed as Home Defence Squadron, specifically for the protection of the Firth of Forth. Flying a variety of aircraft, which included the Avro 504, the squadron had three detached flights plus the use of several landing grounds. Its most southerly was called Southfields, and this was same location that Air Ministry officials visited late in 1936 with a view to constructing a more permanent and considerably larger airfield.

Acklington was to become one of five new armament training camps which, unlike other airfields being constructed at the time, were not elaborate, but needed technical and instructional buildings of a specific design. Unique to all armament practice camps were 'F'-type flight sheds. These inter-war hangars were of steel construction, with large side-opening doors; Acklington had a pair, which later on were complemented by a more common 'J'-type hangar.

A lone hangar at Acklington in 1977, dismantled not long after this photo was taken. (A Ferguson)

The camp officially opened in January 1938, although No.7 Armament Training Camp, which was Acklington's official title, was formed on the airfield on 1st December 1937. This was later redesignated No.7 Armament Training School (ATS) on 1st April 1938 and changed again to No.2 Air Observers' School (AOS) on 15th November 1938. The main aircraft types operated by these schools were the Fairey Seal, the Boulton Paul Overstrand and the Hawker Hind. The Seal was a large three-seat biplane that spent most of its career serving with the Fleet Air Arm (FAA) aboard aircraft carriers. Several of them were on charge with 2 AOS but on 17th August 1939 the unit managed to write three of them off in the same day! A group of Seals was practising formation flying when, during a position change, they collided. Both aircraft crashed at Beal, near Berwick-on-Tweed. Sadly one of the aircrew was killed. One of the surviving aircraft from the formation decided to land near the wreckage to provide assistance to the survivors. Unfortunately this aircraft struck an obstruction on landing next to the wreck, thus to become the third loss of the day for 2 AOS.

On the outbreak of the Second World War, 2 AOS left for Warmwell in Dorset, and Acklington was immediately transferred to Fighter Command and the control of 13 Group, whose headquarters were at the Blakelaw Estate, Ponteland Road in Newcastle-on-Tyne. In terms of area covered, 13 Group had one of the largest compared to all others in Fighter Command. Under the command of Air Vice Marshal R E Saul DFC, who took over on 24th July 1939, the group's area of responsibility stretched from Catterick in North Yorkshire to southern Scotland.

The action began quickly when 607 Squadron from Usworth made the short flight in their ageing Gloster Gladiators to Acklington on 9th October 1939. They went into battle on 17th October, when three aircraft of 'B' Flight, led by Flt Lt Sample shot down a Dornier Do 18 flying boat, 40 miles east of Berwick. The squadron's stay was short; by the beginning of November the unit was sent to Merville in France (via Croydon) in support of the British Expeditionary Force (BEF). They would suffer dearly at the hands of the Luftwaffe. This pattern of short staying fighter squadrons continued throughout the Second World War, and the majority were successful at shooting down at least one enemy aircraft.

Gladiators returned on 2nd October with the re-formation of 152 Squadron, which was actually earmarked for Spitfires. By December

The Fairey Seal was a rare aircraft and was certainly more at home operating with the FAA rather than 2 AOS at Acklington.

A Dornier Do 18 flying boat, similar to the aircraft shot down by Flt Lt Sample's Gloster Gladiator on 17th October 1939.

the squadron had replaced their biplanes with the state of the art fighter and quickly became accustomed to all of the advantages the Spitfire brought.

On 27th October, 111 Squadron Hawker Hurricane Mk.Is arrived from Northolt in confident mood. The squadron had the privilege of becoming the first RAF unit to receive a high-performance eight-gun monoplane, and, since its arrival in December 1937, a steep learning curve had been climbed. The squadron's stay at Acklington was only a staging post in preparation for another move to Drem in Scotland. Only days before departure, the Commanding Officer, Sqn Ldr H Broadhurst AFC took off alone after receiving a report that enemy aircraft were approaching the coast. The weather was atrocious, but Broadhurst pressed on, flying on instruments only through thick cloud. On clearing an iced-up windscreen, he spotted a group of Heinkel He 111s of KG 26, inbound from their base in Schleswig, North Germany. A single aircraft was picked out at a range of 500 yards. The bomber dived into cloud, but Broadhurst remained focused and continued to close until he was just 150 yards from the Heinkel. A quick burst of fire from the Hurricane put the ventral gunner out of action and the second burst sent the Heinkel into a flaming spiral dive into the North Sea. This was the first of many victories for 111 Squadron and it seemed quite appropriate that this popular CO took the victory. Broadhurst was awarded the Distinguished Flying Cross (DFC) for his action that day, preferring to risk himself rather than his squadron.

Known throughout the RAF as 'Broady', Harry Broadhurst was one of the great characters of the Second World War. He joined the RAF in 1926 and by the time of his retirement from the RAF in 1961, he had attained the rank of Air Chief Marshal, becoming en route the youngest Air-Vice Marshal in British history.

Another Hurricane squadron, 43 Squadron, arrived at Acklington on 18th November 1939. It was nicknamed 'The Fighting Cocks', a name it had gained by becoming the first unit to operate a post First World War fighter, the Gloster Gamecock. A fighter squadron from birth, this unit was very keen to show how good the Hurricane was. Before its departure to Wick in Scotland on 26th February 1940, the squadron managed to shoot down five enemy aircraft, all Heinkel He 111s. Three of these kills were achieved in a single day and one in particular made history as the first enemy aircraft to crash in England.

On 3rd February 1940, the weather was particularly bad, and, virtually without exception, Acklington was the only airfield open for operations in the north-east of England. 'B' Flight, with three

A flight of Hurricane Mk.Is, similar to those operated by Sqn Ldr Broadhurst's 111 Squadron.

Hurricanes, was 'at readiness'. Their pilots, Flt Lt Peter Townsend, Flying Officer Folkes and Sgt Jim Hallowes were trying to keep warm in a dispersal hut near their aircraft. Suddenly the phone rang and the order to 'scramble' was given. The three pilots ran to their fighters and within minutes were airborne, heading east to meet the enemy. There was a report that two enemy aircraft were attacking a trawler off Whitby but on arrival only one aircraft was spotted, an He 111H of KG 26. Townsend attacked first, instantly killing one member of the crew and hit the starboard engine. Folkes followed with a concentrated attack from the rear, which caused smoke to pour from the German bomber. The pilot, who was the only crew member not to have been hit, made a dash for the clouds in a last ditch attempt to survive. But the aircraft was so badly damaged that it was inevitable that the pilot would have to crash land, as no surviving member of his crew was capable of bailing out. With the coast only two miles away, the Heinkel made a copybook crash landing near to Bannial Flat Farm, north of Whitby. The pilot, Fw H Wilms, and the radio operator/dorsal gunner, Uffz. K Missy, survived, but unfortunately Uffz. R Leuschake and Uffz. J Meyer were killed in the encounter with the Hurricanes.

On 6th January 1940, 152 Squadron became operational with the Spitfire Mk.I, gaining experience flying coastal and convoy patrols up and down the east coast. First contact with the enemy came on 29th January with a brief combat against a group of Ju 87 Stukas, which managed to escape into the clouds. A few days later, the squadron recorded its first kill by shooting down a He 111 off the North Yorkshire coast, followed by another He 111 on 27th February.

The experienced pilots of 72 Squadron descended upon Acklington on 2nd March 1940. The unit had been equipped with the Spitfire Mk.I since April 1939, but Acklington's runways were in such poor condition that the squadron could only operate their old mount, the Gloster Gladiator. It was a great relief that this situation lasted only a fortnight, by which time conditions had improved and the squadron settled into the routine of convoy patrols. Very little action was experienced until the squadron was hastily moved down to Gravesend on 1st June so that they could carry out patrols over the Dunkirk beaches. One of the few accidents involving a 72 Sqn aircraft is worthy of note, as the aircraft involved is preserved in the RAF Museum at Hendon in north London. Spitfire Mk.I K9942 was bellylanded on the airfield after returning from a patrol on 5th June 1940. The aircraft was quickly repaired and served with another ten units before it was selected for preservation on 28th August 1944.

Sqn Ldr Peter Townsend (crouched) poses with pilots and the mascot of 85 Squadron, which he went on to command on posting from 43 Squadron.

65 Heinkel He 111s attacked the North-East on 15th August 1940. Thankfully Acklington's squadrons were ready for them.

The evacuation of Dunkirk, more officially known as Operation 'Dynamo', signalled the end of the Battle of France, and Britain now stood alone. To quote Churchill: 'The Battle of France is over. I expect that the Battle of Britain is about to begin.' The battle can be broken down into four phases: firstly the Channel battles, which simply tested our defences in the vain hope that we might sue for peace following the fall of France; secondly, the crucial attacks on Fighter Command airfields, a strategically logical attempt at destroying the RAF before an invasion of southern England could be attempted; thirdly, in a switch in tactics, German bombers were sent to damage civilian cities, mainly London, in revenge for Bomber Command's ineffective attacks on Berlin. The fourth and final phase was when the main bomber force was withdrawn due to mounting losses, only to be replaced by fighter-bomber operations.

As the focus for a potential invasion was obviously the south of England, many airfields in the north were simply used by resting squadrons who were involved in the intense action over the Channel. The first squadron to arrive during this new period of hostility was 79 Squadron on 13th July 1940. Equipped with the Hurricane Mk.I, the squadron scored 11 Group's first victory on 21st November 1939 by shooting down a Dornier Do 17 near Manston. They were then sent to France on 10th May 1940 and in only ten days managed to shoot down 25 enemy aircraft, only suffering five aircraft and two pilots lost.

By August 1940, all the fighter squadrons based in the North-East were either fully rested or had quietly become very experienced and efficient fighting units. This caused some disquiet; 72 Squadron was itching for a fight and starting to become frustrated that it had not been moved south so as to take on the Luftwaffe, and 79 Squadron, which had already tasted action, was also ready for a move. Their anxious wait was soon over, however, as Acklington was about to be thrust into the heart of the Battle of Britain.

13 Group's day came on 15th August 1940, when the Luftwaffe launched a massive force of aircraft. Airfields were selected as their main targets, although industrial targets were also always on the agenda.

65 Heinkel He IIIs of KG26, escorted by 34 Messerschmitt Bf 110s of ZG76, were steadily crossing the North Sea, initially setting course for the Scottish coast. A group of Heinkel He 115C floatplanes was also heading for the Scottish coast. The intention was for them to fly a slightly different course from the main bomber force and hopefully draw the attention of 13 Group's fighters. This feint failed to work because of poor navigation, with both groups ending up together as they approached the coast.

At 12:08 hrs, one of the many radar stations positioned along the east coast began to plot a large group of 'bandits' approaching the Firth of Forth. The enemy force then turned south-west, directly towards

Tynemouth. It was now decision time for Air Vice-Marshal Saul; he immediately scrambled the Spitfires of 72 Squadron, sending them directly at main force, with the plan of meeting the enemy near to the Farne Islands, off Bamburgh. The Hurricanes of 79 Squadron were positioned to the north of the incoming raiders, while 607 Squadron from Usworth supported 72 Squadron. Saul had to be convinced that Tyneside was the target and that this was the only wave of bombers because he made the daring move of bringing the Hurricanes of 605 Squadron from Drem south to protect Tyneside.

Time was on the defender's side and, by the time 72 Squadron's eleven Spitfires had arrived off the Northumberland coast, they were in the excellent position of being 3,000 ft higher than the attackers. Flt Lt E Graham was leading the small band of fighters that day and his group of Spitfire pilots was initially numbed by the sight of nearly 100 enemy aircraft. Graham hesitated while he tried to work out how to attack the vast force and from which direction. During those few seconds of thought one of his wingmen said: 'Haven't you seen them?' His stuttered reply was to go down in Fighter Command history.

'Of course I've seen the b-b-b-bastards. I'm trying to w-w-w-work out what to do.'

Aircraft were refuelled and re-armed at lightning speed. This Spitfire's engine is still ticking while the squadron armourers reload the Browning machine guns.

Graham positioned his flight with the sun behind, and, still with the height advantage, left each pilot to choose his own target; two-thirds of the group attacked the bombers while the rest descended upon the Bf 110s. The Bf 110s were fitted with external fuel tanks, which were quickly jettisoned once the aircraft were under attack. The flight for this twin-engined fighter was at the very maximum of its range and, to save weight, a decision was made to leave the rear gunners at home. This proved fatal for many of the German pilots. In 'Custer's Last Stand' fashion, the Bf 110s formed a defensive circle in a vain attempt to protect themselves, although many dived for sea-level and headed east for home, leaving the He 111s to fend for themselves. Enemy aircraft spiralled in flames towards the sea as chaos ensued, and Graham's small band tore into as many aircraft as they could. Several He 111s dumped their bombs into the sea and headed back to Norway while the remainder split into two groups; one headed for Tyneside, with the intention of bombing Usworth, while the rest turned south-east, with orders to bomb Linton on Ouse and Dishforth, both bomber airfields in North Yorkshire.

The Hurricanes of 79 Squadron joined the fray just as the force split into two and continued to harry and attack the bombers all the way to their intended target. Once over Tyneside, the area's effective anti-aircraft guns claimed more victims, while the combined force of 79, 605

The Messerschmitt Bf 110s that escorted the He 111s on 15th August left their rear gunners at home. A fatal mistake for many of them.

and 607 Squadrons' Hurricanes deterred the enemy from scoring a single hit on their goal: Usworth. The bombers continued to jettison their deadly cargos, causing limited damage to a number of properties, none of them of military importance.

The tactics of AVM Saul and the skill of all the pilots involved in the fighting that day were classed as an overwhelming success. The Luftwaffe had no idea that so many fighter squadrons were in the area and never again attempted a raid in daylight on that scale against the North-East. The 15th of August was a pivotal moment in the Battle of Britain. Over 160 enemy aircraft were brought down all over the country, 40 of them claimed by aircraft in 13 Group, with six credited to 72 Squadron.

The experience gained by 72 and 79 Squadrons would stand them in good stead, because, by the end of August 1940, both units were moved to Biggin Hill, experiencing more action for the remainder of the Battle of Britain.

On 27th August, 32 Squadron, flying the Hurricane Mk.I, was ordered north to Acklington for a rest and 610 Squadron, flying Spitfire Mk.Is, was also removed from the battle. Both were based at Biggin Hill. While 'resting', 32 Squadron was ordered to carry out night fighting duties. This role was in its infancy in 1940 and, frustratingly, during the squadron's stay at Acklington it did not achieve a single kill despite the fact that night raids were on the increase. However, the squadron did manage to write off a pair of Hurricanes within days of each other. The first, flown by Pilot Officer Sniechowski, crashed on the airfield, and another, on 3rd November, force-landed near Wooperton, with Pilot Officer Waskiewicz at the controls. Both pilots survived.

610 Squadron was also allocated a more defensive role, performing coastal and convoy patrols with the occasional scramble, a far cry from the hectic four sorties per day at Biggin Hill. The loss rate was high for this experienced unit during their stay at Acklington. The first casualty, on 30th September 1940, was Flying Officer C H Bacon, who crashed on the beach at Alnmouth and was killed. Pilot Officer Ogilvy belly landed his Spitfire at Acklington on 2nd November, and this was followed by the loss of two pilots on 4th and 5th of November, with a final machine damaged in a belly landing on the airfield in December.

Both 32 and 610 Squadrons departed from Acklington in mid December to be replaced by yet another Hurricane squadron, although this time it had travelled south. 258 Squadron had only spent a few days at Drem in Lothian after moving there from Leconfield. The purpose of the trip to Scotland was to collect 263 Squadron's Hurricanes, as that unit was to become the first to be equipped with the Westland Whirlwind twin-engined fighter.

Since leaving Acklington at the end of August 1940, 72 Squadron had moved no less than seven times. They returned to the airfield on 15th December 1940. The squadron had been very successful during the Battle of Britain, claiming over 60 enemy aircraft destroyed plus 14 probables and 26 others damaged. However, the fight had not been won easily: the squadron had lost 27 aircraft; eight pilots were killed and many others wounded.

As expected, the air over the North-East was less hostile for this battle-hardened squadron, but the enemy was still encountered and on a few occasions successfully shot down. On the evening of 14th March 1941, the Luftwaffe launched an attack that extended from Newcastle to Hull and targeted mainly civilian populated areas. Acklington's own anti-aircraft batteries were in action as well as a flight from 72 Squadron. Flt Lt D Sheen, flying a Spitfire Mk.I managed to shoot down a Junkers Ju 88A-5 from KG106. The twin-engined bomber went down in a sheet of flame off Amble. The crew stood no chance, and only one of the bodies of the four-man crew was ever recovered.

On 9th/10th April 1941, the North-East and Newcastle in particular suffered a very heavy bombing raid that continued for nearly five

The Junkers Ju 88 was a very good aeroplane and by the end of the war was the most common bomber to be seen over the North-East. However, it was no match against a determined attack by a Spitfire or Hurricane.

hours. After the raid, on the evening of 10th April, Luftwaffe reconnaissance aircraft were sent to evaluate the damage caused. One of the aircraft, a Ju-88A-5 from 3(F)/122 was caught prowling off the coast of Alnmouth by Sgt Casey and Sgt Prytherch, who were part of a flight of Spitfires from 72 Squadron. The German aircraft stood no chance and was sent into the sea in flames. Similarly all four on board were killed.

72 Squadron had been operating its trusty Spitfire Mk.Is since April 1939. One year later the squadron began to re-equip with the Spitfire Mk.IIa and Mk.IIb. The Mk.IIa was fitted with more powerful Rolls Royce Merlin XII engine, which developed 1,175 hp. The Mk.IIa retained the original armament layout of eight 0.303in guns, but the Mk.IIb was equipped with four 0.303in guns plus the added punch of a pair of 20mm cannons.

The squadron experienced a loss of its own on 29th April while a trio of Spitfire Mk.IIa's was practice flying. Pilot Officer Pocock, Sgt B Collyer and Sgt Perkins intercepted a Ju-88 of 1(F)/120 off Blyth. Pocock and Perkins managed to fire at the bomber before it entered a gap in the cloud, closely followed by Collyer in his Spitfire P8231. Collyer was heard on the radio, saying that his engine had failed and that he was ditching in the sea. Despite a desperate search by the other two aircraft, no trace of Collyer or his Spitfire was found. The same day Sgt Collyer's body was recovered from the sea. He is buried in East Chevington Cemetery, south of Amble.

The following day brought another victory with a Ju-88A-1 being shot down into the sea off the Farne Islands by Sgt White and Sgt Harrison of 72 Squadron. The aircraft had been part of a force which had attacked Whitley Bay, and no crew member survived the impact as the bomber hit the sea.

Only days before 72 Squadron was due to head south again, another new fighter began to arrive. The Spitfire Mk.Vb had gained even more power and was fitted with a Merlin 45 that produced 1,440hp. On 8th July 1941, the squadron left Acklington for the last time and would go on to become one of the RAF's longest serving squadrons.

258 Squadron moved to Acklington on 17th December 1940, becoming operational a few days later as part of Newcastle's defences. The squadron's stay was brief; by February 1941 it had moved to Jurby on the Isle of Man.

January and February 1941 saw the formation of a pair of Polish fighter squadrons. 315 'Deblinski' and 317 'Wilenski' Squadron were both equipped with the Hurricane Mk.I. 315 Squadron moved to Speke in Cheshire before becoming operational and 317 Squadron moved to Ouston, where it began to achieve a certain amount of success against the enemy.

May 1941 was a particularly miserable period for the civilians of the North-East because of the increased ferocity of the Luftwaffe attacks. In response to this, the region's defence was bolstered by the arrival of a flight of night fighters from Ayr in Strathclyde. Detachments of 141 Squadron, who were equipped with the Boulton Paul Defiant, were sent to Drem and Acklington on 1st May.

First flown on 11th August 1937, the Defiant introduced a new tactical concept that later proved to be fatally flawed. Although classed as a fighter, all of the Defiant's offensive armament was positioned in an enclosed turret behind the pilot's cockpit and was therefore incapable of firing forward. After entering service in December 1939, the aircraft enjoyed a brief period of success in combat against the Ju 87 and Ju 88 but the problem came when confronted by enemy fighters, in particular the Messerschmitt Bf 109. In one particular engagement during the Battle of Britain on 19th July 1940, 141 Squadron's Defiants were confronted by a group of Bf 109s of JG 51. Bravely, the Defiant crews managed to shoot down four enemy fighters, but tragically six out of nine Defiants were shot down, with a seventh crash landing at Hawkinge. A few days later, 141 Squadron was withdrawn from the battle and by September all Defiant squadrons were transferred to the night-fighter role.

Hopelessly outclassed against German fighter opposition during the day, the Boulton Paul Defiant achieved some success as a night fighter.

43

The first detachment of 141 Squadron Defiants arrived at Acklington during the first week of May 1941. The squadron was equipped with the Defiant Mk.I, which, unlike the Mk.II and all night fighters to follow, was devoid of any kind of airborne radar. Therefore spotting the enemy was a combination of good use of the weather, good eyesight of the crew and a large slice of luck.

On the night of 6th/7th May, Tyneside was suffering yet another heavy raid, when, at 23:25 hrs, a Defiant, crewed by Flying Officer R Day and Pilot Officer F Lanning, was scrambled from Acklington. The Defiant was over Ashington at 11,000ft when the crew spotted an aircraft, which turned out to be a He 111, over 1,000ft below them. The usual tactic was to position the Defiant underneath the bomber, allowing the gunner to fire into the belly of the aircraft. Day slipped undetected behind and below the bomber; then, sliding back the canopy to get a better view, he positioned the Defiant approximately 100ft below the raider. Lanning fired three short bursts, all of which found their target. The port engine was knocked out and a small fire started in the wing. The He 111 took evasive action, almost colliding with the Defiant as it dived away from its attacker. After considering a long single-engined flight back to France, the pilot of the He 111 made the wise decision to force land in England. After jettisoning its bomb load, the bomber made a forced landing in the grounds of St George's Mental Hospital, Morpeth.

Flying Officer Day returned to Acklington to refuel and re-arm before taking off again at 01:15 hrs. One hour later they found themselves in a good position to attack a Ju 88. The German bomber was from 5/KG 30, which was based at Gilze-Rijn in Holland and was briefed to attack Glasgow, crossing the British coast near Berwick-upon-Tweed. There is confusion as to exactly where the following engagement took place, but at exactly 02:30 hrs Day and Lanning spotted the Ju-88A-5 at 9,000ft, directly ahead. The Defiant did have a good turn of speed, catching the Ju 88 quickly and giving Day plenty of time to get into position for the attack. Lanning fired a quick burst, noticing that all the bullets seemed to strike home but had little effect on the progress of the bomber, although it did turn gently from left to right in a vain attempt to shake off its attacker. The Defiant attacked for a second time with little apparent effect, frustrating Day into make a final point blank range attack on the Ju 88. Day once again threw back his canopy for a better view, only to jam one of the muzzles of Lanning's Browning machine guns. The frustration was overwhelming and, by the time the Defiant crew had sorted out the problem, the Ju 88 had fled. Day and Lanning returned to Acklington, made their combat reports and mulled over the missed opportunity of shooting down two bombers in one night.

The crew of the Ju 88 now headed for home unaware that, in fact, a few of Lanning's bullets had found their mark. The pilot noticed that the temperature of the port engine was rising rapidly, giving no option but to shut it down. The bomb bay doors were also stuck open and the combination of this and a dead engine meant they had no chance of making it back to base. A crash landing was inevitable and the pilot skillfully put the Ju 88 down on the beach of Holy Island's North Bay. Both crews of the German aircraft survived and Day and Lanning were awarded DFCs for their successful combat that evening.

Another new squadron was formed at Acklington on 10th May 1941. 406 Squadron became the Royal Canadian Air Force's (RCAF) first night fighter unit, initially under the command of an RAF officer, Wg Cdr D G Morris DFC. The squadron badge was adorned with a lynx, an animal which had a reputation for keen eyesight. Their motto, 'We kill by night', certainly set the tone for this new unit. At first the Canadian crews trained with the Bristol Blenheim Mk.IF and Mk.IVF but its main equipment was to be the superb Bristol Beaufighter, which it began to receive in early June 1941. 406 Squadron, like eight other night fighter squadrons at that time, received the Mk.IIF variant, powered by a pair of Rolls Royce Merlin XX engines delivering 1,280

One of the earliest dedicated night fighters, the Blenheim Mk.IF was initially operated by 406 RCAF Squadron.

The Bristol Beaufighter Mk.IIF was the only variant of this superb aircraft that was fitted with the Rolls Royce Merlin engine.

horsepower apiece. The Mk.II was the only version to use the Merlin engine; all others were fitted with the powerful Bristol Hercules. Demands for increased production of the Short Stirling bomber, which also used the Hercules power plant, meant that a temporary alternative was needed for the Beaufighter.

The power of the Beaufighter also provided the perfect platform for the highly secret Airborne Interception (AI) radar, which was fitted into the nose of all MK.IIs. The squadron achieved its first success during a heavy air raid on Newcastle on the night of 1st/2nd September. Despite the fact that the squadron had not been declared operational, Flying Officer Fumerton and Sgt Bing took off from Acklington determined to test the ability of the Beaufighter. Just after 22:00 hrs they closed in on a Ju 88 and clinically shot it down with the loss of all on board. By the end of the year, the squadron had claimed five enemy aircraft destroyed. Four more were damaged before the squadron moved north to Ayr on 1st February 1942.

74 Squadron's Spitfire Mk.Vbs arrived from Gravesend on 9th July 1942 for a well-earned rest. The squadron reverted to its old Spitfire Mk.IIs but saw very little action while at Acklington and by the beginning of October had left for Llanbedr in Gwynedd.

A break in the tradition of fighting units at Acklington was formed in August 1941. 13 Group Target Towing Flight (TTF), equipped with

Lysander Mk.IIs and Mk.IIIs, provided air gunnery refresher training to all fighter units operating from within the Group. The unit was renamed 1490 Flight (Target Towing) Flight on 8th December 1941, by which time it had received Hawker Henley target tugs as well.

43 Squadron returned to Acklington for a second tour of duty on 4th October 1941. Equipped with the Hurricane Mk.IIa and Mk.IIb, the squadron now had the capability to perform as a day and night fighter unit. The squadron saw a limited amount of action but the formation of an innovative new unit brought hope of an improvement in the situation.

Several American-built Douglas Havoc Mk.Is, Havoc Mk.IIs, Boston Mk.IIs and Boston Mk.IIIs were heavily converted to carry a large and powerful searchlight, originally known as the Helmore light, after its inventor. The aircraft were actually called Turbinlites. The object of the exercise was to illuminate enemy bombers while an accompanying night-fighter squadron would carry out the attack. Acklington's Turbinlite unit was called 1460 Flight and was formed there on 15th Dec 1941 with nine Douglas Havocs.

The whole concept worked well on paper, but achieved virtually no results in the air and was eventually abandoned after only nine sorties

1460 Flight operated the Turbinlite Douglas Havoc. Like all other units equipped with this novel idea, it achieved no success against the enemy.

from Acklington. However, the concept of the searchlight was later developed into the Leigh Light, which, when fitted to the Vickers Wellington, was very effective in attacking surfaced U-Boats.

141 Squadron had been on detachment at Acklington throughout 1941 but on 29th January 1942 the whole unit moved down from Ayr. The Beaufighter Mk.IF had replaced the Defiants, and on 15th February the squadron achieved its first kill with the big twin engined night fighter. Flying Officer J G Benson and Sgt L Brandon shot down a Dornier Do 217E-4 of III/KG 2 during an air raid on Blyth, the aircraft crashing four miles off the coast. The squadron lost several Beaufighters in flying accidents at Acklington before its departure to Tangmere on 23rd June 1942. It joined 43 Squadron, which had also moved to Tangmere on 16th June after converting to the Hurricane Mk.IIc.

Detachments during the year included Spitfire Mk.Vbs of 167 Squadron from Scorton in North Yorkshire and 410 Squadron's Beaufighters, also from Scorton, which used Acklington throughout the summer before the entire squadron moved in later in the year.

Room was now available for another Beaufighter night-fighter squadron, namely 219 Squadron, a unit that had become very proficient at shooting down the enemy. The squadron's appropriate motto was 'From dusk till dawn', and the first of their Beaufighter Mk.IFs began to arrive on 23rd June 1942. The squadron had been flying nocturnal sorties since its re-formation at Catterick on 4th October 1939 and its kill rate did not decline during its stay at Acklington. By the end of August, the squadron score stood at 44 enemy aircraft, and, before they left Acklington on 21st October, a Do 217E was shot down into the sea off Tynemouth.

On 8th July 1942, 1 Squadron joined them, complete with a new fighter. With a heritage that dated back to its formation as a 'lighter-than-air' squadron on 13th April 1912, the unit had had a very busy war up to its arrival at Acklington. Equipped with the Hurricane, the squadron had seen action in France, had taken part in the Battle of Britain, and then become a night-fighter unit before specializing in the art of intruder patrols near enemy bases in France.

1 Squadron was chosen for conversion to the Hawker Typhoon, an aircraft that certainly had its early problems. The Typhoon had its roots in a specification that was drawn up in 1937 for a fighter that would eventually replace the Spitfire and Hurricane, even before they had reached squadron service. During peacetime it is traditional to plan the replacement for an aircraft as soon as it has been accepted for service.

During wartime, however, the development rate of aircraft was so fast the intended replacement often outlived the newer machine.

The Typhoon first entered service with 56 Squadron at Duxford but early troubles included unreliable engines, fumes entering the cockpit, and, most serious of all, catastrophic failure of the rear fuselage (basically the tails were breaking off!). Thankfully all these problems were ironed out, despite calls to scrap the whole Typhoon project. The aircraft matured, quickly becoming a useful addition to Fighter Command's armoury. Originally intended as an interceptor and capable of over 400 mph, the Typhoon was more at home at low level, as it did not perform well at higher altitudes and had a poor rate of climb.

1 Squadron received the Mk.Ib, armed with four 20mm Hispano cannons and capable of carrying a pair of 1,000lb bombs and up to sixteen 60lb three-inch rockets. The experienced squadron pilots quickly tamed the new aircraft, which was often described as a machine that would 'sort the men from the boys'. The pilots first proved the aircraft's worth on 6th September 1942 during one of several experimental raids by 16/KG6 operating the unimpressive Messerschmitt Me 210. During an attack on Middlesbrough, Pilot Officer D P Perrin scored 1 Squadron's first Typhoon success by shooting down an Me 210A-1 near to Fell Briggs farm, New Marske, near Redcar. Seven minutes later, Pilot Officer T G Bridges claimed a second kill, sending down a second Me 210A-1 near Sunnyside Farm, Fylingthorpe in North Yorkshire. The squadron lost a few aircraft of their own in general flying accidents, the most tragic occurring on 21st

The Hawker Typhoon Mk.Ibs of 1 Squadron shot down a pair of Me 210s whilst stationed at Acklington. Unfortunately they lost several aircraft in accidents as well.

October when a pair of Typhoons collided off Amble with both pilots lost. 1 Squadron saw no further action over the North-East, departing for Biggin Hill on 9th February 1943.

410 RCAF Squadron was no stranger to Acklington. Canada's third night-fighter squadron moved in from Scorton on 20th October 1942, equipped with the Beaufighter Mk.IIF. By the end of the month, another new aircraft began to arrive at Acklington and this time it was a true classic. The de Havilland Mosquito was a remarkable aircraft in all respects. Unique in its all-wood construction, impressive performance and load carrying capability, it was head and shoulders above the majority of designs of the time.

410 Squadron received the MK.II night-fighter variant, which was systematically replacing the Beaufighter as the standard home defence night fighter. The Mk.II was the first fighter variant of the Mosquito to enter RAF service in May 1942. Fitted with a combination of a powerful AI Mk.IV radar and an impressive armament of four 20mm Hispano cannons and four 0.303 Browning Mk.II machine guns, the Mosquito packed quite a punch. After many frustrating patrols, the squadron's first Mosquito kill came on the night of 21st January 1943 when Flt Sgt B M Heigh and Sgt T Kipling shot down a Dornier Do 217 near Hartlepool.

Five days later, the last of the 410 Squadron's Beaufighters left Acklington, by now fully converted to the Mosquito Mk.II and on 21st

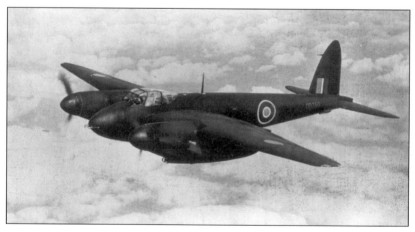

The de Havilland Mosquito Mk.II became the RAF's standard night-fighter during the mid war period and was operated by 410 Squadron RCAF at Acklington.

February the unit flew south to Coleby Grange in Lincolnshire.

Immediately, the defensive baton was handed to 409 RCAF Squadron on 23rd February, the second of Canada's night-fighter squadrons and once again equipped with the Beaufighter, although this time the Bristol Hercules powered Mk.VIF. With the lack of enemy activity at night the squadron was sent on a series of detachments that included Drem, Coleby Grange, and Peterhead. Ranger sorties were flown from Middle Wallop and Coltishall. They involved low-level daylight attacks on German airfields, and several 409 Squadron aircraft were lost on these dangerous raids. The unit temporarily moved to Coleby Grange in December but returned to Acklington to convert to the latest version of the Mosquito night-fighter, the Mk.XIII, in March 1944. Before becoming operational on this new mark, the squadron was moved south to Hunsdon on 1st March 1944.

The Typhoon Mk.Ib returned briefly to Acklington during February and March 1943. In preparing for operational readiness, 198 Squadron practised scrambles before moving to Manston in Kent in support of Westland Whirlwind operations. During this busy period the squadron managed to write off two aircraft: one crashed on landing and another made a forced landing near Radcliffe, south of Amble.

Acklington's northern location did not lend itself to operations undertaken by the USAAF. This is reflected in the fact that in its entire

409 Squadron received the Beaufighter Mk.VIF, but spent most of its time on detachment at several different airfields in the south of England. Note the aerial of the AI radar in the nose of the aircraft.

history the airfield housed only one American unit, and that just temporarily. The 416th Night Fighter (NF) Squadron was formed at Usworth on 14th May 1943 and was hastily equipped with the Bristol Beaufighter Mk.VI. The USAAF was severely lacking any kind of serious night-fighter units, and the 416th NF was one of several formed early in 1943. These new units relied heavily on the experience of the RAF and RCAF squadrons in this field, and all were trained by RAF Instructors, not only on the Beaufighter but night-fighting tactics as well. It was not unusual to see American aircraft in RAF markings, however the reverse was uncommon. The 416th arrived at Acklington on 10th June and along with the 414th, 415th and the 417th became one of the first units to complete its training. Protests from squadron commanders claimed that the American crews had not received sufficient training on the Beaufighter. Senior staff simply replied that they would gain the necessary experience in combat! The unit lost three Beaufighters in serious accidents while at Acklington and by 4th August the 416th NF Squadron had left for North Africa. Within days they were in combat as part of the 12th Air Force, eventually re-equipping with another British type, the Mosquito.

Since 1490 Flight's departure on 4th September 1942, Acklington had had no provision for a target towing unit or the facilities to service such aircraft. On 1st June 1943, a new unit, which was effectively a target towing flight, was formed under the name of No. 6 Anti-Aircraft Practice Camp, Acklington. Under the command of Flying Officer Copeland, the unit was re-designated 1630 Flight a few days later, on 17th June. It was another two weeks after its formation before the first aircraft arrived in the shape of four Westland Lysander TT.IIIs. The first practice target tow was carried out on 8th July, and within days 1630 Flt was flying co-operation exercises with the 416th NF Squadron. The airfield's station commander, Wg Cdr Graham, approached the flight on 18th July 1943 with a view to converting the station flight Miles Martinets to target tugs. This task involved the fitting of winches, cables and drogues to the Martinets, which would eventually supersede the ageing Lysander in the role.

The work of 1630 Flt was carried out with great efficiency and accidents were thankfully rare. However, one spectacular incident involving a Lysander did occur on 23rd July. On return from an air-firing sortie it was the normal procedure to release the target over the airfield so that the attacking pilot's score could be calculated quickly. Pilot Officer Finbow in Lysander TT.III T1747 was returning from one such sortie when, after a low pass, the target drogue caught on the roof of a Blister hangar. The Lysander was dragged to the ground, striking the edge of the perimeter track and smashing the port undercarriage leg to pieces. Incredibly, the towing cable broke free and Finbow was able to gain control and claw the Lysander back into the air. Finbow flew a circuit and carefully landed the Lysander on the surviving starboard undercarriage leg, keeping the wrecked one off the ground until the last second. At a relatively slow speed, the undercarriage dug in and the Lysander gently turned over on its back without injury to Finbow or the winch operator in the rear. Pilot Officer Finbow was eventually promoted and became the officer in command of 1630 Flt on 5th October 1943. The flight continued to serve all fighter units based at Acklington as well as 6 AAPC at Whitby and ground to air co-operation with RAF Regiment squadrons, including 2803 Sqn. The unit was dissolved into 219 Squadron on 30th November 1943. It was a unit that would return to Acklington in a completely different form.

The first all-Belgian fighter squadron was formed at Valley in November 1941. The unit was 350 Squadron, which visited Acklington twice during 1943 with Spitfire Mk.Vcs. The squadron had seen action while stationed at more southerly stations, but while in the North-East, the monotonous convoy patrols yielded very little contact with the

The Lysander was a common sight at airfields throughout the country and Acklington was no exception. 1630 Flight operated the TT.IIIA, very similar to this machine.

enemy. The squadron first arrived on 23rd March, then going a few miles south to Ouston, only to return for the last time on 20th July before leaving for Digby on 25th August 1943. The same day, the second Belgian fighter squadron to be formed replaced it.

349 Squadron arrived with the Spitfire Mk.Va and had only become operational on the type on 13th August at Digby before it was moved north to Acklington. Originally formed at Ikeja in Nigeria during 1942 with Curtiss Tomahawks, it saw little action, being relegated to ferrying fighter aircraft rather than fighting in them. 349 Squadron sent several detachments to Digby during its stay, re-equipping with the Spitfire Mk.Vb before its earlier equipment saw any action. The Belgian squadron left Acklington for Friston in Sussex on 22nd October 1943, and, like 350 Squadron, it still exists today within the modern Belgian Air Force, flying the F-16 Fighting Falcon.

The resident fighter squadron was taken over by a Polish unit on 22nd September. 316 'City of Warsaw' Squadron was not operational when it arrived with its Spitfire Mk.IXs. While at Acklington, the squadron re-equipped with the Spitfire Mk. LF Vb, but not long after the squadron's departure on 15th February 1944 the unit re-equipped again: this time with the North American Mustang Mk.III, an aircraft they would use until their disbandment in December 1946.

Delivery of new and refurbished aircraft was the responsibility of the Air Transport Auxiliary throughout the early years of the war. As

Two Belgian pilots of 350 Squadron pose in front of a Spitfire Mk.Vc at Acklington in 1943.

demand for fighter aircraft increased, however, four Aircraft Delivery Flights (ADF) were formed to support the work of the Air Transport Auxiliary (ATA). No.3 ADF arrived on 8th November 1943, only to be disbanded on 22nd November. No.4 ADF was first formed at Grangemouth in Stirlingshire on 13th April 1941 and was responsible for the re-supply and delivery of fighter aircraft throughout 13 and 14 Group. The flight arrived at Acklington on 25th November 1943, equipped with a Dominie, an Oxford, an Anson, a Defiant and a Mustang Mk.I, although this strength may have been increased by the addition of aircraft from No.3 ADF. As the demand for fighter aircraft in the north of the country subsided, No.4 ADF was transferred to 12 Group control, and a move to York followed on 8th March 1944.

On the night of 1st/2nd December 1943, 19 Stirlings and 12 Halifaxes were dispatched on Gardening operations. This involved dropping mines off the enemy coast, always a dangerous job, as the aircraft had to fly very low and slow over the sea, making them vulnerable to enemy flak and fighter defences. Three aircraft were lost on the raid and on their return several aircraft discovered that their home bases were fog bound. Several Stirlings from 75 Squadron, based at Mepal in Cambridgeshire, and Halifaxes of 466 Squadron, based at Leconfield in North Yorkshire, were diverted to Acklington. One particular Stirling Mk.III EH880, piloted by W/O G J S Kerr, was lining up with the main runway, when, possibly because he misjudged his approach to an unfamiliar airfield at night, the huge bomber undershot the runway, crashing into a farmhouse on the edge of Togston. Seven of the bomber's crew were killed instantly. Only the mid-upper gunner, Sgt K Hook, survived but with serious injuries. The farmhouse was occupied at the time and tragically five children were killed. Their mother and father were rescued from the rubble badly injured. This type of accident highlights how dangerous living near a busy airfield could be.

Acklington provided a safe haven for Bomber Command aircraft again on the morning of 3rd January 1944. Three hundred and eighty three aircraft took part in a disastrous raid on Berlin, losing 27 Lancasters in the process. Once again the weather had removed the option of landing at their home stations and at least 17 Lancasters found safety at Acklington.

25 Squadron had become one of the RAF's most successful night fighter squadrons and had become expert both in the operation of their equipment and tactics. Their current aircraft were the Mosquito NF.II and Mk.VI, both of which would be replaced at Acklington by the very last night variant, the Mosquito NF.XVII. The squadron arrived from

Church Fenton via a detachment in Cornwall on 19th December 1943. The NF.XVII was a conversion of the NF.II and it was the first Mosquito to be equipped with the American-built centrimetric radar. 25 Squadron was the first unit to receive the new mark and also to claim the first kill. Flt Lt J Singleton and Flt Lt G Haslam shot down three Junkers Ju 188s in one sortie over the River Humber on 19th March 1944. 25 Squadron was one of the longest users of the Mosquito, retaining it for nearly ten years in various marks. The squadron left for Coltishall on 5th February 1944, but would return to Acklington in peacetime.

The Spitfire Mk.Vb returned to Acklington again on 21st December 1943. 130 Squadron arrived from Scorton in Yorkshire purely to wind down and eventually disband. What was left of the squadron departed on 4th January 1944, returning to Scorton. Acklington was rapidly becoming a station for various squadrons to wind down, re-equip or re-organize. The latter applied to the airfield as well.

On 16th February 1944, Acklington became part of No.24 (Base) Defence Wing, housing the headquarters, which also controlled Drem in East Lothian. Simultaneously, the airfield was given the title No. 147 Airfield HQ; it operated within 24 Wing and controlled the resident 409 Squadron for night operations and eventually 322 Squadron, which would operate the Spitfire as day cover. These new titles were however short lived at Acklington: by March, 24 Wing moved to Newcastle, followed by 147 Airfield HQ, which moved to Zeals in Wiltshire on 11th May 1944.

Since arriving at Acklington, 409 Squadron had spent most of its time on detachments, taking part in many costly operations over occupied France. The squadron had worked their Beaufighters hard and on 5th February 1944 returned to Acklington to re-equip. The new aircraft was the Mosquito Mk. XIII which it would retain until the squadron disbanded on 1st July 1945. Acklington's longest wartime resident headed south for Hunsdon in Hertfordshire on 1st March, continuing its successful night fighter patrols into the heart of Germany.

The Hawker Typhoon briefly re-appeared during February and March 1944. 56 and 266 Squadrons brought their Typhoon Mk.Ibs on detachment, followed on 8th March by 164 Squadron, which had not long converted to the Typhoon from the Hurricane Mk.IV. All three of these squadrons made use of the good local range facilities to practice rocket projectile attacks. It was a method that the Typhoon would eventually excel at over northern France.

The Spitfire Mk.XIV had a new Griffon engine and a five-blade prop, which not only produced a new sound but even more performance. The Dutch 322 Squadron operated it from Acklington from early 1944.

It was no secret that the Allied invasion of Europe was not too distant, and the throughput of fighter squadrons reflected this, with an increase in squadrons passing through for a few weeks to hone their fighting skills in the relatively safe skies over the North-East. 222 Squadron arrived on 25th February in a non-operational state to carry out air-to-air firing exercises over the coastal ranges. Now operating the Spitfire Mk.IXb, the squadron suffered heavily during the Battle of Britain, at one point having only three serviceable aircraft available to the squadron. Departing on 10th March, they were immediately replaced by 322 Squadron, a Dutch squadron under the command of Major K C Kuhlmann DFC. The squadron was formed in June 1943 at Hornchurch with the Spitfire Mk.Vb, arriving at Acklington with the Mk.Vc. Their new equipment produced a new sound over the airfield, a Spitfire with a Rolls Royce Griffon engine. This powerful machine was the Mk.XIV, which had only entered service with 610 Squadron in January 1944. The Mk.XIV was intended for high altitude combat and was powered by 2,050hp Griffon 65 driving a large, five-blade Rotol propeller, a combination that produced a top speed of nearly 450 mph. The Griffon was longer than the Merlin; so the new Spitfire had a longer nose and a larger fin and rudder to compensate. 322 Squadron completed their conversion training on 24th April, departing for Hartford Bridge (Blackbushe) in Hampshire.

The airfield now fell unusually silent with no squadrons of any shape or form in residence. With D-Day approaching, plans began to upgrade Acklington with tarmac and asphalt runways and perimeter tracks, although one more unit did arrive at Acklington before reconstruction began. With all focus on the Normandy landings, it was realized that Tyneside had no fighter defence whatsoever. Even though any immediate threat had subsided, it was decided to send to Acklington a group of Typhoons of 'C' Flight, No.3 Tactical Exercise Unit, usually based at Honiley in Warwickshire. Arriving on 29th May 1944, the unit was given a temporary operational number of 555 Squadron during this period and operated the Mk.Ib. While operational squadrons massed in the south of England, 555 Squadron was kept on daily readiness but never scrambled during its time at Acklington. Unfortunately, the squadron lost one aircraft on a training sortie on 5th June, when Typhoon Mk.Ib R7822 caught fire and crashed near Long Newton-by-the-Sea, not far from Brunton airfield.

Work now began at Acklington, initially on three new runways, the longest being just under 2,000 yards. Laid out in a traditional 'A' pattern, they were linked by a perimeter track but no permanent dispersals were built around the edge, only temporary planking which would suffice to the war's end. Acklington would remain a practice camp airfield and so dispersals would have been seen as surplus to requirements in future years. 5022 Airfield Construction Squadron (ACS), one of twenty formed during the Second World War, carried out the bulk of the work. 5022 ACS was under the control of 5357 Airfield Construction Wing, which had its HQ at Jesmond Dene in Newcastle. Its area of responsibility not only covered Northumberland and Durham but stretched into North Yorkshire as well.

Construction on the airfield was complete by the end of November 1944, and the only aviation activity that occurred during that time was a few emergency landings. One of the more interesting visitors was a squadron of Royal Navy Chance Vought Corsairs, which took part in an Army exercise during December. The squadron was from HMS *Gannet*, otherwise known as Eglinton in Londonderry.

It was not until 26th February 1945 that a unit once familiar to the North-East was re-formed at Acklington. 59 OTU was disbanded into the Specialized Low Attack School and the Fighter Leaders School at Milfield on 26th January 1944. The unit was re-formed at half strength to train fighter-bomber pilots and its main equipment was the Typhoon Mk.Ib. Even at half strength, the unit had 54 Typhoons on charge, supported by the Miles Master Mk.II, Martinet Mk.I and a Percival Proctor. Usually OTU aircraft have seen quite a lot of action before being relegated to training duties. All of the Typhoons used by 59 OTU were brand new, having been delivered from the makers in January 1945. They were not destined to see a lot of use at Acklington either; only one course was completed before 59 OTU was disbanded for a second and final time on 6th June 1945.

The Station Commander of Acklington who saw the airfield move from war to peace was Wg Cdr G W Gordon Willie Petre. He had been a pilot with 19 Squadron in 1940. It was a particularly poignant moment for him when his old squadron arrived at Acklington on 23rd May 1945. The squadron had gained a very impressive war record and was now equipped with the North American Mustang Mk.IV, the RAF equivalent of the USAAF P-51D, possibly the greatest American-built fighter of the war. Under the command of Sqn Ldr P J Hearne, the squadron had a busy tour at Acklington that did not go without loss. During a practice interception over the North Sea on 12th June, Flt Lts Clayton and Young had to descend through cloud. After coming out of the cloud, Clayton found himself alone, and Young was never seen again. His Mustang Mk.IV KH897 was spotted by the crew of a

Norwegian ship, who saw an aircraft dive into the sea and explode. A second Mustang was lost eight days later when it flew into high ground in fog near Berwick; the pilot, Flt Lt Robson was killed. At the end of July, the squadron took part in an exercise with the Royal Navy. Six Mustangs simulated strafing HMS *Glasgow* to give their anti-aircraft gunners some practice. The squadron left for Bradwell Bay in Essex on 13th August, re-equipping a few weeks later with the Spitfire Mk.XVIe. With this in mind, it may not be a coincidence that Mustang Mk.IV KH642 was left behind at Acklington and used by station flight.

The immediate post-war years saw many changes within the RAF: not only a steady reduction in personnel and aircraft but also an unsettled period of reorganization for the airfields. While the majority closed, Acklington's future looked bright, and, during 1945, the airfield became a forward airfield in the new Newcastle Sector, which had its headquarters at Blacklaw in Newcastle. The intention was that Acklington would house one day-fighter squadron and one night-fighter squadron. The latter role was taken on by 219 Squadron on 14th August 1945, a squadron that was already familiar with the area, having previously served at Acklington in 1942 with Beaufighters. It was now equipped with the Mosquito NF.XXX, which was fitted with Rolls Royce Merlin 76 engines, giving a high altitude capability of up to 39,000ft. The squadron moved several times on detachments to Lubeck in Germany and Spilsby in Lincolnshire before departing for Wittering in Northamptonshire on 1st May 1946.

263 Squadron became the day squadron, equipped with the first jet to arrive at Acklington, the Gloster Meteor F.3. Their stay was brief, as

263 Squadron brought the first jet to Acklington in early 1946 in the shape of the Gloster Meteor F.3.

they had departed for Church Fenton in Yorkshire by 2nd April 1946. They returned again in 1949 and 1950, having re-equipped with the Meteor F.4 and then again with the Meteor F.8.

The airfield's original role was reinstated on 1st May 1946. Acklington became No.2 Armament Practice Station, a title transferred from Spilsby. This was changed to the Fighter Armaments Trials Unit (FATU) in November 1946 and remained so until disbandment in July 1956. The FATU employed many different aircraft for target towing duties during its ten-year stay at Acklington. They included the traditional Master and Martinet, plus, in later years, several converted Mosquitos, which proved very capable target tugs.

Another variant of the adaptable Mosquito returned with 29 Squadron on 26th February 1947. The Mosquito NF.36 was the penultimate version of this most successful night fighter and, apart from a brief period with the Mosquito NF.30, would become the last piston aircraft used by the squadron and the RAF's first jet night-fighter.

Fighter squadrons of the RAF and RCAF made use of Acklington's excellent facilities for air-to-air firing practice. When this came to an end, Acklington was elevated to a front line fighter station and its first occupant was 29 Squadron with the Armstrong Whitworth Meteor NF.11, on 14th January 1957. During its stay, the squadron re-equipped twice, firstly in November 1957 with the Gloster Javelin FAW.6 and then again in February 1958 with the Meteor NF.12. On 22nd July 1958 the squadron departed for Leuchars in Fife, bringing an end to night-fighter operations from the airfield.

One of the most attractive jet fighters ever designed provided the day fighter cover at Acklington when 66 Squadron arrived on 14th February 1957 with the Hawker Hunter F.6. The squadron took part in several detachments to the Middle East during its stay, but, on 30th September 1960, 66 Squadron was disbanded as a fighter squadron. Acklington's fighter days were finally over, but the arrival of 6 Flying Training School (FTS) on 4th August 1961 kept the flying alive. Initially Percival Piston Provost T.1s were used, but these were quickly replaced by the Hunting Jet Provost, which operated from the airfield until its disbandment on 30th June 1968. During its time at Acklington, 6 FTS used both Ouston and Boulmer as Relief Landing Grounds (RLG).

Helicopters were destined to become the last aircraft that would operate from Acklington. 18 Squadron moved in from Gütersloh in Germany on 5th January 1968 with the Westland Wessex HC.2, leaving Odiham on 8th August 1969. 'B' Flight of 202 Squadron was the local

It seems incredible that such a busy airfield, rich with history can disappear. This lone pillbox is one of the few indications of its existence. (Author).

search and rescue flight and had been located at Acklington since 1957. One of the flight's Whirlwinds was written off near Acklington in spectacular style on 16th April 1967. Whirlwind HAR.10 XK990 suffered an engine failure during landing practice a quarter of a mile north of the airfield. After hitting the ground heavily, the rotors flexed to such an extent that the tail of the helicopter was sliced clean off! With 18 Squadron's departure, the flight's Westland Whirlwind HAR.10s were the only aircraft to be seen at Acklington and, like so many other RAF airfields at that time, Acklington would become a victim of Government cuts.

The Whirlwinds moved to Boulmer in early 1972 and Acklington was placed in a state of Care and Maintenance before its rapid rundown and closure later in the year. The old airfield was purchased immediately by the Home Office, which quickly converted the site into a Category 'C' prison, opened a year later. The airfield itself did not survive for much longer, becoming an open cast mine, which has now removed all trace of a very busy station. Acklington as an airfield has been effectively removed from the map and anyone visiting the site today will discover a solitary pillbox as the only connection with a military past. While many disused airfields throughout the country leave behind some memory of its existence, Acklington can only hope that present-day historians continue to record the events that happened there for future generations to appreciate.

3
BOULMER

Boulmer had a rather inauspicious career during the Second World War; despite this it is the only remaining active RAF Station recorded within this book. Re-opened in 1953 as an Air Defence Centre, radar station, it was later re-designated as a Group Control Centre, becoming responsible for the radar at Buchan (Scotland) and Killard Point (Northern Ireland). It continued to be developed into a Sector Operations Centre and served at the front line of detection of Soviet aircraft during the Cold War.

Back in 1940, several Luftwaffe bomber units based in Norway were causing havoc around the area. They were not only targeting industry but also local airfields such as Acklington, which had proved to be a thorn in the side of the enemy attackers.

A decoy airfield was needed and a location was chosen just inland and south-west of the village of Boulmer, ten miles north of Acklington. A typical decoy airfield had runways painted onto the grass, dummy aircraft parked all around and a limited number of mock buildings. Usually manned by a few resident airmen, whenever a potential attack materialized, the mock airfield could be lit in order to draw in the enemy bombers. By the time this site was completed, Acklington would have become very familiar to the enemy and consequently there were very few deliberate attacks on the Boulmer decoy. On the night of 16th/17th September 1940, the decoy was hit by a pair of HE (High Explosive) bombs, which damaged a nearby cottage. The airfield came close to being bombed on 3rd June 1941. An enemy plane apparently passed low over the airfield but chose to bomb and machine-gun the village instead.

The neighbouring coast near Boulmer lent itself perfectly for the location of an aerial gunnery range, first used by aircraft of 4 Air Gunners School (AGS) in early 1942. The Morpeth-based unit's Lysanders and Bothas also made use of their own permanent range near Amble to the south. On 18th August 1942, Lysander TT.III T1506 piloted by Flying Officer Carter was towing a target during an aerial gunnery exercise. The 'attacking' aircraft was Botha I W5155, which misjudged its approach to the target drogue, striking the cable in the process. The twin-engined crew trainer stood no chance, plunging into the sea off Boulmer, with all five crew lost. The Lysander, with its airframe damaged, managed to crash-land near Boulmer. Flying Officer Carter was trapped in the wreckage and was subsequently rescued by his target tow operator, A.C. Dickinson.

Twelve miles to the south of Boulmer, Eshott became the home of 57 Operational Training Unit (OTU), which arrived from Hawarden in Cheshire. This was a very large unit, which quickly overwhelmed Eshott with its Spitfire Mk.Is and Mk.IIs, Master Mk.Is, Master Mk.IIIs and 6 Fairey Battle Target Tugs, all of which made full use of Boulmer's facilities.

The decoy site at Boulmer was the prime candidate to become the satellite airfield for Eshott and was quickly pressed into use as a Relief Landing Ground (RLG). RLGs could only take so much aerial activity; so it was quickly arranged that Boulmer should be upgraded to a

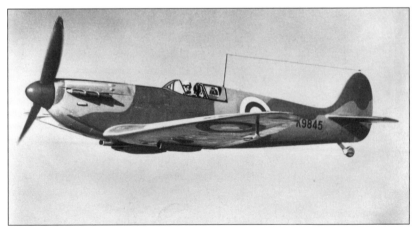

The first resident aircraft at Boulmer were the Spitfires of 57 OTU. This Mk.I would have been a common sight.

standard three tarmac-runway layout, complete with 25 hardstandings, perimeter tracks and temporary accommodation for over 700 officers and airmen.

With great pressure to finish Boulmer because of the amount of aircraft operating from Eshott, the airfield was officially taken over by 57 OTU as its satellite airfield on 1st March 1943. The unit's Advanced Training Squadron was the first to make use of Boulmer's new tarmac runways, followed by a flight of Miles Masters. The latter were used as a stepping stone conversion to single-seat fighters, and congestion began to subside at Eshott.

The sky around Boulmer, however, quickly became congested and mid-air collisions were always an associated risk. A pair of 57 OTU's Spitfires were practising dog-fighting skills on 10th July 1943. An inevitable collision took place off Boulmer; Spitfire IIa P8071 suffered the worse fate – it crashed into the sea – while Spitfire IIa P7836 managed to crash land on Boulmer airfield. Between November 1943 and February 1945 a further 13 Spitfires of various marks from 57 OTU crashed on or near the airfield. The nature of operational training made this rate of attrition acceptable.

Although never officially recognized as such, Boulmer was used by 4 AGS as a forward operating base. Ground crew from the AGS were in residence from early 1943 through to September 1944 when the unit disbanded. The Lysanders and Bothas would be turned around at Boulmer, refuelled and re-armed ready for exercises at the Amble and Boulmer ranges.

The ubiquitous Miles Master operated out of Boulmer with both 57 and 59 OTU. This prototype of the Mk.III was the first of over 600 built.

Milfield, to the north, suffered the same congestion problems as Eshott, and on many occasions during 1943 and 1944 Hurricanes and Masters from 59 OTU also used Boulmer.

With regard to airfield defence, Boulmer was well protected by the usual Anti-Aircraft Units and resident RAF Regiment Squadron. The airfield was also the home of 9 Group Battle School, whose task was to train airmen for the defence of the north-west coast. The local fields and beaches offered a perfect terrain for training, and the sound of gunfire could be heard continually through to the school's departure after D-Day in June 1944.

Visits from Fleet Air Arm fighter squadrons were rare and, although 808 Squadron only stayed at Boulmer for a single day, it is worthy of mention. The unit operated the Seafire L.III, the naval version of the Spitfire, and arrived at Boulmer from Hawarden in Cheshire on 25th September 1944. It is possible that this is the only time a Seafire squadron used an airfield in the North-East in any capacity, and by the following day the unit had left for Eglinton in Northern Ireland.

The largest recorded aircraft ever to land at Boulmer arrived on 4th October 1944. Handley Page Halifax B.III LW590 diverted to the airfield after returning from a successful raid against the U-Boat pens in Bergen. The Halifax belonged to 425 (Alouette) Squadron RCAF, based at Tholthorpe, 16 miles north of York. On departure at approximately 15:10 hours, with Pilot Officer W D Corbett at the controls, the Halifax began to roll down the runway. At a critical moment, both starboard engines cut, sending the bomber into an uncontrollable swing. The Halifax struck a shed used for storing wood and was destined never to fly again. No one onboard was hurt and a local Maintenance Unit eventually dismantled the aircraft.

57 OTU remained at Boulmer until its disbandment on 6th June 1945. Eshott was also being closed down; so Boulmer was placed under Care and Maintenance, becoming a satellite for Acklington. The latter briefly became the home to 2 APS (Armament Practice Station) and some of this unit's more unusual aircraft, including an Albemarle and Mustang IV, used Boulmer for circuits.

Still retained by the Air Ministry, Boulmer was re-activated in 1953, having been chosen as an Air Defence Control Centre. A new site for this complex collection of buildings was chosen, next to the B1339 north of Lesbury. Within a year the building was completed and the station officially re-opened as 500 Signals Unit.

The airfield's runways were in sufficiently good condition for use by 6 Flying Training School (FTS), which moved to Acklington on July

1961. Boulmer became a Relief Landing Ground (RLG) for the Jet Provosts of the FTS until the unit's disbandment in 1968.

'B' Flight of 202 Squadron, with the Westland Whirlwind HAR.4, had originally moved to Boulmer in 1972 after Acklington's closure but never made Boulmer its permanent home. The airfield's first

Modern-day equipment at Boulmer is the Westland Sea King HAR.3 operated by 202 Squadron.

permanent flying unit arrived in 1978 in the shape of 'A' Flight of 202 Squadron with the Westland Whirlwind HAR.10. 'A' Flight re-equipped with the more capable Westland Sea King HAR.3 in 1979 and continues to operate this highly efficient and safe helicopter today. 'A' Flight provides search and rescue for a vast area which stretches through northern England, southern Scotland and the Lake District, and as far as the Norwegian coast. The Flight's aircrew have received many awards over the years, including a George Medal. The Flight was called to the Alexander Kielland platform in March 1980 after it capsized and it was also involved in the tragic Piper Alpha fire in July 1988.

Boulmer is now the home of the School of Fighter Control and is one of the control and reporting centres in the UK ASACS (Air Surveillance and Control System). Its future at Boulmer is in doubt, as a move to Scampton in Lincolnshire looks like a distinct possibility in 2006.

Boulmer's layout is very unusual because the station is divided into two modern camps, neither of which encroaches on or utilises the flying area of the wartime airfield. Large sections of the runways and perimeter track remain, all best viewed from the minor road that joins Lesbury and Boulmer. This road follows the line of the eastern perimeter track, and another minor road, that leads to Seaton Point and Marmouth Scars, was also part of the wartime airfield.

The original airfield was accessed from the Long Houghton/Boulmer road and this is the location of 202 Squadron and its Sea King helicopters. The helicopter station is a self-contained RAF camp, complete with its own hangar, tower, technical and domestic buildings, and like ASACS is surrounded by a very high secure fence. Behind this fence, a connection with the Cold War role of the airfield is represented by a 56 Squadron Phantom FGR.2.

4
BRUNTON

Positioned nine miles north of Alnwick, the location for an airfield near to the village of Brunton seems rather isolated. However, with links to the Great North Road and the main east coast railway line, Brunton was not as inaccessible as it appears at first sight.

Aviation in the immediate area can be traced back to the First World War, as a small airship station was constructed at Chathill, a few miles to the north-west. It was under the control of the much larger airship station at East Fortune in Lothian until 1920, when the site was abandoned.

Construction of the new airfield began in mid 1941, with 600 acres of land being requisitioned for the site stretching north of Brunton across to the small village of Tughall. Simultaneously a Q decoy site was constructed six miles to the north, near the village of Elford. The threat of invasion was still a possibility up until 1943, when military advisers steadily began to see the tide of war go in their favour.

Work on the airfield was briefly disrupted on 6th September 1941 with the unannounced arrival of a 10 Squadron Whitley Mk.V. The aircraft, Z6932, was on air test from its home base of Leeming, Yorkshire when the crew became lost in bad visibility following a failure of their navigational instruments. With the plane low on fuel, the pilot, Flt Sgt W Stuart RCAF had been attempting to find Acklington. Soldiers from a nearby searchlight unit ran over to the crew and gave them instructions to follow the railway line south to find Acklington. The Whitley promptly taxied to the end of one of the completed runways and took off in a southerly direction. The aircraft was airborne only briefly, when it struck a steamroller, causing the nose to rise sharply. Out of control, the Whitley careered through some high-tension cables before hitting the ground and bursting into flames. With ammunition going off and fuel tanks about to explode, local

69

workmen and the same soldiers from the searchlight unit rushed to the scene, managing to rescue the tail gunner, Sgt. Whitlock, who was the only survivor.

In direct response to this unfortunate accident, the airfield contractors blocked all of the runways with oil barrels and various obstacles. Less than two weeks later, a Hurricane made a wheels-up landing near to Brunton, the pilot complaining he could not land on the airfield because the runways were blocked!

Construction of the airfield was disrupted again on the night of 1st September 1941, although this time by the enemy. A force of 25 long-range bombers attacked a variety of targets throughout Northumberland and Durham with specific attention paid to Newcastle. The attack lasted for only an hour and the relatively small force caused considerable damage throughout the area. At 23:05 hrs Brunton was singled out by an enemy bomber, which managed to drop eight high explosive (HE) and several incendiary bombs (IB) onto the middle of the airfield. They were dropped in a line 230 yards long; one of the HEs caught the side of a runway with the remainder falling in open ground. Luckily there were no casualties and no serious damage was caused.

Brunton was built in a traditional triangular pattern with two short runways of 1,100 yards and a main runway of 1,600 yards in length. Accommodation was only temporary and, by the end of June 1942, the airfield was ready for use.

The first occupants of Brunton were the Hurricanes of 59 OTU. This is an example of a Hurricane Mk.I.

On 2nd August, 59 OTU, equipped mainly with Hurricanes, moved from Crosby-on-Eden, Cumbria to Milfield, and, simultaneously, the latter became the parent airfield of Brunton. Two days later, 17 Hurricanes arrived from Longtown, Cumbria (Crosby's satellite), beginning their first training sorties the following day.

59 OTU was earmarked to become the main training unit for the Hawker Typhoon.

The Miles Martinet replaced the Lysander as the primary target towing aircraft for the majority of OTUs.

As mentioned earlier, the threat of invasion was always in the minds of the military planners. One contingency plan was called the *Saracen Scheme*, a method of quickly converting OTUs into fighter squadrons. In 59 OTU's case, the unit would become 559 Sqn and in the event of an invasion could be quickly re-allocated to a different airfield, in this case, Woolsington. The title of 559 Sqn was actually used at Brunton in March 1943, briefly transferring to Milfield and later returning to Brunton as an independent squadron flying the night fighter variant for the Hurricane on 7th July.

59 OTU had been operating the Hurricane since it began flying training in March 1941. However, the unit was earmarked to become the main OTU for the Hawker Typhoon. The transition between the two fighters was very slow because of early teething problems with the Typhoon. By May 1943, the big Hawker fighter began to arrive at Milfield and in turn started to use Brunton's facilities as well.

Aircraft movements at Brunton were very high and the condition of the airfield began to reflect this in the summer of 1943. Contractors began to make repairs without causing any major disruption to the training programme. Considering how busy the airfield was, accidents involving aircraft of 59 OTU were unusually rare. Only four Hurricanes were written off, with only one of a serious nature. Hurricane Mk.I W9121 was returning from a night navigation exercise on 27th March 1943 when the aircraft struck some trees on approach. The fighter hit the ground and overturned, seriously injuring the pilot. Brunton provided a relatively safe location for the ferry pilot of a Boulton Paul Defiant to crash land on 15th October. Defiant Mk.I N1635 suffered an engine failure; the pilot was able to crash land the aircraft on the airfield, wrecking the aircraft beyond repair.

59 OTU was disbanded on 26th January 1944 and was absorbed into No.1 Specialized Attack Instructors' School, which in turn was absorbed into the Fighter Leaders' School (FLS). Brunton remained a satellite, but the majority of FLS operations were flown from Milfield.

57 OTU, based at Eshott and Boulmer, was also active in the area, and on 17th March 1944 the emergency services from Brunton were involved with one of the unit's Spitfires. Two aircraft, Spitfire Mk.I X4595 and Spitfire Mk.I R6596, were practising dog-fighting techniques when one of the aircraft misjudged its attack and they collided high over the village of Wandylaw. X4595 came down on Hepburn Moor while R6596, under partial control, managed to crash land near to Brunton, where the airfield's rescue team attended the scene quickly and efficiently. If the option was available to crash land near an airfield

or military base, help was never far away, increasing your chances of survival!

The airfield was quiet for much of 1944, although the FLS did use Brunton for refuelling and re-arming exercises as well as using the airfield as a miniature bombing range. Later in the year, Milfield received another unit, 56 OTU, which had been disbanded in October 1943 and was re-formed on 15th December 1944 with over 130 Typhoons, Tempests, Masters and support aircraft on strength. Brunton was first used by 56 OTU in January 1945 for its Typhoon and Tempest operations, as it would have been impossible to operate effectively from one airfield despite the fact that the FLS had left Milfield at the end of 1944.

The powerful Hawker Tempest Mk.V was a fairly common sight at Brunton during the last few months of the Second World War. The Tempest Mk.V was one of the fastest aircraft operated by the RAF during the last year of the war. A vastly improved development of its predecessor, the Typhoon, the aircraft first entered service in April 1944. It proved to be a very effective fighter both in the ground-attack and high-altitude combat role. It also excelled, because of its impressive

Brunton remains virtually intact with many buildings remaining, including this air raid shelter, one of many around the airfield's perimeter. The Coastal Emitter Site can be seen in the distance on the right-hand side of the photograph. (Author)

73

speed, at chasing and destroying the V-1 Flying Bomb. Capable of nearly 430 mph, the Tempest laid claim to shooting down 638 of the 1,771 flying bombs destroyed by RAF fighters.

All aircraft operated by 56 OTU at Brunton were training pilots in their last stage of the course syllabus; so that may explain why only one incident involving a Tempest occurred on the airfield. On 9th April 1945, a Tempest V EJ845 swung on take-off and left the runway, destroying the windsock in the process. Sadly, Flt Lt I W Smith RCAF, an experienced pilot, was killed. A few weeks later, all OTU operations

An aerial view of Brunton shows how complete this disused airfield is. All three runways, perimeter track and the majority of 'pan handle' dispersals are intact. The airfield is best viewed from the railway bridge which crosses the main line (see lower left-hand side of the photograph). (Crown Copyright)

came to a conclusion at Brunton and a very swift closure of the airfield came at the end of May 1945.

Aviation has since returned to Brunton, which remains virtually intact with most of the main runway still in use. Light aircraft operate occasionally from Brunton and the Border Parachute Centre has made the old wartime airfield its home.

The best way to view Brunton is probably from a railway bridge, accessible via a wartime road on the western side of the airfield. From this viewpoint, it's easy to imagine wartime aircraft operating, and the line of air raid shelters that can be seen are in excellent condition. In the distance several period buildings remain, the majority being utilized by the local farm, which owns the bulk of the site.

In 2002, a large coastal emitter site was built at Brunton, encased in a camouflaged dome. The site is under the control of RAF Spadeadam, which is located on the edge of Wark and Kielder Forests. The radar provides aircrews with an electronically controlled area off the Northumbrian coast where they can practise manoeuvres and tactics, specifically involving the use of chaff and flare. A typical military sign with a red border tentatively indicates the presence of the military after an absence of 57 years.

5
ESHOTT

Since the first prototype took to the skies in 1936, the Spitfire has become an iconic aircraft, which remains as strong in people's minds today as it did in the Second World War. Admittedly promoted by many British propaganda films, it was not until 1941 that the Spitfire began to take on the role as a 'war winner', continually out-classing its main opponents as the aircraft was developed. The majority of pilots who joined the RAF from 1938 wanted to fly it, although the thought of fighting and surviving in it crossed few of their minds.

All potential single-seat fighter pilots underwent a rigorous training programme, which usually began at a Flying Training School with students cutting their teeth on de Havilland Tiger Moths followed by Miles Magisters. Many young airmen trained in the USA, Canada and later South Africa, usually learning their skills on the North American Harvard. If successful, the pilot would then be posted to an Operational Training Unit (OTU), which would be equipped with Miles Masters and the type the fighter pilot would eventually fly, which in Eshott's case was the Spitfire. On arrival at the OTU, the training was just as relentless until the day that the individual pilot was posted to a front line squadron.

A site for an airfield at Eshott was first surveyed in early in 1941, initially intended as another fighter station for the protection of the North-East. The location was very accessible, as the Great North Road ran along the western boundary. The rest of the airfield was located between the villages of West Thirston to the north and Eshott to the south-east. A close proximity to the already established airfield at Acklington meant that disciplined air traffic control was imperative to avoid mid-air collisions. Even while under construction, Eshott drew the attention of the enemy. On the night of 11th/12th May, bombs landed nearby, followed by another raid in the early hours of 25th May 1941. An enemy bomber just missed the part-built airfield with a line of high explosive and incendiary bombs which stretched almost as far as neighbouring RAF Acklington.

Construction began in early 1942, and, as the war progressed, the role for Eshott was downgraded to training. Three runways were constructed in the usual triangular pattern, although the main runway, at over 1,900 yards in length, was more than sufficient and could quite easily operate larger, bomber type aircraft. Accommodation was classed as temporary, but there was plenty of it, with numerous Nissen huts which could accommodate nearly 2,000 officers and airmen. The luxury of a T1 hangar was added plus eight Blister hangars, which could accommodate a pair of fighters, making maintenance more comfortable for the engineers.

Eshott's close proximity to Acklington helped a pilot of a Lysander of 4 AGS make an emergency landing on the part-built airfield on 1st October 1942. Although usually based at Morpeth, the Lysanders had been visiting Acklington and only minutes after take off the engine of Lysander TT.III T1521 failed. This particular aircraft had a busy career

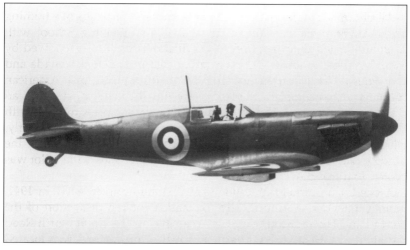

57 OTU spent nearly three years at Eshott, operating several different marks of Spitfire the entire time. This particular aircraft is Mk.I K9787, the first production Spitfire built.

and was eventually written off while serving with 8 AGS at Evanton in Ross-shire.

With work still to be carried out on the airfield, the first and main unit to operate from Eshott began to arrive on 10th November 1942. 57 OTU was formed at Hawarden, Flintshire (now in Clywd) on 1st November 1940 to train single-seat fighter pilots using the Miles Master and Supermarine Spitfire. A re-shuffle of units resulted in 41 OTU, which trained pilots in the role of tactical reconnaissance, moving from Old Sarum in Wiltshire to Hawarden. Eshott was the only airfield available at such short notice, and it fell far short of what the unit had been used to at its Welsh home.

57 OTU had a good cross-section of aircraft, including Spitfire Mk.Is and IIs, Master Is and IIIs, plus three Fairey Battle TT Mk.Is. The Battles were employed by the unit for target towing duties over the local aerial ranges. The TT Mk.I was the last production variant of the ill-fated three-seat light bomber and many remained in service until 1943 when the Miles Martinet replaced them. With over 100 aircraft on strength, life and operations were quite cramped until Boulmer became the airfield's satellite on 1st March 1943. This not only eased the amount of traffic in the circuit but also meant that certain stages of the training syllabus could be carried out at the satellite.

Because of the rate of development of the Spitfire, there was always a good supply of early marks available for use by the OTUs. Virtually all had seen action, many in the Battle of Britain and all had served with a multiple of units. For example, Spitfire Mk.I L1028 was built in June 1939 and served with five front line squadrons and four OTUs. It was later converted to a Mk.Va before being unceremoniously overturned and wrecked at Eshott on 21st April 1945. Many early marks did not last as long as this once assigned to an OTU.

Despite being obsolete, the Spitfire Mk.I was a perfect introduction to the challenges of flying a single-seat fighter. Powered by a Rolls Royce Merlin producing over 1,000 hp, this ground-breaking aircraft was capable of speeds in excess of 350 mph. By the end of the war, the Spitfire had matured into an aircraft with nearly twice the power and a top speed of over 450 mph. By late 1940, the improved Mk.II entered service, and, less than three months later, the Mk.V was introduced, each mark becoming more powerful as the design improved. It was these three marks that equipped the majority of fighter OTUs and 57 OTU in particular had a large throughput of Spitfires with many of them ending their flying careers in Northumberland.

On arrival at any fighter OTU, the student pilot spent many weeks undergoing a variety of ground instructions and aviation related subjects without stepping into an aeroplane. 'Bull' was high at Eshott, typical of a training station. An average course lasted three months and, although the pilots were introduced to the Spitfire while on the ground, many tests and exams had to be taken before that first magical flight could take place.

Ground studies included exercises in survival and making good your escape if you had to bail out over enemy territory. An escape kit was issued that was packed with a host of ingenious items. They included several different compasses, a bar of soap that contained a very efficient hacksaw, maps and a high quality 'Commando' style dagger. Traditional 'Teddy Bear' fur-flying boots were replaced with fur-lined boots, complete with leather soles. The top part of the boot was designed to be cut off, producing a more civilian looking shoe that drew less attention to the owner when in enemy territory. The survival pack included 'iron rations' in very thin tins, aspirins, bandages and water treatment tablets, which made the water almost undrinkable, but would keep you alive. Plastic bags filled with sulphanilamide were also included in the kit; the theory was that these would protect and help heal burned hands.

Physical survival training was carried out at Eshott by a detachment of Commandos. They taught the aircrew the art of survival, camouflage and several ways of crossing a river, for the latter making use of the local Longdike Burn.

Spitfire Mk.IIa P8437 of 57 OTU pictured at Eshott. This particular aircraft served with six different units before being struck off charge in November 1944.

79

Before any flight took place, the student pilots had to work through five broad sections of the course; these were as follows: Knowledge of Spitfires, Handling the radio, Cockpit drill and Emergency procedures, Oxygen system on Spitfires, and Readiness to fly Spitfires. With regard to the oxygen system, a decompression chamber was used at Eshott. Even the Spitfire Mk.I was capable of reaching 34,000ft; so it was essential that oxygen drills were learnt. One of the most important exercises on the course was to show the students the effects on the body when oxygen failure occurs. This was done by placing a group in the decompression chamber, half with oxygen masks on, the other half without. Air was pumped out of the chamber to simulate an increase in altitude. Those without masks began to show the effects by becoming very self-confident, with the slightest thing making individuals laugh and giggle for no apparent reason. Simple tests involving writing with a pen and combing their hair at the same time were set. As altitude increased, hair was combed with pens and messages were written with combs! This exercise was one of the most important on the course and drove home the importance of checking personal and aircraft oxygen equipment.

Usually three to four weeks into the course, the trainee pilot was allowed to fly a Spitfire. The final check out and flying test were carried out with an instructor in one of the unit's Miles Masters; the luxury of a two-seater Spitfire was not available until 1948! Only once the instructor was satisfied would the student be allowed to take the controls of a Spitfire.

Once in the air, the Spitfire was a truly phenomenal performer and those first flights must have been an amazing experience for many, fulfilling the dream of a lifetime. On the ground, the Spitfire could be quite difficult to handle, mainly because of its design. With its long nose, which removed all forward vision because of the tail dragger design of the fighter, the aircraft could only be taxied by swinging from side to side. Only once the tail had lifted during the take-off run could the pilot see over the nose and from that point all criticism of the aircraft disappeared. The controls were light and positive and the stable design meant that hands and feet could be removed from the controls without the machine plunging out of control. With an impressive rate of climb, top speed and good handling qualities on landing, the jump from a Master to a Spitfire must have surprised many young pilots.

The course now progressed to actually fighting in a Spitfire and pairs of students were encouraged to practise dog-fighting tactics both at high and low altitudes between themselves, sometimes resulting in fatal aerial collisions. Aerial gunnery was practised against targets towed by the unit's Battles and Martinets as well as 4 AGS Lysanders which provided this service to any unit operating in the area. Bombing skills were also honed both on ground and sea targets; once again, misjudged attacks resulted in many pilots being lost.

With Acklington in such close proximity to the airfield, it was not uncommon to receive visitors, some planned and others mistaking Eshott for its older neighbour. Eshott's emergency services were also called upon to deal with accidents from Acklington as well as their own. The 416th Night Fighter Squadron USAAF was formed at Acklington with the Beaufighter Mk.VI, a very capable aircraft that did take some getting used to. On 4th August 1943, Lt Jack L Brewer was returning to Acklington from a practice sortie when one of the aircraft's Hercules engines burst into flames. Beaufighter Mk.VI KV904 was quickly engulfed in flames and Brewer had no time to escape before the big fighter dived into the ground one mile west of Eshott.

57 OTU averaged two fatalities a month, with at least four to five aircraft damaged or written off in accidents. The latter also includes the loss of six Miles Masters, all of which were described by Training Command as 'acceptable losses'.

The remains of 1st Lt Anthony L. Serapiglia's P-47D after the mid-air collision on 12th April 1944.

Spitfire Mk.IIa P7350 is the oldest airworthy example of its type in the world. 57 OTU was its last unit; today it is operated by the Battle of Britain Memorial Flight at Coningsby in Lincolnshire.

The instructors who were posted to Eshott had a great deal of experience, many in combat and several during the Battle of Britain. It has been suggested that many of these individuals resented being on a training unit and were always itching to get back to a front line squadron. This may have been the case, but their experience and knowledge was invaluable, and it was essential that it was passed onto and 'drummed' into these potential fighter pilots.

The majority of OTUs had a large spread of nationalities, Eshott being no exception. As well as the British, pilots arrived from Canada, Australia, Poland, France, Czechoslovakia and Norway.

It was a Norwegian pilot who was tragically killed in a dramatic aerial collision over the airfield on 12th April 1944. A flight of four Republic P-47s stationed at Milfield was carrying out a simulated dive bombing and strafing attack on a military convoy that was travelling along the Great North Road south of Felton. Colonel Glenn E. Duncan, who witnessed the accident, was leading the flight. The group had split into pairs and Duncan noticed that the other two aircraft had strayed very close to the edge of Eshott. Duncan only spotted the Spitfire at the moment of collision, unable to warn either aircraft. 1st Lt Anthony L. Serapiglia, the pilot of P-47D 42-25530, had no chance of avoiding Sgt Kai Ather Knajenhjelm, aged only 19, who in Spitfire Mk.I R6762 was completely oblivious to the American fighter. They collided head on at only 800ft. The Spitfire entered an inverted spin while the P-47 lost a wing and plunged earthbound, disintegrating on impact. The incident was later blamed on inaccurate maps that did not even show the existence of the aerodrome and a policy was introduced whereby such exercises should be conducted in 'local flying areas', away from airfields.

As mentioned earlier, the rate of attrition was incredibly high at Eshott, but as always there were a few exceptions to the rule. Two Spitfires in particular still survive today. Spitfire Mk.Ia R6915 arrived on 57 OTU's strength on 13th June 1943. R6915 served with distinction throughout the Battle of Britain, and in the hands of Pilot Officer N le C. Agazarian and Flying Officer J Dundas had a Bf 109, a He 111 and a Bf 110 to its credit. On 21st September 1943, the Spitfire was damaged in a flying accident at Eshott; then after repair it was transferred between several Maintenance Units before arriving at the Imperial War Museum in London on 28th August 1946. R6915 survives today and is suspended from the ceiling of the museum by cables.

Another survivor is Spitfire Mk.IIa P7350, the oldest airworthy example in the world. After surviving several skirmishes with Bf 109s during the Battle of Britain, P7350 passed through several units unscathed before arriving at Eshott on 31st March 1944. On 22nd April 1944, while lined up on the end of Eshott's main runway, another Spitfire taxied into P7350. Then began an epic journey of repairs before it was sold to a scrap merchant called John Dale & Co. Luckily, the Spitfire was donated back to the RAF in 1967 and was restored to flying condition so that it could appear in the epic film *Battle of Britain*. In 1968, P7350 joined the Battle of Britain Flight, which became the Battle of Britain Memorial Flight a year later. P7350 continues to entertain crowds every year throughout the United Kingdom and will hopefully go on for many years to come.

From the beginning of 1944 to the end of the Second World War, 57 OTU's workload was always very high and usually just beyond the resources of the unit, which is how the senior staff preferred it. On 26th January 1944, both 55 and 59 OTU, based at Annan in Dumfriesshire and Milfield respectively, were disbanded. Their demise meant that 57 OTU's throughput of fighter pilots would have to increase. The population of aircraft also rose, with the Spitfire Mk.Vb and later Mk.Vc being the most prolific types on station. More training exercises were carried out at Boulmer, a role that never decreased until the end of the war.

As well as the plethora of Spitfires on charge with 57 OTU, the unit was atypical in the fact that it also had an interesting collection of support aircraft. By mid 1944, they included three different marks of the Miles Master, which were mainly employed for familiarization duties, at least half a dozen Miles Martinets for target towing, an Airspeed Oxford, two Miles Magisters, a single Tiger Moth, a Hurricane Mk.I and a de Havilland DH.89 Dominie.

The long main runway at Eshott served a particularly useful purpose on the evening of 31st December 1944. On return from a raid in northern Germany, a group of 2nd Air Division Consolidated B-24 Liberators was diverted to northern England, as its home base in Norfolk was fog bound. The group became lost north of Newcastle and by using the 'Darky' position-fixing system was able to locate Eshott. Twenty-six of the large four-engined bombers landed safely, and all departed early the following morning.

On 15th May 1945, the hammer fell on 57 OTU and all training was suspended. Student pilots who had yet to complete their course were transferred to the few surviving OTUs. On 6th June 1945, the unit was officially disbanded and Boulmer ceased to be a satellite of Eshott on the same day. The only task that remained was the ferrying of the

OTU's aircraft to other units, although the majority would end up at Maintenance Units for storage and ultimately scrapping.

On 18th May 1945, 289 Squadron arrived from Acklington with an assortment of aircraft that included a type that was rarely seen in Britain. Formed at Kirknewton in November 1941 as 13 Group Anti-Aircraft Flight, 289 Squadron operated from various airfields in the south and north-east of England. The unit was equipped with the powerful Spitfire Mk.XVI, powered by the American-built Packard Merlin, and the Vultee Vengeance Mk.IV. The Vengeance was the only aircraft to enter RAF service specifically designed as a dive-bomber that could operate in close support with Army operations. The aircraft entered service with 82 Squadron at Karachi in August 1942. The aircraft performed very well as a dive-bomber despite its cumbersome appearance and was not replaced in this role until mid 1944 by the capable Mosquito. The later marks were converted by Cunliffe-Owen into target tugs, all serving with anti-aircraft units. The Vengeance remained in RAF service until May 1947.

A few days later, another target-towing unit arrived on detachment. 291 Squadron was formed in December 1943 from three different flights, spending their entire existence at Hutton Cranswick a few miles south-west of Driffield in Yorkshire. The squadron also possessed the Vengeance, plus the Miles Martinet Mk.I and the Hurricane Mk.IIc. 289 and 291 Squadron had left Eshott by the beginning of June, and by 26th both units had been disbanded.

Between June and October 1945, Eshott was placed under Care and Maintenance, although little movement was ever observed on the rapidly deteriorating airfield. Activity returned on 1st October 1945 with the arrival of 261 Maintenance Unit, which used Eshott as a sub-site for its main home at Morpeth. The unit was formed as a Ground Equipment Depot at Long Benton, north of Newcastle, in June 1945, moving to Morpeth not long after. Eshott remained a sub-site until 1st January 1948 brought an end to its RAF service.

It was 35 years before flying returned to Eshott. The majority of its wartime buildings have disappeared; those that still exist are located on the southern side, on private property. Large sections of the original runways remain, making the airfield a very attractive proposition for light aviation. It is now the home of Eshott Airfield Flying Club, and this enthusiastically run group will ensure that aviation will remain in this area for many years to come.

6
MIDDLETON ST
GEORGE

Positioned on the very edge of Yorkshire, which became home to many bomber stations and squadrons throughout the Second World War, Middleton St George has all too often been recorded amongst this group of airfields, many overlooking the fact that the airfield is actually located in County Durham, therefore qualifying it for a chapter within this book. The flying activity of this airfield has continued almost unabated for 65 years, today in the guise of Durham Tees Valley Airport. The destinations that can be visited from the airport today are considerably safer and far more inviting than what was on offer for the aircrew back in 1941.

In the July of 1934 a huge RAF expansion programme was launched, which included an increase of both airfields and squadrons. Fighter, Bomber, Coastal and Training Commands were all reorganized; Bomber Command in particular was to consist of four controlling groups. In peacetime these groups played an administrative role; this would change to an operational one on the outbreak of war.

The site of one of these new expansion airfields was selected on land belonging to the Middleton Hall estate, five miles east of Darlington, which is where the airfield was to gain its official name. However, locally it was known by a different name, in this case, Goosepool. The criteria for these type of airfields were generally as follows: a grass flying field of approximately 250 acres prepared with three runways, four aircraft hangars (referred to as aeroplane sheds at the time) of C Type standard (steel framed, brick walls and steel doors), all technical buildings, workshops and stores built of brick; and all messes and barrack blocks made of brick or concrete, flat roofed and centrally heated. No forethought was given to dispersing the buildings with regard to enemy attack.

By the time construction of Middleton began in 1939, the expansion criteria had changed slightly. Wartime rules dictated less elaborate building work and, although many technical buildings were built to the pre-war specification, the hangar types and positions were changed. Only one C Type was constructed and a slightly less costly J Type accompanied this; both had a span of 150ft and were 300ft long. They still exist today. Later on in the war, a pair of Teesside-produced Type T2 hangars and a single Type B1 made the airfield complete. Several planned 'H' style barracks were also cancelled and less comfortable Nissen huts were built in dispersed areas. As Bomber Command and heavy bombers had been allocated Middleton, the original grass runways were changed to concrete by the end of 1940, and the main runway had been extended to 2,100 yards. A complex perimeter track was also constructed and this linked 36 hardstandings and a bomb dump on the south side of the airfield.

Officially opened on 15th January 1941, Middleton was now a bomber station and would remain so for the entire war. Allocated to 4 Group, whose headquarters was at Heslington Hall near York, it was initially under the command of Australian born Air Vice Marshal A

The first to arrive at Middleton were the Armstrong Whitworth Whitley Mk.Vs of 78 Squadron.

Coningham. In July, Coningham was replaced by a New Zealander, Air Marshal Sir Roddy Carr CB, DFC, AFC, who remained in this post until 1945. Twelve other bomber airfields in Yorkshire were controlled by 4 Group; Middleton was the most northern of all the bomber stations.

On 7th April 1941, 78 Squadron arrived, under the command of Wg Cdr B V Robinson. They were equipped with the Armstrong Whitworth Whitley Mk.V, an aircraft that they had been operating since July 1937. The squadron had already seen a lot of action including very long range attacks on Berlin, a round trip of around 10 hours in an aircraft that was only capable of 230 mph.

Often criticized by post-war historians, the Whitley was a capable bomber for that period of time. It could carry a bomb load of 7,000lbs – 3,000lbs more than the Wellington – and deliver it into the heart of Germany. The Mk.V had a range of 1,500 miles, and on 27th/28th October 1940 a group attacked the Skoda works at Pilsen in Czechoslovakia. The aircraft was eventually superceded by the new four-engine bombers such as the Stirling, Halifax and, later, the Lancaster. However, its excellent range meant that it was well suited for Coastal Command operations and it became the first aircraft to locate and destroy a U-boat. The Whitley remained in service until at least July 1943 and it is a shame that no examples of this early linchpin of Bomber Command exist today.

There was no time for the 78 Squadron to settle in at Middleton and no working up period was needed; so the squadron was straight into action from the airfield on the night of 8th/9th April 1941. The target was Kiel, and the squadron joined a force of 160 other aircraft, to carry out a reasonably successful attack, which fell mainly on the dock and other areas of the town. More importantly the squadron all returned safely.

Targets during May included Dortmund, Bremen, a return to Kiel and the heavily defended city of Cologne. It was on their return from Cologne that the squadron lost its first aircraft while operating from Middleton. In the early hours of 4th May, Sgt L Hatcher in Whitley Mk.V Z6483, along with his crew of four, had to abandon the aircraft near Leominster in Herefordshire. The combination of low fuel and a failed radio gave them no choice and luckily all managed to escape without injury. Sgt Hatcher rose to the rank of Squadron Leader, and earned the DFC and the AFM before losing his life flying an 83 Squadron Lancaster from Coningsby, Lincolnshire in December 1944.

It was not long before the first of many casualties, not only for the squadron but for Middleton also. Sgt L Thorpe in Whitley Mk.V T4147 was part of a raid on Bremen, which itself was a major diversion raid for a larger attack on Hamburg. The A G Weser submarine yard was the main focus of the Bremen attack, although local reports claim it was not damaged in the raid. Flak defences brought down Thorpe's aircraft near Heisfelde on the outskirts of Leer; however, it is possible that a night fighter claimed the Whitley as well. The five crew members were all killed.

May finished with two more aircraft lost, one claimed by a night fighter, the other by flak; once again there were no survivors.

Middleton got busier on 4th June 1941 when a new unit arrived on base. 76 Squadron was re-formed in April 1937 with the Vickers Wellesley, although by the start of the Second World War it had re-equipped with the Handley Page Hampden and Avro Anson. Before seeing any action, the squadron was absorbed into 16 OTU and from April 1940 no longer existed. Re-formed again in May 1941 at Linton-on-Ouse in Yorkshire, 76 Squadron became the second unit to operate the Handley Page Halifax Mk.I and later the Mk.II.

76 Squadron's operations began from Middleton on the night of 12th/13th June. Eleven Halifaxes were joined by seven Stirlings on an attack against the Hüls chemical works. Fires were started near the plant and all of Middleton's aircraft returned home safely. The first aircraft lost by the unit was demonstrated in full view of all on the station that day. Pilot Officer A E Lewin was carrying out circuits and bumps in Halifax Mk.I L9514 on one of the shorter secondary runways. The bomber swung during landing and ran off the runway, causing the undercarriage to collapse. The Halifax was damaged sufficiently for it to be written off.

The Halifax was a bomber aircraft that was only over-shadowed in later years by the Avro Lancaster. First flown in October 1939, the production Mk.I was powered by four Rolls Royce Merlin engines, each developing 1,145hp. Capable of carrying up to 13,000lbs of bombs, the aircraft was protected by three powered turrets with a minimum of two Browning machine guns each; this would increase to ten guns in total. The Mk.II, which began to arrive at Middleton in the summer of 1942, had slightly more powerful engines. This gave it a greater speed and it could climb slightly higher, but it made no difference to the size of the bomb load. The first Halifaxes entered service with 35 Squadron at Linton-on-Ouse in December 1940, becoming operational on 1st March 1941. During that month, additional aircraft were delivered to the squadron in order to create a 'C' Flight, which would go on to form the nucleus of 76 Squadron under the command of Wg Cdr G T Jarman.

Both squadrons at Middleton operated side by side throughout 1941. 78 Squadron in particular suffered high losses with their Whitleys. Four more aircraft were lost in June, all with the loss of their crews. One of 78 Squadron's losses was Whitley Mk.V Z6661, which was shot down by a 3./NJG3 on a raid to Bremen on 18th/19th June. One of the roundels was cut from the wreckage by the crew of the night-fighter, who then displayed it outside the operations room of their home airfield of Werneuchen near Berlin. German night-fighter crews often visited the remains of their victims, as well as any survivors from the crew.

After taking off as part of an attack on the *Tirpitz* in Kiel Harbour on the evening of 20th June 1941, a 76 Squadron Halifax unintentionally flew into the middle of the Middlesbrough balloon barrage. The pilot, Sqn Ldr T Sawyer had been concentrating on his duties, and, after a warning from his wireless operator, realized that the balloons, all of which were another 800 ft above the Halifax, surrounded him. Still climbing, the pilot skilfully wove his way through the cables, completed the sortie and returned safely to Middleton. After this incident, it was arranged that the barrage would be winched down to 500ft during the take off and landing times of the bombers.

76 Squadron had its first operational loss on the night of 23rd/24th June. The squadron was taking part in a raid on Kiel, when a night-

A Rolls Royce Merlin powered Handley Page Halifax Mk.I of 76 Squadron.

91

fighter attacked Halifax Mk.I L9492. Pilot Officer W K Stobbs was at the controls when the Messerschmitt Bf 110 of II./NJG1, flown by Oblt Reinhold Eckardt, tore into the Halifax. Only one of the crew, Sgt J S Lipton, managed to bail out before it plunged to the ground near Eilendorf, 14 miles south of Hamburg. Not only was this the squadron's first loss, but it was also the first Halifax to be reported missing from air operations.

July 1941 continued badly for 78 Squadron: another five Whitleys were lost, three of them on the same raid. Twenty-eight Whitleys joined 45 Handley Page Hampdens on a raid to Hamm, located on the eastern edge of the Ruhr. The raid was hampered by poor weather and as a result only 31 aircraft managed to bomb the target, which suffered only moderate damage. Sgt O W McLean RAAF and his crew crashed in the North Sea with the loss of the crew, and Flying Officer Wright managed to crash-land his Whitley near to Bircham Newton airfield in Norfolk without injury to his crew. However, the story of the night occurred when Sgt W M McQuitty RAAF had to ditch his flak-damaged Whitley off the east coast. The navigator, Sgt J F Hafferden swam nine miles to shore and raised the alarm. A search of the area was carried out immediately, but unfortunately no trace of the aircraft or the remaining four crew members was ever found.

76 Squadron lost another Halifax on the night of 5th/6th August. Six members of the crew survived to become POWs and one, the flight engineer, Sgt C B Flockhart, managed to escape captivity. The tail gunner, Flt Lt T B Leigh, an Australian, was one of 50 who were shot by the Gestapo on 30th March 1944 after escaping from Sagan (The Great Escape). The month continued badly for both squadrons: five aircraft were lost by 76 Squadron and a disturbing nine Whitleys were lost or written off by 78 Squadron. This was one of the worst months in Middleton's short history.

On one particular raid on Berlin, on the night of 12th/13th August, 76 Squadron sent out twelve Halifaxes as part of a force of 70 aircraft, which included Wellingtons, Stirlings and Manchesters. The raid was a shambles with flak and night-fighters claiming nine aircraft including three from Middleton. Lt Hans Autenrieth of 6./NJG1, who at the time had no idea that he was closing in on a 76 Squadron Halifax, carried out one particular attack. His controller guided him to a four-engined aircraft which was 10 km away and 3,000ft below him. He caught up with the bomber quickly, as it was being held in a searchlight, closed to 300ft and fired his machine guns and cannons into the starboard engines. After making a 180-degree turn, Autenrieth temporarily lost his prey. The night-fighter stumbled across the bomber for a second time and managed to press home another attack. Ten minutes later, Autenrieth spotted burning wreckage, presuming correctly that it was his bomber and the first kill of the war for the young fighter pilot. The Halifax was L9531, piloted by Sgt C E Whitfield, and after the second attack all of the seven-man crew managed to bail out safely. Unfortunately, only two survived to become POWs, while the five others had inadvertently parachuted into a swamp and all drowned. Another Halifax was brought down by flak near Parnewinkel, a town between Bremerhaven and Hamburg. The pilot of this particular aircraft was Flt Lt C Cheshire, brother of Leonard Cheshire VC, who would eventually become the commanding officer of 76 Squadron. Cheshire and four others became POWs, but sadly two air gunners were killed in the ensuing crash. The tragedy of war was brought home to Middleton when Halifax Mk.I L9562 was in the circuit returning from the same Berlin raid. The Halifax was on approach to land when the bomber stalled and crashed in flames near the airfield with all seven men perishing. Although aircrew fatigue took its toll so close to home, it was discovered after examination of the wreckage that enemy action might have caused or contributed to the crash.

The Messerschmitt Bf 110 quickly became vulnerable when operating in daylight. However, as a night-fighter, it was deadly. This aircraft is the G-4 standard night-fighter variant.

Targets for both squadrons were becoming more varied and challenging. One in particular lay in Brest harbour. Three of Germany's capital warships, namely the *Scharnhorst, Gneisenau* and *Prinz Eugen* had been bottled up in Brest harbour for some time, impatient to cause as much havoc to Allied shipping as possible. 76 Squadron became involved in the ongoing process of trying to put these deadly warships out of action, for the first time on 13th/14th September 1941. Even at night, the German defences were capable of producing an effective smoke screen, which was the case on this raid. Out of 147 aircraft taking part, 120 managed to bomb but none of them actually saw the target. Only one aircraft was lost: a 76 Squadron Halifax experienced problems on the homeward leg over Bedfordshire. All of the crew successfully bailed out, but the pilot, Pilot Officer R E Hutchin, remained with his aircraft and perished in the ensuing crash near the River Ouse close to Renhold, three miles north-east of Bedford.

78 Squadron's time at Middleton came to an end on 20th October 1941 with a move to nearby Croft in North Yorkshire. The squadron continued to operate the Whitley until March 1942, when they were replaced by the Halifax, an aircraft that it would fly until the war's end.

The Halifax Mk.II equipped both 76 and 78 Squadrons during their tours at Middleton.

94

A common sight at Bomber Command stations throughout the country were small units of Airspeed Oxfords carrying bright yellow triangular markings on their fuselage and wings. These triangles were to warn other pilots that an aircraft from a Beam Approach Training Flight (BATF) was performing blind approaches to the runway. 1516 BATF arrived from Topcliffe in North Yorkshire on 17th November 1941 with eight Oxfords and continued to operate from the airfield until it moved to Croft on 16th September 1942. Despite the Flight's vivid markings, accidents would happen, usually in the airfield's circuit. One such incident occurred on 25th June 1942 between Oxford V4140 and 76 Squadron Halifax Mk.II W7661. Sgt J H G Bingham was flying his Halifax at 2,000ft, slightly below the cloud base, when the Oxford suddenly appeared on a rapidly converging course. Sgt F R Mason, the pilot of the Oxford, tried to dive under the bomber but unfortunately the tail of the Oxford struck the rear of the Halifax, causing both aircraft to plunge out of control to the ground near the airfield. In all, eight valuable aircrew were killed in this tragic training accident.

With training still in mind, in late 1941 there was a need for an additional stepping-stone for new bomber crews from an Operational Training Unit to a front line squadron. Too many crews were being lost in needless accidents before even attempting to fly on operations. From December 1941 onwards, the majority of Bomber Command squadrons began to form Conversion Flights (CF). No.76 CF was formed at Middleton on 20th January 1942, with four Halifaxes on strength. All new crews arriving on the squadron would now pass through the CF, rather than going straight onto operations with often fatal results. By the end of 1942, all of the CFs were disbanded into the new Heavy Conversion Units (HCU), which provided a more comprehensive training on specific aircraft, resulting in an even more efficient bomber crew ready for operations.

German naval sea-power was never far down the list of Bomber Command's targets in early 1942. Thanks to the Royal Navy, the battleship *Bismarck* was sunk in the Atlantic in May 1941. However, its sister ship, the *Tirpitz*, was still at large. Hitler was convinced that the invasion of Europe would come via Norway, and with this in mind the *Tirpitz* spend her entire war sailing from fiord to fiord. On her arrival off the Norwegian coast, the RAF began a series of bombing raids against her, the first of which 76 Squadron took part in. The squadron had sent a detachment of Halifaxes to Lossiemouth in Morayshire and on the night of 29th/30th January, nine Halifaxes and seven Stirlings set out to attack the giant ship near Trondheim. The raid was a failure, as only two aircraft actually reached the Norwegian coast, although both did bomb shipping in the area. More operations were flown from Tain in Ross-shire on 30th/31st March. Twelve Halifaxes were involved in this attack but once again the giant battleship remained hidden. The squadron lost Halifax Mk.II R9453 on the return leg of this raid. Sqn Ldr A P Burdett and his crew were last heard on the wireless transmitter at 02:15 hrs and it is presumed that they came down in the sea approximately 16 miles south of Sumburgh Head in the Shetland Islands. Sadly, only Burdett's body was ever recovered from the water.

The squadron took part in their final attack on the ship on 27th/28th April. On this occasion, the *Tirpitz* was found and bombed, but no hits were recorded and unfortunately a single Lancaster and four Halifaxes were lost, although all participating 76 Squadron aircraft returned home safely. After a relentless series of attacks carried out by the Royal Air Force, the Royal Navy and the Fleet Air Arm, the *Tirpitz* was finally sunk by 9 and 617 Squadron Lancasters with 12,000lb 'Tallboys' on

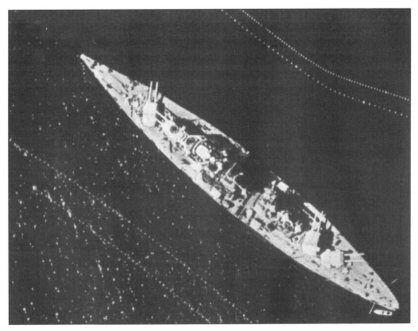

Bird's-eye view of the elusive German battleship Tirpitz *in a Norwegian fiord. 76 Squadron were involved in attacking the ship in early 1942.*

12th November 1944. Despite having never left Norwegian waters, the *Tirpitz* had presented a constant threat to Allied shipping for over two and half years.

78 Squadron returned to Middleton on 10th June 1942, now equipped with the Halifax Mk.II, while 76 Squadron contributed aircraft and crews to detachments in the Middle East whilst still committing its resources to operations over Germany. Flying from various bases throughout Egypt, the squadron's aircraft made a series of attacks against Tobruk, supported by 454 Squadron, who were non-operational. An eventual combination of several squadron detachments, including 10 and 227 Squadron resulted in all of the Middle Eastern Halifaxes forming a new unit called 462 RAAF Squadron. This became the first Middle East Halifax squadron, eventually returning to England in August 1943.

78 Squadron's own CF joined the main squadron from Croft on 30th June, bringing more Halifaxes into the increasingly busy airfield. Personalities began to grow throughout Bomber Command and both of Middleton's squadrons would receive Commanding Officers (CO) of significant stature. 78 Squadron's new CO was Wg Cdr J B 'Willy' Tait DSO, DFC who arrived on 10th July 1942. Coincidentally, Tait, via 467 Squadron, was to become the CO of 617 Squadron from July to December 1944 and leader of the raid which destroyed the *Tirpitz* in Tromsö fiord. In August, 76 Squadron also received a new CO on promotion in the shape of Wg Cdr G L Cheshire.

Leonard Cheshire was an extraordinary individual, whose leadership qualities and bravery were recognized very early on in his RAF career. 76 Squadron was only his second posting and he rose from pilot officer to wing commander in just over two years. In March 1943, he was posted to Marston Moor in Yorkshire to become the station commander and the RAF's youngest group captain, at just 25 years of age. Desperate to return to operational flying, Cheshire voluntarily reverted to the rank of wing commander and became the CO of 617 Squadron in November 1943. He was personally involved in the squadron's low-level marking technique, which was to make 617 Squadron the envy of the specialist Pathfinder Force. Removed from flying operations in July 1944, he went on to become the official British observer of the second atomic bomb drop on Nagasaki on 15th August 1945. This event affected him in such away that, along with his second wife, Sue Ryder, he dedicated his life to the care of the physically handicapped and terminally ill. The first Cheshire home opened in 1948. Today 85 are open in the United Kingdom and the organization operates in 57 countries around the world. Group Captain G L Cheshire VC, DSO Bar x 2, DFC, Order of Merit, passed away on 31st July 1992 at the age of 74.

A major reorganization of Bomber Command airfields in the north of England brought about the combined departure of 76 and 78 Squadron on 16th September 1942 to Linton-on-Ouse in North Yorkshire, though still remaining in 4 Group. Both squadrons had suffered heavy losses while operating from Middleton and they would continue until the war's end. Both would also achieve great distinction, especially 76 Squadron, which went on to carry out the most bombing raids of any Halifax unit, with 396 raids flown. 78 Squadron managed to fly the most sorties in 4 Group, and it is believed to have dropped the highest tonnage of bombs by the group, although this record was reflected by the fact that it suffered more losses than any other Halifax unit and the third overall loss rate within Bomber Command. Both Conversion Flights departed the same day to another 4 Group airfield, at Riccall in North Yorkshire.

Aircrew from the Royal Canadian Air Force (RCAF) had been flying with the RAF since the beginning of the war. As their numbers rapidly increased, it was only a matter of time before they began to form into squadrons of their own and eventually operate within a RCAF Group. Several airfields in North Yorkshire, including Middleton, were selected for use by the RCAF and on 25th October 1942, 6 (Bomber) (RCAF) Group was formed at Linton-on-Ouse. The unenviable task of forming, from scratch, a complete bomber group on foreign soil

Vickers Wellington Mk.III was the main variant to serve within Bomber Command. 420 (Snowy Owl) Squadron RCAF brought them to Middleton in October 1942. This is the prototype at Boscombe Down in Wiltshire.

followed by organizing it into a fighting force fell upon Air Vice Marshal G Brookes CB, OBE. Yorkshire-born Brookes emigrated to Canada when he was 16, later serving in the Royal Flying Corps with 13 Squadron, flying the BE.2. Brookes joined the new RAF as an instructor and then transferred to the Canadian Air Force in 1921. Despite reservations voiced by Air Chief Marshal Sir A Harris about Brookes' ability to take on the new 6 Group, the Canadian managed to bring the group to an organized state of operational readiness in record time.

The first Canadian unit to arrive at Middleton was 420 (Snowy Owl) Squadron RCAF, flying the Vickers Wellington Mk.III, on 15th October 1942, under the command of Wg Cdr D Bradshaw. Affectionately known as the 'Wimpy', the Barnes Wallis designed Wellington was not expected to be still in front-line Bomber Command service by this time. The Mk.III entered service in 1939 and was to remain the standard 'heavy' bomber until the arrival of the Short Stirling and Halifax. These aircraft entered service in 1940 and 1941 respectively and while the demand for bomber aircraft continued there was still room for several Wellington squadrons. In total, 17 squadrons were equipped with the Mk.III, many serving until late 1943, mainly in the Middle East. The Wellington went on to become the most produced multi-engined British bomber in history, with 11,460 aircraft built, and several trainer versions remained in RAF service until the early 1950s.

420 Squadron was formed at Waddington on 19th December 1941, becoming the fourth RCAF bomber squadron to be formed overseas. It was equipped initially with the Handley Page Hampden, its capability increasing with the arrival of the Wellington Mk.III. This aircraft was the first RAF bomber capable of carrying the 4,000lb High Capacity bomb, more commonly known as the 'Cookie'. On arrival from Skipton-on-Swale in North Yorkshire, the squadron immediately prepared for its first raid from Middleton that same evening. The target was Cologne and the bulk of the attacking force was made up of Wellingtons, including 420 Squadron. The raid was not successful, as large decoy fires lit by the Germans drew away the majority of the RAF's bombers. Eighteen aircraft were lost, including 420 Squadron Wellington Mk.III X3808 with Flt Sgt L E White RCAF and his crew, who were never found.

The Canadian feel around the station was increased on 10th November 1942 with the arrival of 419 (Moose) Squadron RCAF from Croft, commanded by Wg Cdr M Fleming, and a return of the Handley Page Halifax. The unit gained its name from its first CO, Wg Cdr John 'Moose' Fulton DSO, DFC, AFC, who was a native of Kamloops in

British Columbia. Sadly, Fulton failed to return from a raid on Hamburg on 28th/29th July 1942. The unit had only just received the Halifax Mk.II, having operated the Wellington Mk.III like its Canadian colleagues. Also like 420 Squadron, it began operations on arrival at Middleton, with little time to settle in.

1516 BATF had visited Croft on detachment during September 1942, returning to Middleton on 14th October. The flight's distinctive Oxfords flew south to Hampstead Norreys in Berkshire on 12th December. A new Canadian BATF was formed three days later at Middleton, also equipped with the Airspeed Oxford. 1535 BATF was equipped with eight aircraft and provided beam approach training for both resident Canadian squadrons until its departure to Dalton in North Yorkshire on 3rd June 1943.

A corner of the airfield was filled with aircraft of a different type in December and January 1943. An assortment of machines, including Lysanders, Blenheims and Martinets from 6 Anti-Aircraft Co-Operation Unit were on detachment from Cark in Lancashire. The aircraft were working with 15 LAAPC at Whitby, providing target-towing facilities for trainee gunners.

The headquarters of 6 RCAF Group moved to Allerton Park, near

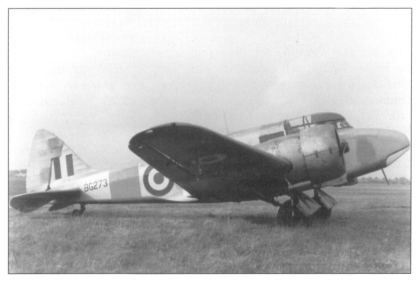

The Airspeed Oxford was a common sight around most bomber airfields, Middleton being no exception.

Knaresborough, Yorkshire on 1st December 1942 and Air Vice Marshal G Brookes declared the group operational. At 00:01 hours on 1st January 1943, the group was officially recognized and over the following three days the RAF handed over six airfields, including Middleton, for the use of RCAF squadrons. The other airfields were Leeming, Dishforth, Croft, Dalton and Skipton-on-Swale, all in North Yorkshire. The group would grow as the war progressed, with more airfields and units being added.

The airfield did not have to wait long for the first casualty of the new year and the first under RCAF control. Wellington Mk.III BJ604 of 427 (Lion) Squadron RCAF, based at nearby Croft, overshot the approach to one of Middleton's short runways and ended up with its starboard wing overlapping the Darlington to Eaglescliffe railway line. The crew managed to escape the aircraft unhurt, but unfortunately it was too late to warn a passenger train, which ploughed into the wreckage. Sadly, one person died and another was injured in the train.

As well as industrial targets in occupied France and Germany, mining operations or 'gardening' were carried out by both squadrons. Equally as dangerous as operations against mainland targets, mine laying was an essential task in the effort to contain and disrupt the activities of the German Navy. At this stage of the war, the mines had to be dropped at the relatively low level of 6,000ft or less, making aircraft particularly vulnerable to enemy ground defences. Each mining area was given an area code, the majority of which were named after fruit, vegetables and flowers, hence the term 'gardening'. For example, the Frisian Islands code was 'Nectarines' and St Malo was 'Hyacinth'. One of the war's biggest mining operations took place on 9th/10th January, when 121 Halifaxes, Wellingtons and Stirlings placed their ordnance around the Frisian Islands, the German Bight and the Kattegat, the latter being the large expanse of water between Denmark and Sweden. Ninety-seven of the group managed to drop their mines, but, once again, the operation did not go without cost to Bomber Command. Four aircraft were lost, including Halifax Mk.II W7857, piloted by Sgt F H Barker RCAF of 419 Squadron, which became the first aircraft lost on operations whilst at Middleton and the first since converting from the Wellington. It is presumed that the aircraft crashed into the Kattegat, as at least one of the crew is buried in a Swedish cemetery.

By the end of February, 420 Squadron began to receive replacement aircraft for the Wellington Mk.IIIs. Athough still a Wellington, the Mk.X was the most powerful version produced. Fitted with a pair of

101

1,675 hp Hercules XVIII engines, over 3,800 were built, eventually serving with 29 squadrons, the majority of which would go to serve in the Middle East.

Described by the Commander in Chief of Bomber Command, Sir Arthur Harris, as his 'main offensive', the Battle of the Ruhr began on the night of 5th/6th March 1943 and would continue until the end of July. Housing the most powerful flak and searchlight defences, any target selected in the Ruhr would make the most hardened bomber crew groan with apprehension. Both of Middleton's squadrons took part in the first raid of the battle, which involved 442 aircraft against the heavily defended industrial city of Essen, with specific attention being paid to the giant Krupps works.

Led by Pathfinder Mosquitos, which would mark the target for the main force, the raid got off to a faltering start. Aircraft suffering from mechanical failure were not an uncommon occurrence, but, on this evening, 56 aircraft had to return early with a variety of problems, including three of the lead Mosquitos. Despite this, the raid continued and the remainder of the Mosquitos managed to mark the target for the main force, which attacked in three waves. An area of damage totalling 160 acres was later recorded on reconnaissance photographs. Most of the bombs fell on the centre of Essen, with only a few hitting the Krupps factory. Fourteen bombers were shot down, two of them from

As a night fighter, the Junkers Ju 88 shot down many aircraft of Bomber Command.

Middleton. First to fall was 420 Squadron's Wellington Mk.X HE280 with Pilot Officer Graham RCAF at the controls, brought down by flak over the target, the first of this type to be reported missing from the unit. Sgt L Bakewell of 419 Squadron was beginning the long flight home when his Halifax Mk.II DT646 was intercepted by a night-fighter over Arnhem in Holland. Already damaged by flak, the Halifax was easy pickings and Lt Walter Schön in his Bf 110 of 3./NJG 1, based at Twente, scored his first victory by sending the bomber earthwards in flames between Nijmegen and Arnhem. All seven crew managed to parachute to safety, but unfortunately the rear gunner, Flt Sgt J R Couper, is believed to have landed in the River Waal and drowned. Of the survivors, five ended up in captivity but the Flight Engineer, Sgt A C Turner, managed to evade detection and eventually returned to England with the help of the local resistance.

Despite this period of Bomber Command operations being called the Battle of the Ruhr, targets all over Europe were still being attacked. It would have been suicide for Harris to concentrate all his forces every night against the same target. Enemy night-fighter units would have concentrated their attacks and Bomber Command would have been quickly removed from the war. Two thirds of all raids were focussed on the Ruhr while the remainder were spread from Stettin on the edge of the Baltic to Pilsen in Czechoslovakia. Middleton's squadrons were also involved in raids on Berlin, Frankfurt, Stuttgart and comparatively local targets such as St Nazaire on the French coast.

420 Squadron's time at Middleton was coming to an end and a signal was received indicating a move overseas to join the North African campaign. The ground party left Middleton in early May 1943, arriving at Beaufarik in Algeria the following month. The squadron's Wellingtons followed on 15th May. In just six months of operations from the airfield, the squadron had suffered 15 aircraft lost. Six months later, the squadron returned to 6 Group, although this time it was based at Dalton and later Tholthorpe, both in North Yorkshire, and flew from the latter until the war's end.

The Wellingtons of 428 (Ghost) Squadron RCAF arrived from Dalton on 4th June 1943 under the command of Wg Cdr M Fleming. Like its predecessor, the unit was flying a mixture of Mk.IIIs and Mk.Xs, but both were due for replacement soon after their arrival at Middleton. By now, the majority of Canadian squadrons were flying the Halifax, and 428 Squadron would be no exception.

Originally intended for use with Coastal Command, the Halifax Mk.V first entered Bomber Command service in October 1942, with 408

103

(Moose) Squadron, another Canadian unit. Five squadrons within 6 Group would become equipped with Mk.Vs, including 428 Squadron, whose new aircraft began to arrive at Middleton only days after their own arrival. Still powered by Merlin engines, the Mk.V was essentially the same as the Mk.II. However, one of the areas that was seen to be slowing the production rate was the excellent, but complicated, Messier undercarriage of the earlier marks. The Mk.V incorporated a new levered-suspension Dowty undercarriage that could be produced at a considerably faster rate and eventually 904 of this version were produced.

In a short time, 428 Squadron became operational, joining 419 Squadron for its first raid from Middleton on 19th/20th June 1943, a position that would remain the same until the end of hostilities. The target was the Schneider armaments factory and Breuil steelworks at Le Creusot, 50 miles south-west of Dijon in France. The raid was carried out at the relatively low-level of between 5,000 and 10,000ft. Despite this, the main factory targets were left unscathed, the majority of bombs falling into a nearby residential district. 428 Squadron returned unscathed to Middleton after its first operation with the Halifax, although a few aircraft landed at airfields in the south of England through shortage of fuel.

One of 428 Squadron's most experienced airmen, and its first aircraft loss, occurred in an unsuccessful attack against the Ruhr target of Gelsenkirchen on 9th/10th July. Halifax Mk.V DK229 was part of a force of 418 aircraft, led by ten Pathfinder Mosquitos.

A Halifax Mk.V of 408 (Moose) Squadron RCAF powers down Middleton's main runway.

Equipment failure and poor marking was blamed for the poor bombing, most of which fell in the neighbouring towns of Bochum and Wattenscheid. Piloted by Sqn Ldr F H Bowden, DFC and Bar, DK229 was struck by flak at least twice at the beginning of the return leg for home. With two engines failing, Bowden gave the order to his crew to bail out while he kept the crippled bomber steady. Bowden's bravery cost him his life but the remaining six members of his crew survived, five becoming POWs and a sixth evading capture, which, considering they all landed in the vicinity of Cologne, was quite an achievement.

The Battle of the Ruhr was nearing its end, but this meant little to the individual aircrew, who were just thinking about surviving one raid to the next. Aachen was singled out on 13th/14th July for a relentless and swift attack, which almost razed the town to the ground. However, the attackers did not have it all their own way and, despite a diversion raid by Mosquitos on Cologne, local defences brought down 23 aircraft, 18 of them by night-fighters. The skies over Germany that night seemed to be filled with enemy aircraft, and both squadrons from Middleton were heavily involved. 419 Squadron's Halifax Mk.II JD270, piloted by Sgt W Cameron, was heading for home at 20,000ft when he heard a shout from his rear gunner, Sgt R Boos. A Bf 110 was closing fast on the bomber but was unable to attack as Cameron threw the Halifax into a defensive corkscrew manoeuvre. The enemy fighter broke away, but at the same time came into the range of Boos' machine guns, giving him the opportunity to fire a three-second burst at the night fighter. Sgt Boos later reported seeing small red flashes on the Bf 110 as his rounds appeared to hit the cockpit area of the fighter, the Flight Engineer later confirmed this and the night-fighter was claimed as damaged.

With the adrenalin still pumping, Boos spotted a second night-fighter closing on JD270. This time it was a Junkers Ju 88 and again Boos shouted to his pilot to corkscrew the aircraft in what was proving to be a particularly useful defence. With his guns at a difficult angle, Boos fired a long burst at the Ju 88, only to see his tracer rounds skim over the top of the night-fighter, but it was enough to convince the German pilot to break off his attack. Minutes later, another Ju 88 closed in on JD270, possibly the same aircraft, but by now Boos was in no mood to find out and the call was given to Cameron for a third time to push the Halifax into a spiralling dive. Boos fired at 500 yards and immediately the Ju 88 returned fire but luckily it passed over the top of the bomber. Seconds later, with the Ju 88 now even closer, the determined night-fighter pilot fired again, but once again missed and dived away and was not seen again. All of this was a mere seven minutes of combat and Sgt Boos had managed to expend over 500 rounds of ammunition.

Another Halifax from 419 Squadron was not so lucky, neither was its rear gunner. Halifax Mk.II BB323 was being flown by an American pilot, namely 2nd Lt B J J Furey USAAF, when it came under attack by Oblt Heinz Strünning in his Bf 110. The experienced Strünning had already claimed 35 bombers shot down and Furey's aircraft would become his 36th. The guns of the night-fighter clinically killed the rear gunner, Flt Sgt W C Batkin, before he had a chance to fire and the attack was so effective that Furey immediately ordered his crew to bail out, which they did, becoming POWs.

Three aircraft from 428 Squadron did not return to Middleton that night either. Flt Lt W G Weeks RCAF and his crew were all killed by a night-fighter attack, their aircraft, Halifax B.V DK228, crashing near Dinant in Belgium. Halifax Mk.V DK257, piloted by Flt Lt D S Morgan RCAF, suffered the same fate near Tilburg in Holland; both rear and mid-upper gunners were killed in defence of their bomber from an attack by Lt Rolf Bussmann of 1./NJG 1 in his Bf 110. The remainder of the crew managed to bail out.

Finally, this costly attack claimed Halifax Mk.V ED209, flown by Pilot Officer W D F Ross. After leaving the target, the aircraft was hit by flak and was later abandoned near Marche-en-Famenne in Belgium. All survived after abandoning the crippled bomber. Five of the crew became POWs but the Flight Engineer and Rear Gunner with the help of the local resistance managed to evade capture.

Despite its having been attacked 98 times previously, Sir Arthur Harris focussed his forces on Hamburg on the night of 24th/25th July 1943. Harris had already prepared his senior commanders for the Battle of Hamburg, conceived many months before, a campaign that would last until 3rd August. The attacks on Hamburg have caused a lot of controversy over the years, especially the claim that a needless amount of incendiary bombs were dropped in follow-up raids, causing the infamous 'firestorms'. No more incendiaries were carried on this raid than any other involving Bomber Command. A combination of unexpected factors including high local temperatures, low humidity and an inability for fire vehicles to pass through the city contributed greatly to the firestorms.

Both squadrons took part in the first raid of the Battle of Hamburg and all returned safely to Middleton. With 791 aircraft involved in this particular raid, the risk of aerial collision or being struck from above by another aircraft's bombs was always a possibility. Pilot Officer A Reilander of 428 Squadron brought his Halifax home with holes in the wings and tailplane, not as a result of enemy action but from a stick of incendiary bombs from a friendly aircraft above! Both squadrons went on to lose aircraft over Hamburg; it was a brief battle of just nine days which cost Bomber Command 130 aircraft.

Since late 1942, it had been no secret to the British Intelligence Service that the Germans had been experimenting with rockets propelled by liquid fuel. Agents in neutral countries had gathered significant information that indicated that experiments had reached an advanced stage at a place called Peenemünde on the Baltic coast. The previous May, a Spitfire from 1 Photographic Reconnaissance Unit (PRU) had by chance photographed strange circular objects in the wood near Peenemünde. The photographic interpreters simply noted them as 'heavy constructional work' and they were filed away. As reports increased from Germany, more focus was given to Peenemünde and many more photographic sorties were flown until, in May 1943, a Mosquito of 540 Squadron confirmed the potential existence of large rockets and their launchers. These rockets were later known as the infamous V-2.

Churchill immediately ordered their destruction along with all evidence of the V-1 Flying Bomb, which was already close to becoming fully operational. The first of many raids was launched on 17th/18th August 1943 as part of Operation *Crossbow*, which would involve 596 aircraft; for the first time a Master Bomber would control the whole raid. The attack would also be the first time that Bomber Command had attempted a precision raid on such a small target at night. Peenemünde was not a big target; so a well-executed concentrated attack should have ensured its total destruction and, under the control of Gp Capt J H Searby of 83 Squadron in the role of Master Bomber, success was anticipated.

The whole raid was made up of three waves; 5 and 6 Group aircraft were in the last, a position never favoured by aircrews. It was the first time that the Lancaster operated with 6 Group. 426 Squadron, based at Linton-on-Ouse, had recently received the Lancaster Mk.II and it was a sign of things to come for the Canadians. Under a moonlit sky, the raid started well and a Mosquito diversion raid on Berlin managed to draw away virtually all enemy night-fighters for the first part of the raid, the first two waves of bombers all being left unscathed. However, by the time the third wave attacked, the night-fighters arrived en masse and this is where the raid suffered most casualties. 5 Group lost seventeen out of 109 aircraft, and the Canadians, despite only having 57 aircraft involved, lost twelve of them to the guns of the night-fighters, including two of the newly arrived Lancasters. With the combination of a moonlit night, the Mosquito diversion over and no fighter protection, the enemy fighters, now equipped with a new upward-firing twin machine gun called *Schräge Musik*, reeked havoc amongst the bombers. Many Halifaxes, especially in 6 Group, had an added ventral gun position to combat such attacks; whether it would have proved effective is open to question but it would certainly have raised morale.

The attack against Peenemünde had been a success; 560 of the bombers managed to drop over 1,800 tons of bombs onto the target. Many scientists and senior staff were killed in the raid, but sadly 500 to 600 foreign workers also paid the ultimate price when the main labour camp was hit. The rocket programme was later estimated at being put back by at least two to three months, potentially reducing the threat of the V-2. Forty bombers were lost on the raid, Middleton's squadrons in particular suffered more than most. Both 419 and 428 Squadron lost three aircraft each, with the total loss of 38 aircrew killed and only five surviving to become POWs. Such was the ferocity of the night-fighter attacks that the majority of aircraft were simply blown out of the sky.

Raids against distant targets deep in Germany were now becoming more frequent, Berlin in particular receiving regular attention from large groups of bombers. These operations played into the hands of the night-fighters, whose efficient tactics and seemingly limitless resources took their toll on the RAF's bombers. By this stage of the war, the Germans were also employing less traditional aircraft as night-fighters. Single seat fighters such as the Messerschmitt Bf 109 and Focke-Wulf Fw 190 also joined the fray. The raid on Berlin on 23rd/24th August was only partially successful and the force was decimated by the loss of 56 aircraft, the majority at the hands of the night-fighter crews. This was the most aircraft lost by Bomber Command in a single night since the beginning of the war. Despite this, W/O F Edwards and his crew from 428 Squadron made sure that the night-fighters did not have everything their own way. Edwards' Halifax was attacked twice by the combined efforts of a Ju 88 and a Bf 109. The enemy fighters knocked out the starboard outer engine, put several holes in the starboard wing and fuel tanks and damaged the aileron as well. In their brave defence, the Bf 109 was shot down and the Ju 88 peeled away, probably to attack a less determined victim. Edwards skilfully brought the damaged bomber home, landing safely on three engines at Little Snoring in Norfolk.

A few nights later, over Nuremberg, the night-fighters were enjoying another harvest of bombers. Sgt C Coutlee's 419 Squadron Halifax was singled out by a Ju 88 but was met with a hail of bullets from both its rear and mid-upper gunners, sending the twin-engined fighter down in flames. Almost simultaneously, a Ju 88 was attacking Pilot Officer R Eaton in his 428 Squadron Halifax. The Halifax gunners struck the night-fighter several times before it was seen diving away; it was later claimed as destroyed. On return to Middleton, Eaton's Halifax had nearly 60 cannon and bullet holes in it!

A trip to Mönchengladbach on 30th/31st August, saw no let up in the night-fighter activity or their success rate. But once again the Canadians from Middleton fought back. Sgt G Marjoram's 419 Squadron Halifax was singled out no less than six times by several enemy fighters whilst returning from the target. To add to the problem, the aircraft's rear turret was jammed, leaving the rear gunner exposed to enemy fire and unable to help. A combination of return fire from the mid-upper turret and skilful evasive manoeuvres meant that the Halifax survived to fight another day. The Halifax of Sgt H Bullis was lucky to survive a very accurate and heavy attack by an Fw 190. The aircraft sustained damage to the fuselage, flaps, ailerons, rudders, the bomb bay, which was empty by this stage, and the port inner engine, which had to shut down. With the aircraft in a very precarious condition, the Halifax gunners still managed to shoot the Fw 190 down in flames. The final story of the evening for 419 Squadron was one worthy of the Distinguished Flying Medal (DFM) for the navigator of Halifax Mk.II JD387. With Flying Officer D Laidlaw RCAF at the controls, the Halifax came under concentrated fire from an unknown night-fighter. The hydraulics suffered the most damage, with navigational aids and flight instruments also knocked out; also a serious fire broke out in the fuselage, turning a delicate situation into a dangerous one. Without hesitation, Sgt J N S Ashton tackled the fire, quickly bringing it under control and possibly saving the Halifax from certain destruction, and earning himself the DFM for his actions. After safely landing back at Middleton, the aircraft was declared a write-off after a technical inspection.

A return to Berlin the following night was another triumph for the enemy night-fighter and its tactics. Five of Middleton's Halifaxes failed to return, three from 419 Squadron and two from 428 Squadron. 419 Squadron's Halifax Mk.II JD270 was actually in collision with a single engine night-fighter, part of the port wing being ripped off by the impact. Considerably less damage was caused to Flying Officer J

Westland's Halifax by a Ju 88, which was claimed destroyed in a combat that only lasted seconds, the only consolation prize for the Canadians that evening.

By October 1943, the German night-fighters seemed to be gaining the upper hand and were not only achieving success against bombers over Germany but were beginning to follow the bombers home as well. On 3rd/4th October, a large force of bombers attacked the industrial town of Kassel, including 75 Halifaxes from 6 Group. The attack itself did not go according to plan but considerable damage was caused in the area, including both the Henschel and Fieseler aircraft factories. Over the target area, 419 Squadron bombed without incident but it was a different story for 428 Squadron. Halifax Mk.Vs EB214 and EB213 were both brought down by flak, while Flt Sgt C R Newton RAAF in EB210 received a mauling by an Fw 190 on the return leg. With a damaged hydraulic system, wings, tail and bomb bay doors, Newton made an emergency landing at Tangmere in Sussex. 419 Squadron seemed to have escaped the attention of the enemy until over Lincolnshire, where Flt Sgt D T Cook's Halifax Mk.II JB967 was intercepted by an enemy intruder. Completely taken unawares, the Halifax was raked with fire and Cook was on the verge of giving the order to bail out, when the attack ceased and JB967 appeared to be still under control. On final approach to land at Middleton, the bomber crash landed, broke into three pieces and the port wing was ripped off. Incredibly, only two of the crew were injured.

419 Squadron's OC, Wg Cdr M Fleming RCAF accepted promotion on 8th October 1943 and therefore he could no longer remain in his current post. His replacement was Wg Cdr G McMurdy RCAF, who arrived at Middleton on 11th October. McMurdy's first operation with the squadron was a return to Kassel on 22nd/23rd October in an attempt to improve on the last attack. This was achieved with devastating effect; the town was virtually destroyed, with over 5,500 people killed. For McMurdy though, it was his first and last operation: a night-fighter shot his Halifax Mk.II JD782 down near Lauenförde, 30 miles north of Kassel. Five, including Wg Cdr McMurdy, were killed, although three managed to bail out, becoming POWs. Three days later, Wg Cdr W Pleasance took over command of 419 Squadron.

Berlin had drawn the attention of Bomber Command since the beginning of the war, but from 18th/19th November 1943 to 31st March 1944, Sir Arthur Harris would launch a new campaign, named the 'Battle for Berlin'. It would be Bomber Command's greatest test of men, equipment and tactics. Harris' plans for Berlin were set back at a very early stage with the withdrawal of the vulnerable Short Stirling, whose Achilles' heel was always its lack of altitude. This now left the Halifax Mk.IIs and Mk.Vs of 4 and 6 Groups equally exposed, as their performance was inferior to the Lancasters and the loss rates for both groups began to soar to an embarrassing level. By February 1944, losses were so high that Harris withdrew ten squadrons of Halifaxes, including several Canadian ones, from the battle.

On the first raid of the Battle of Berlin, the main force attacked the capital while a major diversionary raid was carried out on Mannheim and Ludwigshafen. 94 Halifaxes from 6 Group took part in a scattered bombing raid on a city that was heavily defended. Two of 419 Squadron's Halifaxes were brought down by flak, with several others damaged. 428 Squadron all returned safely, although at least four aircraft had received serious flak damage.

The German controllers on the night of 25th/26th November had plotted a large force of bombers as they crossed the Dutch coast. At first, it could not be decided whether their target was Mannheim or Frankfurt. The latter was eventually chosen and all night-fighters in the area were directed to bombers. No diversion raid was planned and a force of 262 aircraft, the bulk of which were Halifaxes, flew a direct course to Frankfurt. Before the night was over, the night-fighters had claimed 15 bombers shot down, despite the fact that official records

As the war progressed, a wider variety of aircraft were becoming available to the Luftwaffe's night-fighter squadrons, including the Focke-Wulf Fw 190.

111

claim considerably less. Sgt G Scade in his 419 Squadron Halifax was lucky to make it home to Middleton after a relentless night-fighter attack. The underside of the bomber was damaged from its Perspex nose to its port rudder and all the navigation instruments were rendered useless. Sqn Ldr J Beggs RCAF and his crew did not make it home to Middleton that night after Oblt H H Augenstein in his Bf 110 attacked them. Halifax Mk.V LK969 was shot down at 19,000ft and became Augenstein's 23rd kill. The first attack by the Bf 110 set the starboard inner engine alight and the second killed the bomb aimer, Sgt P J Barske RCAF, immediately, and spread the flames to the starboard outer engine. Beggs ordered his crew to bail out, the six survivors spending the rest of the war in a POW camp.

No strangers to mining operations, both of Middleton's squadrons were involved in a unique mine laying sortie on 4th/5th January 1944. Eighteen Halifaxes took part in Bomber Command's first high-level mine laying operation off Lorient and Brest. They were carrying the A Mk I-IV mine, which weighed in at 1500lbs each and up until this particular sortie had always been delivered at various heights not exceeding 6,000ft and an airspeed of 200 mph. On this occasion, the 419 and 428 Squadron crews dropped the mines at the relatively safe altitude between 14,000 and 15,000ft without loss, although two of 419 Squadron's Halifaxes had to return after failing to find the aiming points. Flying a similar operation two days later, Flt Sgt R McIvor in Halifax Mk.II JP119 was at 15,000ft and 200 mph, ready to drop mines off Brest, when a Bf 109 attacked the aircraft. The rear gunner, Sgt R Dujay shouted to his pilot to corkscrew and simultaneously he opened fire on the German fighter at a range of approximately 400 yards. Dujay's guns jammed after only a few rounds and remained so when the Bf 109 attacked for a second time. Once again though, McIvor managed to shake off the attacker and JP119 returned to Middleton, shaken but unscathed.

Despite being the focus of Sir Arthur Harris' current campaign, Berlin became the diversionary target on the night of 21st/22nd January. Magdeburg, the main target, had never been singled out for a major attack before, certainly not an attack that involved 648 aircraft. On this occasion, 45 Lancasters and 69 Halifaxes from 6 Group made up the force, and once again the German night-fighters would dominate the evening's proceedings. By now, with alarming regularity, the German fighter controllers plotted the progress of the bomber force across the North Sea, and, before the actual target destination of the force was worked out, the night-fighters were closing in. Several bombers were shot down before reaching the target and Sqn Ldr E Hamber in Halifax Mk.II JN953 of 419 Squadron nearly joined them. An unidentified twin-engine aircraft attacked the Halifax several times, eventually being driven off by the aircraft's gunners. On reaching the target, JN953 was hit by flak but still managed to drop its bomb load and eventually return to Middleton. The next day over 80 holes caused by cannon fire and flak were found in the Halifax. Flt Sgt J Quinn in Halifax Mk.II JD114 suffered a similar night-fighter attack, but likewise managed to attack the target and return home safely. Flak claimed the squadron's two losses for the evening. Flt Sgt Hawkes RCAF in JD420 was hit by flak in the port outer engine and the resulting shrapnel wounded several of the crew and killed the navigator Flt Sgt W J K Fletcher RCAF outright. The six remaining crew bailed out to safety and became POWs. Less fortunate was the entire crew of Halifax Mk.II JD466, piloted by Flt Lt A G Hermitage. The bomber crashed at Borne, 16 miles south of Magdeburg with the loss of all on board. 428 Squadron lost a single aircraft to a night fighter over the target. Flt Sgt R E Terry RCAF and his crew in Halifax Mk.V DK237 were forced to bail out after the attack, which seriously wounded the mid-upper gunner, Sgt S J Smith RCAF. All except Smith became POWs; the gunner was admitted to a local hospital, where he succumbed to his injuries two days later.

The attack on Leipzig of 19th/20th February proved to be the last operation to Germany for the Halifax Mk.II and Mk.V and the worst for Bomber Command, and 6 Group in particular, since operations began. A diversionary mine laying raid in Kiel Bay and a Mosquito bombing raid against several night-fighter airfields in Holland did not distract the German defences in any way. Once again, the bombers endured relentless attacks from night-fighters from crossing the Dutch coast, combined with heavy flak over the target and more fighter attacks on the return leg.

Fighters attacked three of 419 Squadron's Halifaxes after entering the target area. Recently commissioned Pilot Officer G Scade was in the thick of the action again. A Ju 88 at 18,000ft attacked his Halifax Mk.II JD459 over the target. The rear gunner, Sgt O Lee, spotted the fighter in time and managed to fire a short burst of fire before the Halifax entered a corkscrew. An Fw 190 attacked Flying Officer H Brown in Halifax Mk.II JP200. Rounds were exchanged but neither bomber or fighter were hit after a series of evasive manoeuvres. Halifax Mk.II JP204, with Flying Officer A Byford at the controls, received the attentions of a Ju 88, and, after a brief exchange of fire, the Halifax was hit several times by cannon rounds. The hydraulic motor which powered the rear turret was knocked out, the port tail plane was shot away and several holes were created in the fuselage and port wing. Despite this, Byford and his crew survived the attack and no more fighters were seen that evening. Flt Sgt D K Macleod RCAF and his crew in Halifax Mk.II JD114 were not so lucky, neither was Flying Officer L T Lucas RCAF in LW237. Macleod's aircraft and crew were lost without trace, while Lucas and three of his crew survived to become POWs.

Flying Officer W Blake in his 428 Squadron Halifax Mk.II LW285 was in for a very busy evening. His Halifax was attacked no less than five times over a period of two hours. The first was by an Fw 190 firing its cannons, which were avoided by a corkscrew to port, followed by a second by an unidentified single-engined fighter, once again skilfully avoided by the combined instructions of the rear gunner and pilot. A Ju 88, which fired its cannons at an extreme range from astern, some of which damaged the Halifax, made the third attack but it then peeled away without the rear gunner firing a shot. The fourth attack came while the Halifax was trying to avoid predicted flak which lay in its path. Flak damaged the starboard fin and rudder and destroyed the intercoms to both the mid-upper and rear turret. Unidentified and unseen by all the crew, the night-fighter launched its attack. The rear gunner now had to use light signals to inform the pilot where and when to take evasive action. Before this could be implemented cannon fire ripped into the fuselage, cutting the oxygen supply to the rear turret. Once again, the Halifax outmanoeuvred its attacker, only for another to appear minutes later. A single-engined fighter opened fire with cannons and machine guns at approximately 600 yards, and on this occasion the rear gunner returned fire and claimed that he had seen his rounds strike the fighter. Blake and his crew had experienced more fighter attacks in one night than some crews had experienced in an entire tour of duty – and survived! A single Halifax from 428 Squadron, was lost on the Leipzig raid. Flying Officer A W Woolverton and his crew were all killed when their aircraft crashed into the Ijsselmeer, off Andijk, Holland.

Setting out for a raid on Le Mans on the evening of 13th March 1944, Flying Officer W Barclay RCAF had a close shave with a pillbox after take off. Fully loaded with bombs and fuel, Halifax Mk.II JD459 seemed rather reluctant to get into the air, so reluctant that the bomber struck the top of a pillbox, damaging the main undercarriage, rudders and ventral gun position and tearing off the tail wheel. Barclay clawed the bomber into the air, but, with control just being maintained, the bomber still would not climb above 800ft. The aircraft flew out to sea and jettisoned its bomb load; then flew a steady orbit to use up as much fuel as possible before attempting a forced landing. One hour later, Middleton was free of traffic and Barclay brought the bomber in for a crash landing, which was executed with great skill, only marred by the Halifax colliding with an MT vehicle and injuring the driver in the process. The crew all walked away uninjured but with replacement aircraft in sight, JD459 was declared a write off.

As a nation, Canada had already contributed many air crew and provided the RAF with extensive training facilities throughout the country. With a desire to contribute further, an agreement was reached with the Canadian Government to build Lancasters under licence. In early 1942, the Victory Aircraft Company was formed at Malton, Ontario, and in August of that year ex-44 Squadron Lancaster Mk.I R5727 was sent to the company as a pattern aircraft. Conveniently, the Packard Company, based at nearby Detroit, Michigan, just over 200 miles away, supplied Merlin 28, 38 and 224 engines for the new Lancaster, designated the Mk.X. The first production Lancaster Mk.X KB700 left the Malton production line in September 1943 and the following month it arrived at Woodford in Cheshire for inspection by Avro.

All Lancasters produced by the Victory Aircraft Company were flown across the Atlantic and all Mk.Xs built were delivered to 6 Group. Four hundred and thirty Lancaster Mk.Xs were built in two blocks; the bulk of aircraft in the second did not see action and many remained in RCAF service well into the 1950s and early 1960s.

419 Squadron received its first Lancaster Mk.Xs in early April 1944 and within two weeks had become operational on the type. Nine Lancasters went into action with the squadron for the first time in a raid on the railway yards at Montzen in Belgium on 27th/28th April 1944. This operation was the last that the squadron's remaining Halifaxes would take part in, so it was particularly sad that Pilot Officer R McIvor RCAF and his crew were lost at the hands of an enemy night-fighter over Maastricht. Since arriving at Middleton, 419 Squadron had lost a remarkable 41 Halifaxes on operations.

First introduced in early 1943, the 'Base' system was successfully employed throughout Bomber Command until, in several cases, many months after the end of the war. Usually made up of three airfields, each base had a controlling airfield, generally with good facilities and of pre-war design. This airfield would control all activities, ranging from administration, intelligence gathering and debriefing to operations.

A 419 Squadron Lancaster Mk.X is pictured over a target in 1944.

No.64 (RCAF) Base was formed at Middleton on 1st May 1944, and, unlike the majority of other bases, controlled only one other airfield. Croft, the home of 431 (Iroquois) and 434 (Bluenose) Squadrons RCAF, both still flying the Halifax, was under Middleton's jurisdiction.

The railway yards at St-Ghislain were successfully attacked on 1st/ 2nd May, but two more aircraft were lost from 6 Group, including the first Canadian Lancaster to be lost in Bomber Command service. The increasingly successful Oblt H-H Augenstein attacked Pilot Officer J C McNary RCAF in Lancaster Mk.X KB711 of 419 Squadron at 11,000ft over Ghent. Cannon shells from Augenstein's Bf 110 killed McNary and mid-upper gunner W/O J L E Chartrand RCAF outright. With the Lancaster out of control, six members of the crew managed to bail out, and the crippled bomber crashed less than a mile from Ghent city centre.

Now in a more reserved role, 428 Squadron continued to operate its Halifaxes, mainly performing high-level mine laying operations, although several others included targets in northern France in support of the forthcoming invasion of Europe.

Ten Halifaxes from 428 Squadron were ordered on a mining operation on the night of 14th/15th May. Their objective was around the mouth of the River Seine and off the coast of Le Havre. Each aircraft carried a pair of 1,500lb mines and all except Flying Officer G Gonyou and his crew managed to drop their ordnance without incident. The mines on Gonyou's Halifax would not release, and, while the crew unsuccessfully struggled to release them, the orbiting bomber crept closer and closer to the occupied coastline. Without realizing it, Gonyou had drifted over an enemy airfield south of Honfleurs. The Germans, equally confused by the Halifax's behaviour, presumed it to be their own and lit the flare path in readiness for an emergency landing. At this point several crew members pointed out their delicate position, and the Halifax made a very hasty exit out to sea and the eventual safety of Middleton.

Every squadron from 6 Group, made up of 192 Halifaxes and 32 Lancasters, joined a force of over 1,000 bombers on the night of 5th/6th June 1944. The largest invasion force the world had ever seen was heading for Normandy while huge formations of bombers travelled overhead. Bomber Command's targets that night were ten different coastal gun positions which had to be knocked out if the Allies had any chance of making it ashore. The batteries at Longues, Houlgate and Merville-Franceville were successfully attacked through solid cloud by the bombers of 6 Group and all from Middleton returned home safely.

The following day, 419 Squadron attacked the coastal guns at Longues for a second time. By now the invasion was well under way and the end of the war was in sight.

The continual disruption of the enemy's communication network was the focus of Bomber Command attacks throughout June, the majority of which were railway targets. On 12th/13th June, 92 aircraft from 6 Group, including the Lancasters of 419 Squadron targeted the railway yards at Cambrai. Once again the German night-fighters would rule the skies, and many bombers, including three from Middleton, would not return. Flying Officer R N Wilson RCAF and his crew in Lancaster Mk.X KB714 fell victim to a night fighter and Flying Officer W M Lacey RCAF, in Lancaster Mk.X KB731, was hit by flak near Hazebrouck. Only two airmen survived from Lacey's crew and both managed to evade capture.

The third aircraft lost that evening was the most significant for 6 Group and provides a typical example of the bravery and spirit of the Canadian airmen. Flying Officer A De Breyne RCAF, in Lancaster Mk.X KB726, was subjected to a devastating attack by a Ju 88 night fighter, which immediately destroyed both port engines. Fire spread quickly through the aircraft, setting hydraulic pipes alight in the rear fuselage and thus immobilising the rear turret. De Breyne gave the order to bail out, but, as Pilot Officer A C Mynarski RCAF prepared to leave his mid-upper turret and jump by the rear exit door, he noticed that Flying Officer G Brophy RCAF was trapped in his rear turret. With complete disregard for his own safety, Mynarski rushed to the aid of Brophy, making every effort to free the rear gunner but without success. Brophy waved him away, realizing that nothing could be done. By now Mynarski's clothing and parachute were well alight, and, as a parting gesture, he saluted Brophy as he jumped out of the door.

Several French people saw Mynarski's descent and later reported that both his parachute and clothing were on fire. Sadly, despite efforts by local doctors, he died of severe burns. Meanwhile, with Brophy still trapped in his turret, KB726 crashed to the ground, throwing the rear gunner clear, and, along with three other crew members, he managed to evade capture. Brophy later described Mynarski's actions in attempting to save his life with complete disregard for his own. With this in mind, Mynarski was awarded the most conspicuous award for heroism, a posthumous Victoria Cross, the only such honour bestowed on a Canadian airman of 6 Group, Bomber Command.

Throughout June, brand new Lancaster Mk.Xs were beginning to arrive for 428 Squadron, its Halifaxes now at the end of their operational lives. The squadron flew its last Halifax operation on 27th/28th June 1944; a small group dropped mines off Brest and all returned home safely. 39 Halifaxes had been lost on operations and training sorties since arriving at Middleton. Hopes were now raised that the arrival of the Lancaster would change the squadron's fortunes.

The first all-Lancaster operation from Middleton took place on the night of 4th/5th July against the railway yards at Villeneuve. Despite being in retreat, the night-fighters were as prevalent as ever, and as usual the majority of losses fell to them. At least six of 419 Squadron's Lancasters returned home riddled with holes from determined attacks and three more failed to return. Out of the 21 airmen who did not return that evening, only three were killed, and, as a guide to the progress of the Allied advance, eight others managed to evade capture and make it to the Allied lines. 428 Squadron lost its first Lancaster with Pilot Officer W C Gray RCAF at the controls. Sadly, Gray and his rear gunner, Flt Sgt S J Stewart RCAF, were killed, but the remaining five crew members survived, three of them evading capture.

It is interesting to note the comparison of claims, which would often be exaggerated on both sides. On the night of 4th/5th July, when Bomber Command flew 702 sorties and lost 28 bombers, the German night-fighter crews claimed 48 enemy aircraft shot down!

By the end of July, Sir Arthur Harris resumed his attacks on German cities, firstly Kiel on 23th/24th, followed by a series of attacks against Stuttgart on 24th/25th July. The latter, in particular, was a very eventful night for both of Middleton's squadrons.

Three 419 Squadron Lancasters suffered damage by night-fighters and Flt Sgt J A Phillis RCAF in KB719 was shot down. It was later reported by the surviving crew that rockets were fired by the night-fighter. 428 Squadron suffered similar incessant attacks. Pilot Officer S Huston's Lancaster had its starboard inner engine burst into flames, but the crew managed to extinguish the flames and return home safely. On the journey to the target Lancaster Mk.X KB740, with Pilot Officer Corbet RCAF at the controls, collided with another bomber over France. Both bomb bay doors were torn off, the starboard inner engine burst into flames, all the propellers were bent and the landing gear was rendered useless. Thinking the aircraft was doomed, the rear gunner, Sgt J Sanduluk RCAF, bailed out. However, KB704 flew on and Corbet turned for home, dumping the bomb load into the English Channel. After some very skillful flying, Corbet nursed the Lancaster to the emergency-landing airfield at Woodbridge in Suffolk, where he performed an impeccable belly landing without injury to his remaining crew.

Daylight operations, mainly over France, were becoming more common, and, with Allied airfields now in the region, fighter escort was at last available. On 5th August a concentrated effort was made to destroy the V-1 Flying Bomb storage sites at Forêt de Nieppe and St-Leu-d'Esserent. Enemy fighter opposition was non-existent but the useful flak would never go away. The 419 Squadron Lancaster of Flying Officer J Tees was hit by flak over the target, knocking both port engines out. Six of the Spitfires which had been providing escort for the main force descended, shooting up light flak positions in order to detract attention from the bomber. The Spitfires continued to escort the bomber until Tees managed to restart the engines and return safely home.

Setting out for another raid against a V-1 site on 27th August, WO L H MacDonald RCAF, the pilot of 419 Squadron Lancaster Mk.X KB724, was in trouble soon after his wheels left the runway at Middleton.

Lancasters of 419 Squadron lined up at Middleton. In the immediate foreground is the tail of Lancaster Mk.X KB711, the first Canadian Lancaster to be lost in Bomber Command service.

121

Three minutes after take-off, both starboard engines failed; with a full bomb load and no height the crew's situation was perilous. However, MacDonald managed to keep the aircraft airborne long enough to make a smooth belly landing in a field east of Appleton Wiske, six miles south of the airfield. While MacDonald and his shaken but uninjured crew quickly vacated the fully armed bomber, the irate farmer whose land they had just churned up greeted them. With no thought to the fact that the bomber could explode any second, the farmer tore into the crew for destroying his garden and crops!

Being the only Lancaster-equipped squadrons in 6 Group at that time, only 419 and 428 Squadrons joined an all-Lancaster operation against the town of Stettin on 29th/30th August. The attacking force of 402 Lancasters and a single Pathfinder Mosquito inflicted the worst damage of the war so far on the town, but once again suffered at the hands of the night-fighters and defensive flak. 419 Squadron took quite a mauling, although all returned safely to Middleton. Incendiary bombs from another aircraft struck the Lancaster being flown by Pilot Officer R Mansfield. The port outer engine was put out of action and caught fire, making the mid-upper gunner, Sgt B Jigursky RCAF, bail out, thinking the aircraft was about to explode. The fire was quickly extinguished and the Lancaster returned home safely. No such luck for Flying Officer L S Plunkett RCAF, who was on his second tour of duty in Lancaster Mk.X KB709 of 428 Squadron. Plunkett and his experienced crew were presumed lost over the Baltic.

It was not unusual for Middleton's squadrons to be diverted to more southerly airfields, due to lack of fuel, or poor weather at their home base. After a successful attack on Stuttgart on 19th/20th October, both squadrons received signals that Middleton was closed due to poor weather. The whole of 419 Squadron diverted to Stradishall and 428 Squadron landed at Chedburgh, both in Suffolk, returning to Middleton later that day.

Another big effort by 6 Group, made up of eleven Halifax squadrons and three Lancasters, attacked the town of Oberhausen on 1st/2nd November 1944. The Lancasters of 428 Squadron escaped unscathed. However the 419 Squadron crews received special attention from the defending night-fighters. Flt Lt A Warner and crew in Lancaster Mk.X KB744 (an aircraft borrowed from 428 Squadron) were attacked by a Me 410, and Flt Lt J Bell returned to Middleton on three engines. It was Flying Officer R L Cox RCAF and crew, in KB767, that fell victim to the worst attacks of the night. After successfully bombing at 20,500ft, the Lancaster was instantly hit by flak, causing damage to the mid-upper turret, and shrapnel had punctured both main wheels. Cox then descended to 15,000ft, and the bomber was attacked by a Fw 190, cannon and machine gun fire damaging the fuselage and tail. Another flak hit damaged the starboard wing, intercom, hydraulics and instruments, and the port inner engine was damaged and shut down. Unbelievably, the bomber survived a second Fw 190 attack, and it was only after this that Cox realized that his navigator, wireless operator and rear gunner had all been wounded. After managing to restart the port inner engine, Cox set course for the emergency landing airfield at Manston in Kent, where he made a successful forced landing. Cox and several crew members were decorated for their actions that evening. KB767 unsurprisingly never flew again!

As the Allied advance moved steadily westward, Bomber Command aircraft not only encountered an increased number of fighters, as a result of their more concentrated positions, but also met with the new jet-powered variants, which were initially seen as almost impossible for a bomber to shoot down. The rear gunner of Flying Officer H Walker's Lancaster Mk.X KB763 had different ideas during a raid on Bochum on 4th/5th November 1944. KB763 was attacked by a Messerschmitt Me 163, more commonly known as the 'Komet'. Developed from a pre-war glider design, this tiny fighter was powered by a Walter rocket engine that could push it along at nearly 600 mph. Limited by its short endurance of only 7.5 minutes, the Komet was extremely effective at attacking Allied bombers. At only 18ft long and with a wing span of a mere 30ft, the Me 163, aided by its amazing speed, was a difficult target to hit. However, the rear gunner of KB763 hit the Komet several times during its attack; the tiny fighter caught fire and dived straight into the ground exploding in a fireball.

Under the orders of the Chief of Air Staff, Air Marshal Sir Charles Portal, the important task of destroying oil targets was always presented to Sir Arthur Harris. Despite post-war accounts to the contrary, Harris always bombed such targets when the weather and resources were available. One such occasion, which involved 6 Group, was on the large oil refinery at Castrop-Rauxel in the heart of the Ruhr. Though in an area not popular with aircrews because of the concentrated flak positions, the raid was carried out with great efficiency and the refinery was to produce no more for the remainder of the war. Both of Middleton's squadrons returned home safely, although not without several aircraft receiving holes from flak and night-fighter attacks. 419 Squadron Lancaster, being flown by Flying Officer L Blaney, experienced an unnerving moment when they thought the aircraft had been hit from below, lifting the bomber a further 400 to 500ft into the air. It was later confirmed that another bomber, probably a Halifax, had exploded below them and the resulting blast had caused Blaney's Lancaster to rise so fast.

The risk of aerial collision not only presented itself over enemy territory but also in the relatively safe skies over England. Whilst outbound on a raid to Soest on 5th/6th December, Halifax Mk.VII LW200 of 426 (Thunderbird) Squadron RCAF collided with 428 Squadron Lancaster Mk.X KB768 over Rugby in Warwickshire. Sadly, all fourteen crew stood no chance.

Friendly fire has existed since warfare began, and, with the average bomber aircraft being equipped with at least six machine guns each, it was inevitable that air gunners accidentally fired upon their own side. Sqn Ldr C Black in Lancaster Mk.X KB762 had just attacked the I G Farben chemical works in Ludwigshafen on 15th/16th December 1944. Already damaged by flak over the target, the bomber was crossing the North Sea for home when a Coastal Command Boeing Fortress II attacked it. The nose of the Lancaster was hit several times as well as the bomb aimer, Flt Sgt B McKinnon, who was hit in the foot. Black decided to make for Woodbridge, where medical facilities were close at hand.

Although many senior staff promised the end of the war by Christmas 1944, the conflict continued at the same ferocious pace into the new year. Middleton's Lancaster squadrons took part in yet another raid on Nuremburg on 2nd/3rd January 1945, a target that had claimed far too many bombers since it was first seriously attacked in October 1941. On this occasion a combination of clear visibility and accurate marking by the Pathfinders resulted in the most successful attack on the city so far and all of Middleton's bombers returned home safely, although one very famous Lancaster Mk.X met its end at Middleton after landing from the Nuremburg raid.

KB700, nicknamed the 'Ruhr Express', was the very first Canadian Lancaster produced. It had served initially with 405 (Vancouver) Squadron RCAF at Gransden Lodge in Cambridgeshire. After flying just two operations, the Lancaster was transferred to 419 Squadron, where it went on to complete another 47 operations. On the return from Nuremburg, with Flt Lt A G R Warner RCAF at the controls, KB700 experienced hydraulic problems and bounced heavily onto the runway. The Lancaster then ran approximately 50 yards off the end of the runway and while attempting to regain the perimeter track clipped a mechanical digger with the starboard outer propeller. A fire broke out and after the crew all escaped safely the bomber was quickly engulfed in flame and destroyed.

Hannover had not been bombed in any capacity since October 1943 but now it was a prime target as part of Sir Arthur Harris' area bombing campaign. One aircraft was lost from Middleton, once again to the perils of friendly fire. Whilst out bound at 20,000ft, Pilot Officer N D Mallen RCAF and crew in 419 Squadron Lancaster Mk.X KB722 were hit by fire from a corkscrewing Lancaster which was trying to shake off an attacking night fighter. KB722 had been struck in both inner engines by the machine gun fire and within minutes both engines were ablaze. Mallen had no choice but to jettison his bomb load and turn for home, although any hope of making it to Middleton was not on the agenda. A course for the airfield at Brussels was set; then altered to Juvincourt, which was found to be fog bound. Manston was the next option, but, after seeing a gap in the overcast sky, Mallen decided to risk a crash landing. This was successfully achieved in a field near the small French village of Guise, not far from St-Quentin.

Another night-fighter kill was chalked up for 419 Squadron during a devastating raid on Pforzheim on 23rd/24th February. Only Hamburg and Dresden received a more severe raid, which claimed the lives of over 17,600 people. The Master Bomber on this raid was Captain E Swales, DFC who must be given credit for the success of the attack. Despite being attacked twice by a night-fighter, Swales continued to control the raid and as a result of his actions on the return journey he received a posthumous Victoria Cross, the last given to a member of Bomber Command.

Flt Lt M McLaughlin in Lancaster Mk.X KB866 had a night-fighter to deal with as well. A Ju 88 closed in on the bomber, but with the combined efforts of both the mid-upper and rear gunners the night-fighter was shot down in flames. The two gunners, in what could be described as a determined defence, fired a total of 2,600 rounds.

The night-fighter menace was destined never to recede while Bomber Command continued its nocturnal attacks. Another jet was increasingly seen by the Canadian bomber crews: the impressive Messerschmitt Me 262, an aircraft that Hitler, unwisely, insisted on being produced as a bomber, when its strength was always as a fighter. On a raid to Hagen on 15th/16th March, Flying Officer D Lambroughton in Lancaster Mk.X KB851 of 419 Squadron was attacked twice by at least two Messerschmitt Me 262s and was lucky to survive the encounter. Two other Lancasters from the squadron were not so fortunate, both falling prey to night-fighters. 428 Squadron also lost an aircraft after a relentless onslaught which involved nine different attacks from the same night-fighter. Flt Lt J D C Craton RCAF and his crew in Lancaster Mk.X KB846 were over the target area when the attacks began. All but Craton and his rear gunner, Flying Officer B B Gray, were killed in the attack. The only consolation was that Gray claimed the Ju 88 destroyed.

The potential of the Me 262 was only unleashed in the latter stages of the war, and Bomber Command did not expect to see such a strong show of force during a daylight raid on Hamburg on 31st March 1945. Flying Officer Lambroughton found himself up against the Me 262 again, and four other 419 Squadron crews had skirmishes with the jet fighter, including Flying Officer M Martin whose gunners fired upon three Me 262s during one attack. Unfortunately, both Flt Lt H A Metivier RCAF and crew in Lancaster Mk.X KB761 and Flying Officer D S M Bowes RCAF and crew in KB869 fell to the guns of the jet fighters. No less than nine of 428 Squadron's Lancasters were attacked by Me 262s, but Flying Officer D Payne's gunners in KB791 achieved success in the midst of the battle. An Me 262 was attacking another Lancaster when both the mid-upper and rear gunner from KB791 opened fire. Both gunners claimed hits and the jet fighter caught fire at the wing root and began a spiral dive earthwards in flames.

The Me 262 was the nearest the Luftwaffe got to incorporating an operational jet into their armoury.

The extensively fortified coastal guns on the Frisian island of Wangerooge would mark the final sortie of the war for 419 Squadron, 428 Squadron and 6 Group as a whole. The guns controlled the approaches to the ports of Bremen and Wilhelmshaven and were an obvious threat to any future use of these ports. All went well for both of Middleton's squadrons, but it was sad that four Halifaxes from 6 Group were lost with all their crews in mid-air collisions, one of which was witnessed by Flying Officer D Walsh of 428 Squadron.

In recognition of the contribution that Middleton's bomber squadrons made during their wartime operations, Air Chief Marshal Sir Arthur Harris visited the airfield on 3rd May 1945. Both units had paid a very high price for victory. 419 Squadron whilst serving with 6 Group had carried out the most bombing raids and suffered the most losses.

Both squadrons were now stood down until VE Day arrived on 7th May 1945. The following day, like many other bomber squadrons throughout the country, Middleton's Lancasters embarked on Operation *Dodge*. This was the much safer and happier task of ferrying ex-POWs back to Britain; 6 Group aircraft alone brought 4,329 men back home, many of them Canadians.

A fitting memorial located in front of the St George's Hotel (originally the Officers' Mess) for all the Canadian aircrew who lost their lives flying from Middleton. (Author)

It was easy to forget that, despite the end of hostilities in Europe, the war in the Far East was still raging. Bomber Command squadrons throughout the country were being earmarked for operations in the Pacific theatre, including eight squadrons from 6 Group. 419 and 428 Squadrons were part of this group which would return to Canada to train as part of the new *Tiger Force* although the war against Japan came to an end before the force was needed. 428 Squadron began the long journey home on 31st May, followed by 419 Squadron saying farewell on 1st June 1945.

Bomber Command began to shrink at a rapid rate, and many of its squadrons were disbanded and its airfields closed. Middleton was one of the lucky ones but it would no longer remain a bomber station. In early July 1945, the airfield was transferred to Fighter Command for the first time, and, on 27th July, 13 Operational Training Unit (OTU) arrived, equipped with various marks of the de Havilland Mosquito. The loss rate on the Mosquito was particularly high, especially during take-off and landing, when the aircraft was at its most challenging. In April 1947, the unit moved to Leeming in North Yorkshire, but the

Immediate post-war aerial view of RAF Middleton St George with 13 OTU's Mosquitos in residence. (A Ferguson)

128

Mosquito night-fighters of the re-formed 608 (North Riding) Squadron at Thornaby would continue to use the airfield for many months to come. This Royal Auxiliary Air Force squadron would make use of Middleton until its disbandment at Thornaby on 10th March 1957. The Mosquito night-fighters made way for the Spitfire F.22, followed by the de Havilland Vampire, of which 608 Squadron operated four different marks.

In late 1947, the airfield was handed over to Flying Training Command, specifically for the use of 2 Air Navigation School (ANS), which arrived from Bishops Court in Northern Ireland on 1st October. The school's Avro Ansons and Vickers Wellington trainers remained at Middleton until May 1950 and were replaced by a training unit with relatively more modern equipment. 205 Advanced Flying School (AFS) was formed at Middleton on 7th September 1950, with the task of training day fighter-pilots on the Gloster Meteor. The school was equipped with F.3 and F.4 single seaters as well as a host of two-seater T.7s. Both neighbouring Thornaby and Croft were used as Relief Landing Grounds, the latter becoming the school's home during late 1952 while Middleton's runways were resurfaced and its status raised to that of an all-weather airfield.

205 AFS was redesignated as 4 Flying Training School (FTS) on 1st June 1954, and Vampires were now on strength as well. By June 1956, the school moved south to Worksop in Nottinghamshire and the airfield was returned to Fighter Command.

264 Squadron, flying the Armstrong Whitworth Meteor NF.14, was the first to arrive on 26th February 1957, followed by 92 Squadron with the Hawker Hunter F.6 on 1st March. Both squadrons had moved again by September. 264 Squadron moved to Leeming on 26th and 92 Squadron to Thornaby on the 30th to make way for more expansion work for the next generation of jet fighters.

From October 1957 to June 1958, the airfield was closed while the main runway was extended and strengthened and new buildings were added. Whilst at Leeming, 264 Squadron was disbanded and renumbered 33 Squadron. Now equipped with the Gloster Javelin FAW.7, it was 33 Squadron which was the first fighter squadron to return to Middleton on 30th September 1958. On 1st October, the Hunters of 92 Squadron also returned for air defence duties and the more important role of becoming the RAF Fighter Command's official aerobatic team, known as the 'The Blue Diamonds'.

92 Squadron was destined for conversion onto the English Electric Lightning F.2; so, on 22nd May 1961, the squadron left Middleton for

the last time, its destination Leconfield in North Yorkshire, and many years of supersonic operations. 33 Squadron converted to the Javelin FAW.9 in October 1960 but by December 1962 was disbanded and today performs in a completely different role with the Westland Puma helicopter.

For many, the high point of jet operations at Middleton was the arrival of the Lightning. The first examples arrived in August 1961 with the entrance of the Lightning Conversion Squadron (LCS) from Coltishall in Norfolk, which operated the first trainer variant, the Lightning T.4. On 1st June 1963, the LCS was absorbed into the re-formed 226 Operation Conversion Unit (OCU). By now the unit operated every mark of Lightning available except the F.2s. Sadly for Middleton, the Lightning unit was destined to return to Coltishall on 20th April 1964 and all military flying ceased from that moment on. Despite the amount of reconstruction work and modifications carried out on the airfield, the military had no further use for Middleton. The local Teesside authorities, however, did.

Modern aerial view of the airport. The layout has changed little since the airfield was upgraded into an all-weather fighter station in the 1960s.

130

Snapped up at a bargain price, Middleton's potential as a regional airport was immediately recognized and the airfield, Teesside Airport, began civilian operations only days after the RAF had departed. A series of improvements followed, including a new passenger terminal opened in 1966 and in 1971 its own railway station, which was connected to the terminal by electric powered shuttle buses. In September 2004, it was re-named again, as Durham Tees Valley Airport.

Much of the airfield's military past remains. All the wartime hangars are still in place, utilized by a variety of companies, while the majority of technical and domestic buildings also survive. The original Officers' Mess was converted into the St George Airport Hotel in 1966, and in front of this is a fitting memorial to the sacrifice that the airfield's three Canadian squadrons gave during their time at Middleton St George.

7
MILFIELD

Milfield's history almost became that of a typical training airfield, lost in military history with but a passing paragraph being credited to it. However, halfway through its existence, the airfield's status was elevated to that of one of the most important RAF stations in the country with regard to the invasion of Europe and the Allies' eventual victory. Its remoteness lent itself perfectly to turning already experienced pilots into ground attack specialists, who were regularly given the opportunity to actually use live ammunition on realistic targets.

77 Squadron first used the site in 1917 as a landing ground for their BE.2es and RE.8s. Originally known as Woodbridge, the 90-acre field was the most southerly used by the squadron (whose home airfield was at Edinburgh). The same area, next to the A697, south-east of Milfield, was surveyed again in late 1940, although this time the site would use 700 acres. The original intention was to build a typical A Class airfield for a bomber Operational Training Unit (OTU).

Construction began in early 1941, although by now the criteria had been changed and Milfield was to be built as a fighter-training airfield. The same A-Class triangular pattern still applied, but the runways were considerably shorter with a main runway of 1,400 yards and another two of 1,100 yards each. Eight 'Extra Over' Blister hangars and a pair of T2 hangars were built with a plethora of subsidiary buildings, including a Type 518/40 control tower. The airfield continued to gain buildings that were surplus to requirement on a fighter-training airfield. They included an Astral Navigational Trainer, which was a dome-shaped all-concrete building used by trainee navigators to practise recognition of the stars, using a sextant. It also had an unusually large Motor Transport (MT) section which was equipped with 24 bays rather than the traditional twelve. Possibly a large MT section was built because of the airfield's remote location, allowing a bigger fleet of vehicles to be housed there. Accommodation was dispersed over 13 different sites, none of them luxurious, but it was wartime and the majority of servicemen and women who passed through Milfield were happy serving there.

The airfield officially opened on 1st August 1942 and was ready to receive its first unit the following day. 59 OTU was formed at Turnhouse in Midlothian on 16th December 1940 to train single-seat fighter pilots primarily on the Hawker Hurricane. It did not receive its first aircraft until after it moved to Crosby-on-Eden in Cumbria in March 1941. To make way for 9 OTU and Crosby's transfer to Coastal Command, 59 OTU began to move to Milfield on 2nd August, bringing a few Hurricanes and some support aircraft. The main ground party arrived on the 5th, and, by 10th of August, all 71 Hurricanes, 12 Typhoons, Fairey Battles and Miles Martinets had arrived. Brunton was quickly established as a satellite airfield for Milfield, and aircraft from Crosby's own satellite, Longtown, descended upon Brunton on 4th August. Within days the unit lost its first aircraft when Hurricane Mk.I P3620 collided with P3104 during a dummy ground attack near Fenwick. P3620 crashed immediately, killing the pilot, while P3104 managed to make an emergency landing at Brunton. This would set the tone for 59 OTU's stay at Milfield; not a single month would pass without accident, injury or death to a trainee pilot or instructor.

Flying training began immediately at Milfield, as the unit was already experienced in its own methods and techniques. A typical course ran for ten weeks with around 36 students and the hope that at least 30 pilots would pass out qualified. The latter figure compensated for individuals not attaining the required standard or possibly not even surviving the course! A single instructor was allocated to three or four students, although very often more 'challenging' students would be passed to another instructor. The first half of the course involved flying the Miles Master with an instructor in the rear, the students gradually honing the skills they had already learnt in preparation for that first solo on the more powerful Hurricane. The Master was specifically designed as an advanced trainer which represented the majority of fighter aircraft currently in service with the RAF. The plane's low wing, retractable undercarriage, and reasonably good performance was the perfect stepping-stone for the budding fighter pilot. It was imperative that the student became competent on the Master before he could progress. There never was and never would be a two-seat Hurricane available to the RAF; you were literally on your own for that first flight.

A Hurricane Mk.IId of No.1 SLAIS at Milfield with Sqn Ldr J 'Ginger' Lacey talking to a senior officer.

Once converted to the Hurricane, the student pilots would be taught more advanced navigation techniques, sector and formation flying and the all-important air-to-air firing. The unit's target-towing Miles Martinets, whose crews accumulated more flying hours than any other aircrew on the station, provided the latter.

Air-to-air exercises were often conducted between individual aircraft, whose pilots would perform mock dogfights using a gun camera to register hits rather than live ammunition. On 7th October 1942, a pair of Hurricanes were carrying out a camera-gun exercise south of Berwick when the chasing aircraft fired its guns rather than its harmless camera. The power of its eight Browning machine guns knocked Hurricane Mk.I V6849 out of the sky, although the student pilot managed to bail out to safety. The crippled fighter spiralled into the ground near Ancroft.

A sign of things to come at Milfield was when a new unit was formed at the airfield on 7th December 1942. No.1 Specialized Low Attack Instructors School was brought into being in order to train fighter pilots for very low attacks using specialist weapons such as rocket projectiles (RP), heavy cannons and bombs. Like the OTU, its main equipment was the Hurricane, but a few Masters were used and there was a future plan to introduce the Typhoon as well, which at this point was still experiencing problems.

One of the leading characters involved in the formation of the attack school was Wg Cdr D Gillam DSO, DFC, AFC. Born in Tyneside, Gillam was a career pilot who had served with distinction during the Battle of Britain and in March 1942 he became responsible for setting up the RAF's first Typhoon Wing at Duxford, Cambridgeshire. The attack school's first Chief Flying Instructor was another Battle of Britain veteran. Sqn Ldr J 'Ginger' Lacey was one of the highest scorers during the battle, with 15 confirmed kills and quite possibly several others unaccounted for. Despite his aerial experience, Lacey had sampled how ineffective a fighter was against enemy armour back in May 1940 in France. Lacey described how the Hurricane's 0.303 machine guns were virtually ineffective. It was like shooting at elephants with a pea-shooter! The attack school would improve upon lessons learned in those early days.

The main mark of aircraft in the attack school was the Hurricane Mk.IV, which was introduced to the school in May 1943. The Mk.IV was constructed with a 'universal' wing, which could be fitted with a host of ordnance, including 250lb and 500lb bombs, two, four or eight RPs or a pair of 40mm anti-tank guns. The aircraft was, unusually, given clearance to carry different weapons asymmetrically, for example a 40mm gun under one wing and a 250lb bomb under the other. It was not popular with pilots in action because the added weight of armour and multiple stores restricted its performance compared to the earlier marks. The Mk.IV did perform exceptionally well against armoured vehicles both in North Africa and later in Europe, overshadowed only by the Typhoon in the ground attack role.

The attack school provided support for the newly formed 184 Squadron, which arrived on detachment from Colerne in Wiltshire in December. Equipped with the Hurricane Mk.IId, which was the anti-tank version, the squadron was destined to receive the more capable Mk.IV in May 1943. The squadron returned again on 3rd February and left on 22nd February, becoming the only operational squadron to be associated in any capacity with Milfield during the war.

With the arrival of the School, a new ground attack range was constructed at Goswick Sands, north of Holy Island in early 1943. The range would be developed over the coming months with a variety of

A Hurricane Mk.IV loaded with eight rocket projectiles, one of several different combinations of ordnance available to the type.

ground targets, including old tanks and lorries, all of which had live weapons either dropped on or launched at them. Simulated convoys were also laid out on the range; some of the early targets were a pair of Newcastle Corporation double deckers, a removal van and even an old steam lorry.

Milfield's target towing facilities were also increased the previous month. Known as the North and South Tow, they were located between Holy Island and the Farne Islands (North Tow), and between Dunstanburgh Castle and the Farne Islands (South Tow). The Target Towing Flight operated parallel to the coast, approximately one mile out to sea and at between 2,000 ft and 6,000 ft.

In the event of a German invasion, which by 1943 was looking unlikely to happen, all fighter OTUs would have been called to the defence of the country. The number 500 was added to the unit, establishing a new name; in 59 OTU's case of 559 Squadron. Events dictated that this reserve force was never brought into being. However, 559 Squadron was formed at Milfield, moving temporarily to Brunton in March 1943 with 18 Hurricane Mk.Is and IIs. By June, the squadron was operating its aircraft as night fighters at Milfield, and on 7th July the squadron returned to Brunton.

It had been planned for many months that 59 OTU would receive the Hawker Typhoon and eventually be fully equipped with the big ground attack aircraft. The Typhoon never did fully replace the Hurricane, but the first eventually began to arrive at Milfield in April 1943. It was an inauspicious start on 18th April: the first aircraft to arrive, Typhoon Mk.Ib R8867, burst a tyre on landing, damaging it beyond repair.

By May, the 30th OTU Course had passed through Milfield and the 31st would become the first Typhoon conversion course. The title of 559 Squadron was used by the OTU for the third and final phase of the student pilots' training, and the Typhoon accident rate during this time reflects this new phase of the unit's history. Four Typhoons were lost in accidents: one in May, and three in June, two of which were landing accidents attributed to wind shear on approach to a particular runway. Little was known of the phenomenon in 1943, and on 5th July an investigating group visited Milfield to find out why so many aircraft

Hawker Typhoon Mk.Ia R7580, pictured while being assessed by the Air Fighting Development Unit. This aircraft went on to serve with 59 OTU and spun into the ground near Milfield on the 13th June 1943.

were crashing on landing. Once the problem was discovered, the approach patterns were changed and the accident rate began to marginally subside.

The students of virtually all OTUs were made up of individuals from all over the globe, and in June 1943 a rather resourceful Italian prisoner of war who was working on a farm near the airfield suggested making a memorial to Milfield. This was a unique piece of foresight as the majority of military memorials have been put in place many years after the end of the Second World War. The Italian was a stonemason by trade and he skilfully crafted one large globe representing the world with a very impressive eagle standing upon it. Unfortunately, the Italian was moved before he could complete the second. A local airman finished the second globe and eagle, although this one was not up to the standard of the first. However, they both survive today, representing a fitting memorial to all who passed through Milfield.

During September 1943, the airfield was indirectly affected by the operations of the USAAF 8th Air Force. One hundred and forty-seven Boeing B-17F Flying Fortresses were dispatched on 16th September to attack the French port of Nantes and the Chateau-Bougon airfield. On their return, B-17F 42-30030 named 'Old Ironsides' of the 388th Bomb Group, 502nd Bomb Squadron, based at Knettishall in Suffolk, became lost. Low on fuel, the pilot, 1st Lt H O Nagorka, decided to ditch in the sea south of the Farne Islands. All ten crew survived the impact of the ditching, although the aircraft sank so fast that two gunners were drowned. The survivors managed to reach St Cuthbert's Island and were eventually rescued.

The crew, including a severely injured tail gunner who had lost a leg, was transported to Milfield, as it had been decided that another B-17 from 388th BG would collect them. The large American bomber arrived over Milfield a few hours later, with Major Forrest at the controls. Landing safely, the B-17 was the largest aircraft to visit the airfield, but fears were raised that the runways may be too short for the take off. For some inexplicable reason, it was decided to lengthen runway 24, which was only 1,100 yards long, rather than the main one. This was achieved by removing the hedge on the Wooler to Milfield road and extending the runway with pierced steel planking. A fully laden B-17 would use most of a 2,000-yard runway, but, without bombs and with a light fuel load, the American bomber departed from Milfield with little fuss.

By the end of 1943, the future of both 59 OTU and No.1 Specialized Low Attack Instructors School was envisaged by senior staff in a more combined role. Despite a high loss rate, the OTU had produced over

1,200 fully training fighter pilots and accumulated over 100,000 flying hours. The attack school had also formed itself into a very efficient unit, continually improving on its own instructing techniques as well as producing a consistent supply of pilots trained in the ground attack role.

On 26th January 1944, a closing down ceremony of 59 OTU and the attack school was attended by AVM D F Stevenson, AOC 9 Gp who thanked the units for their achievements. Both units were then absorbed into the Fighter Leaders School (FLS), a unit that would become responsible for training virtually all ground attack pilots for the forthcoming D-Day invasion and beyond.

The FLS was formed on 15th January 1943 at Chedworth in Gloucestershire as part of 52 OTU. Equipped with 36 Spitfires, mainly tired Mk.Is and IIs, the school moved again on 9th February, this time to Charmy Down in Somerset but before it could settle in there was another move to Aston Down in Wiltshire, on 16th August. Redesignated 52 OTU (FLS), then changed again to 52 OTU (Fighter Command School of Tactics), on arrival at Milfield on 26th January 1944 it adopted the official title Fighter Leaders School, finally becoming autonomous.

The school had not been entirely successful since its formation, mainly because of too many moves and very little opportunity to fly

A flypast of four Hurricane Mk.IIcs over Milfield in early 1944, possibly when the OTU and SLAIS merged into the FLS.

139

ground attack sorties in the more crowded southern skies. Milfield offered good bombing and gunnery range facilities that would continue to expand with the added use of Doddington Moor, between Kirknewton and Akeld. The airspace over Northumberland was relatively quiet, and the airfield itself was well organized to accommodate several small squadrons of aircraft and had the added bonus of Brunton still being available as a satellite airfield, although it was not used to any great extent.

Having soaked up three different units, the FLS now had a wider and more up to date range of aircraft at their disposal. The Spitfire was still the dominant type, with later the Mk.Vb, Vc, IX and XII joining the school. The Typhoon Mk.Ib and Hurricane Mk.I and IV, supported by the usual collection of lesser types, transformed the FLS into a very capable unit.

The importance of the FLS was reflected by the comments of Air Chief Marshal Trafford Leigh-Mallory on 18th January 1944. While the school was preparing for its move north and the first course at Milfield, Mallory, the then Commander in Chief of the Allied Expeditionary Force, said;

'I want this course to take precedence over current operational commitments and all officers attending to enter into the spirit and urgent purpose for which it has been formed. Nothing could be more important to the success of Operation 'Overlord' than to train to meet the enemy at the outset at the top of our form. There is no doubt that his first impressions at the initial clash will have the most far reaching effect on the final issue.'

The Air Officer Commanding of the 2nd Tactical Air Force (TAF), Air Marshal Sir Arthur Coningham KCB, DSO, MC, DFC, AFC, extended this sentiment by being personally involved in the school, visiting Milfield throughout the year.

The FLS was divided into two wings. These were named the Tactics Wing, under the command of Wg Cdr E H Thomas DSO, DFC, and the Armaments Wing, under the command of Wg Cdr R E P Brooker DFC. The Tactics Wing was made up of three squadrons, each under the command of a squadron leader with a flight lieutenant as deputy; all were very highly experienced. The Armaments Wing was initially made up of two squadrons, with 4 Squadron operating the Hurricane Mk.IV and Typhoon Mk.Ib, and 5 Squadron operating the Typhoon and Spitfire.

It was planned that each course would last for three weeks, weather dependent. In the first week, the Tactics Wing flying syllabus involved

140

training in fighter-bomber attacks using practice bombs, moving on to more substantial live ammunition in the second week. The final week was purely to develop the new skills learned. Intertwined within the course was the Armament Wing syllabus, which involved 4 and 5 Squadron. 4 Squadron specialized in the use of rocket projectiles (RP), using practice heads made of concrete and live rockets with 25lb armour piercing heads and the larger 60lb version. 5 Squadron was dedicated to the delivery of bombs and cannons, using both shallow and steep dive-bombing techniques. The aircraft were capable of carrying either eight 25lb practice bombs or a pair of 500lb live bombs. By now, Goswick range was becoming more complicated, with a variety of targets which included a 200ft beach target and six Churchill Tanks, both for RPs. There was also a live bombing target, a practice bombing target, six 10ft squares for air to ground 20mm cannon and 0.303 in, as well as a 10ft square moving target for 20mm cannon. Realistic gun emplacements and over 50 MT vehicles arranged in convoy for all weapons also provided an inviting target. Finally, a 150ft white circle for camera gun attacks and a section of railway line for RP attacks completed the range.

The army was also involved in providing live moving targets for the FLS aircraft to be vectored to. Major Fraser was in command of a contingent of troops which were based at Milfield but also had a tented camp near East Horton. To the north was Horton Moor and it was here that Major Fraser's 'private' army drove tanks and trucks in staged convoys for the benefit of the attacking fighters.

North-east England was turned into a 'simulated northern Europe' in early February 1944. The FLS took part in a massive land battle tactical exercise, which covered an area from St Abbs Head to Duns, up to Musselburgh near Edinburgh and down to Lauder in the Borders. These large-scale exercises continued all over the country right up to the D-Day Landings in June. The local population were to become quite used to being attacked by their own air force. As well as the facilities at the local ranges, targets representing enemy locations were regularly dummy attacked. Kelso Bridge, Roxburgh Viaduct, Twizel Station, the village of Norham and the small town of Coldstream were all used for practice dive-bombing.

Local exercises also took advantage of the east coast main line for dummy attacks, although the train drivers and passengers were usually completely oblivious to their part in the FLS training programme. Operation Salmon, between 14th and 16th February 1944, involved a single Spitfire flying a reconnaissance sortie along the

From February 1944 the FLS gained a sixth squadron, specifically to train American pilots in ground attack and flight leadership skills. The first USAAF aircraft to arrive was the Republic P-47 Thunderbolt.

main railway line. When the pilot spotted a train he would contact Milfield, which would scramble a squadron of Typhoons as quickly as possible. During this particular exercise, one group of Typhoons managed a dummy attack on a train travelling north out of Newcastle within 21 minutes of receiving the information. Not bad, considering this particular group had to taxi to the opposite end of the airfield to take off!

In late February, the FLS was expanded to a sixth squadron, which would be operated by the USAAF, initially with the Republic P-47 Thunderbolt. On the ground the P-47 never gave the impression of being a nimble manoeuvrable fighter. However, despite being the largest and heaviest single-engined fighter built during the Second World War, the P-47 was a superb fighter. 6 Squadron was equipped with the P-47D with a powerful new engine and a 'teardrop' canopy, which gave 360-degree visibility. Overall command of the new American squadron was performed by Colonel A Salisbury DFC, USAAF. His main responsibility was to coordinate the operation of the unit with Tactics and Armament Wings. The squadron's new commanding officer was Major Paul T. Douglas, posted in from the 368th Fighter Group, based at Greenham Common, Berkshire.

Ground attack sorties were quite possibly one of the most dangerous tasks a pilot would have to face. Not only was the danger level raised by operating so close to the ground, but there was also the additional risk of carrying potentially volatile ordnance. On 9th March 1944, during a demonstration of dive-bombing to Prince Bernard of the Netherlands over the Goswick Range, Flt Lt M Bouquen's Spitfire Mk.Vb P8549 was literally blown apart by its own bomb, highlighting the risks even without enemy fire.

The importance of the unit was raised to another level when discussions were held at Milfield on 11th March to establish the principles of the existence of the FLS, with Air Marshal Coningham in attendance. Special reference was given to the teaching of all current tactics, with specific attention given to close support operations. Facilities on the airfield were to be improved to support the school with new ideas and weapons that could be tested on the local ranges and new tactics that could be passed on for future operations. With the arrival of the Americans, it was suggested that the FLS should work closely with the School of Air Tactics in Orlando, Florida and exchange information and personnel.

Another result of this meeting was that pilots from front-line squadrons were attached to the FLS for short periods in order to maintain an up-to-date tactical outlook from all theatres of the war. This first hand experience was invaluable information that the school could pass on. It was also decided that new staff pilots should join the school direct from operations and that their tour would be no longer than three months. The course length was adjusted to three weeks in summer, with the addition of a week in winter, although there was little opportunity for pilots to return for the extra week.

The final item on the agenda was that the FLS should maintain a regular flow of information to the Operational Requirement Experimental Establishment and that the aircraft manufacturers, specifically Hawkers, should co-ordinate future development of current and new aircraft. The FLS really could make a difference and, with the support of senior officers, was quickly becoming a respected centre for ground attack training.

The USAAF at the time had sufficient resources for their pilots to attend an FLS course at Milfield in their own aircraft. The third course at Milfield not only had the resident P-47s, it also had P-51 Mustang and P-38 Lightning pilots as well. At the end of this course the station commander, Gp Capt J R Adams AFC, thought it would be a good idea to give the American pilots the chance to fly the Typhoon for experience. This comparative exercise went very well, and from then on it was the practice for RAF and USAAF pilots to fly each other's aircraft at the end of each course. However, several pilots recall that it was utter chaos as pilots totally unfamiliar with flying another aircraft type and without any conversion training attempted to fly without killing themselves. Luckily, no incident ever occurred during these moments of madness, which probably reflected just how experienced these particular pilots were.

The casualty rate of the FLS was remarkably low considering the nature of the training, although accidents would happen. A practice 'target of opportunity' saw the demise of Lt Serapiglia and his P-47 on 12th April (see Eshott), and on 2nd May a Spitfire from 3 Squadron FLS was lost off Alnwick. Flt Lt Wilkinson was taking part in Exercise Drier when he lost control and plunged into the sea off Boulmer. Two more pilots were lost in June and September, both while performing air-to-ground firing exercises on the Goswick range. These losses were once again described by senior staff as inevitable and acceptable.

As well as the busy flying programme, the pilots were expected to attend several lectures during their short stay at Milfield. Many were given by highly experienced and senior officers including Wg Cdr W F Blackadder, who led 607 Squadron (see Usworth), from the Air Fighting Development Unit at Wittering, Northamptonshire and Wg Cdr T G 'Hamish' Mahaddie, who on 6th June 1944 gave a detailed lecture on the role of the Pathfinder Force.

Other American units arrived during 1944, including several P-51 Mustangs and the twin-engined P-38 Lightning, pictured here.

The same day, the greatest invasion the world had ever seen took place on the beaches of Northern France, and, by 7th June, Gp Cpt D Gillam was leading a wing of five Typhoon squadrons into battle against German armoured vehicles. Many of the pilots in those squadrons trained at Milfield, and with the invasion the FLS had a new reason to continue producing highly trained ground attack pilots. The Typhoons of the 2nd TAF would play a major role in the defeat of the German Army right up to the end of the war. Losses would be high, averaging two pilots per week, but the enemy would suffer considerably more, especially at the Falaise Gap and, later, in the Ardennes conflict. A high ranking German officer who was inter-viewed after the war was asked what had been the main contributing factor that had brought about his defeat. His reply was quite simply the aircraft of the 2nd TAF.

As if Milfield was not busy enough, another specialist unit was formed there on 6th September 1944. The Day Fighter Development Wing (DFDW) initially comprised a fighter training squadron, a fighter bomber squadron and an air support development squadron and, like its immediate neighbours, it operated a combination of Spitfires, Typhoons and an assortment of support aircraft. The increasingly less hostile skies over Northumberland and southern Scotland were becoming the perfect area for units like the DFDW to experiment with new techniques and tactics.

To help replace the losses of the 2nd TAF, it was decided to re-form 56 OTU, which been redesignated No.1 Combat Training Wing at Tealing, Angus in October 1943. Milfield's facilities and location lent itself perfectly to the OTU, and it was officially in residence on 15th December 1944. The unit was first introduced at Sutton Bridge in Lincolnshire in November 1940 to train fighter pilots on the Hurricane. At Milfield, its new aircraft would be the Typhoon Mk.Ib and the formidable Tempest Mk.V.

The Allied advance through Europe was progressing towards Berlin, albeit at a frustratingly steady pace. The war was still getting further away from Milfield, and meetings were held to discuss the possible relocation of the FLS and the DFDW to a more southerly location. With the arrival of 56 OTU, space had become limited and the inevitable order to move came quickly. On 23rd December, a signal was received by the FLS and the DFDW instructing them to move to Wittering by 27th December 1944. All the aircraft departed that day, followed by a mass exodus of the ground crew, the majority of which travelled by train from Akeld Station, disembarking at Stamford.

Milfield bears little resemblance to its wartime layout, with only remnants of the north-eastern perimeter track remaining. The two grass runways are for the gliding club and neither replicates the position of the originals. (Crown Copyright)

During its stay at Milfield, eleven courses had passed through the FLS with an average of 60 pilots on each. The school had provided an invaluable source of fully trained pilots that certainly made an impact on the war in Europe. The FLS was destined to be absorbed into the Central Fighter Establishment (CFE), while the DFDW remained autonomous until it was renamed the Day Fighter Combat Squadron in 1958 and survived until its disbandment at Binbrook in Lincolnshire in November 1965.

The OTU now had to find space for all of its aircraft, which, at its peak, totalled, over 130. Once again, Brunton served as a satellite airfield and remained in this role until the end of the war. The first course began on 1st January 1945 and was approximately nine weeks long. A new course started every three weeks with the intention of qualifying at least ten pilots at the end of each.

Initially, the introduction of the Tempest Mk.V caused a few problems, as there was a distinct shortage of experienced instructors on that particular aircraft. Many were hastily re-trained on the relatively new fighter and not only was the casualty rate high amongst the students but also several instructors fell foul of the power of the Tempest. A development of the Typhoon, the first Tempest to fly was the Mk.V in September 1942, the earlier marks only flying as prototypes with a variety of engines. The main difference between the Typhoon and Tempest was that the latter featured a thin-section laminar flow wing and a lengthened fuselage, which contained the fuel tanks and increased the aircraft's range to a maximum of over 1500 miles.

At any one time during its existence at Milfield, 56 OTU had 53 Typhoons and as many Tempests on strength. These were supported by at least 16 Miles Masters, with half a dozen Martinets providing aerial gunnery targets. The courses continued unabated right up until the war's end and, unusually, did not come to a grinding halt upon the arrival of VE Day. However, Brunton's use by the OTU as a satellite came to an end on 21st May 1945, and its closure followed not long after.

The airfield now braced itself for an influx of surplus Typhoons and Tempests from front line squadrons which were either being disbanded or re-equipped. 183 Squadron arrived on 16th June 1945 to deliver their tired Typhoon Mk.Ibs; then, the following day, the squadron travelled south to Chilbolton in Hampshire to convert to the Spitfire Mk.IX. The predicted arrival of war weary aircraft never materialized, the majority of Typhoon and Tempest squadrons being disbanded in Germany.

The training programme at Milfield continued at a vigorous pace because it was expected that all new pilots would be transferred to the Far East to continue the war against the Japanese. In August, the combined effect of two atomic bombs and a 1,660 aircraft bombing raid against Tokyo brought a final end to hostilities on 15th August 1945.

The pace of the OTU started to decrease, although the demand for Tempest pilots in particular was seen as enough justification for the unit to continue flying from Milfield. The Typhoon training pro-gramme started to tail off by the end of 1945, although it was quickly replaced with the arrival of the Spitfire Mk.IX, which would now operate alongside the Tempest Mk.V as the main aircraft type.

The powerful Hawker Tempest Mk.V was operated by 56 OTU during its stay at Milfield.

Although a few wartime buildings survive around the edge of the old airfield, the centre is dominated by Milfield Gliding Club's excellent hangar and clubhouse. (Author)

The end came for 56 OTU on 14th February 1946, outliving the majority of similar units by at least nine months. The students on the final course completed their training at Keevil in Wiltshire and within two months the airfield was closed.

The major part of the airfield was handed back to its original pre-war owners, although several buildings on the main site were used to accommodate Latvian soldiers until at least 1950. Several other huts, mainly on the old WAAF site, were converted with approval from the Ministry of Health in 1948. Another 56 huts were converted into one-, two- and three-bedroom houses in 1950 and the old WAAF mess was converted into a school.

Aviation briefly returned in 1977/78 when Air Anglia made a few flights with a Fokker Friendship out of Milfield, but unfortunately the idea of regular flights to larger domestic airports and Europe was never pursued. Not long after, a more permanent aeronautical use for the old airfield manifested itself in the shape of The Borders Gliding Club, which still operates from Milfield today, and its bright blue hangar and clubhouse dominate the centre of the airfield.

Considering how rich its wartime history was, it is very easy to drive past Milfield without realizing it. No runways or original hangars remain and a quarry now dominates the western side of the airfield. The northern and eastern perimeter tracks have now been incorporated into a minor road and a few wartime buildings are now a private dwelling on the eastern side where access to the gliding club can be gained.

8
MORPETH

Aerial gunnery was an art that needed to be taught, and taught well. The survival of a bomber and its crew depended upon the teamwork of the crew and the skill of the pilot. At 20,000ft over Germany, the skills that had been taught while at Morpeth saved the lives of many aircrews.

The site was first surveyed in late 1940 and contractors began preparing it early the following year. The airfield was located three miles south-west of Morpeth, between the village of Tranwell and the hamlet of Silvington. The runways and perimeter track were sandwiched between two minor roads, while the bulk of the living accommodation was built in woods to the north. The traditional triangular layout of runways was built, the longest being 1,400 yards with two shorter at 1,100 yards each; 36 hardstandings were scattered around the perimeter. Morpeth was well catered for with no shortage of hangars: three 100 ft span 'T1' style and 17 Blister type hangars were positioned around the edge of the airfield, the latter being capable of housing a medium sized aircraft.

For Morpeth no official opening date is available, but the first military personnel arrived on 29th September 1941. The Army was the first to arrive, commanded by Major A S C Brown of the 7th Royal Lancers, accompanied by a contingent of soldiers. The RAF began to arrive in limited numbers and a sufficient number must have been in residence by the end of February 1942, as the station had gained a commanding officer, Wg Cdr J Marson. He was replaced by Wg Cdr C H Brandon on 9th April, and by now Morpeth was ready to accommodate its first unit.

RAF Bomber Command's main equipment by the beginning of 1942 was the Short Stirling, Handley Page Halifax and Avro Lancaster. On average at least three of the seven- or eight-man crews were air gunners, making them the most prolific of all aircrew. When these larger aircraft began to enter service it was obvious that training on a grand scale would have to be introduced to meet the demand. From June 1941, all of the original Bombing & Gunnery Schools (B&GS) which had been formed at the outbreak of the war were replaced by new Air Gunners' Schools (AGS). Eventually, ten new schools were formed in the United Kingdom, the majority in the north of England and Scotland.

All aircrew without exception followed the same training route before being posted to a front line squadron. In the case of air gunners, they were initially tested in basic theory and flying training at one of the many Initial Training Wings (ITW) located throughout the country. Drill and a relentless physical training regime prepared the new gunners for their next stage of training, a posting to an AGS. There followed six weeks' intensive training in the art of aerial gunnery before the air gunner was posted to an Operational Training Unit (OTU). It was at this point that the air gunner would find a crew and start to perform with a team that would stick together until the end of their operational tour. After the OTU came the Heavy Conversion Unit (HCU) and this was where the new bomber crew would finally begin to fly their particular aircraft. Finally came a posting to a squadron and an operational flying tour of duty. The odds of actually making it through training were comparable to the chances of making it through an operational tour.

The Blackburn Botha was the first main aircraft operated by 4 AGS at Morpeth. It was not a sad parting when it was replaced by the Avro Anson.

No. 4 AGS was officially formed at Morpeth on 17th March 1942, with an intended establishment of nearly 40 Blackburn Bothas and over 20 Westland Lysander Target Tugs plus a variety of support aircraft that included an Avro Anson and Airspeed Oxford. The unit's first aircraft was supposed to arrive on 11th April but unfortunately crashed en route. Botha Mk.I W5134, piloted by First Officer Preston of the ATA (Air Transport Auxiliary), crashed near South Clarewood, not far from the fighter airfield at Ouston. Preston was uninjured but the Botha was a total write-off, and this did not bode well for the new school.

The Botha was one of three types of new aircraft that were chosen to re-equip the RAF's maritime squadrons before the outbreak of the Second World War. The other aircraft were the Saro Lerwick and the Bristol Beaufort. The latter was the only one that performed well, with both the Lerwick and Botha withdrawn from front line service after a short period of time. The Botha was designed to operate as a general reconnaissance or torpedo-bomber, although it only went on to serve with 608 Squadron, based at Thornaby. Unusually, the aircraft was ordered from the drawing board without any consideration for its potential failings, which were many. Its main weakness was lack of power; its two Bristol Perseus engines were totally inadequate, and the design of the aircraft exposed serious visibility problems, especially downward and laterally. The Botha was relegated to operate with various training schools and was officially declared obsolete in August 1943, although 4 AGS and several other minor units continued to operate it for much longer.

Throughout April 1942, Bothas and Lysanders began to arrive; generally all were delivered by the ATA without incident. On 5th May Air Chief Marshal Sir Edgar Ludlow-Hewitt KCB, CMG, DSO, MC, the Inspector General of the RAF, arrived by air from Acklington. Ludlow-Hewitt's visit was an indication that the airfield and the AGS were nearing readiness to begin a flying programme. Station strength was almost 500 officers, S/NCOs, airmen and airwomen, and more aircraft continued to arrive on a daily basis.

Marshal of the RAF, Viscount Trenchard GCB, DSO, DCL, LLD visited Morpeth on 16th May. Although he had retired from the RAF in 1929, Trenchard retained his senior rank and throughout the Second World War travelled up and down the country visiting virtually every airfield. He managed to visit Morpeth on three occasions, returning on 27th January 1943 and on 30th April 1944. On all of these visits he addressed the officers and airmen separately.

During May 1942, the AGS managed to wreck three of its Lysanders and a single Botha even before the flying programme had been initiated. The most serious of these incidents occurred on 17th May, when the engine cut on Lysander TT.I L4736, piloted by Flt Sgt Szwedowski. Szwedowski was seriously injured and never flew again, and L4736, which had only accumulated a few flying hours from new, was written off.

On 23rd May, No. 1 Air Gunners' Course arrived at Morpeth, consisting of 45 air gunner cadets. The flying training programme finally began at the end of the month, with both air and ground training for the new recruits. 4 AGS had its own air-to-air firing range located to the south of Amble, which extended into the North Sea. Flying sorties were often flown from Boulmer as well as Morpeth, doubling the turn-around capability of the school.

Although the Botha was deemed unfit for many duties, it did serve reasonably well as a gunnery-trainer. The aircraft was fitted with a power-operated turret located along the dorsal spine. The turret was armed with a pair of Browning 0.303-inch machine guns, and the aircraft also had room for at least four pupils and an instructor, allowing several air gunners to operate the guns during a single sortie.

Target towing facilities for the AGS were provided by a fleet of Westland Lysanders very similar to the aircraft pictured. The underside of the target tugs was painted in yellow and black diagonal stripes.

A second course arrived two weeks after the first, and this was the general routine for the school's time at Morpeth. The sudden rise in the work rate can be seen from the flying figures presented. During May the school's Bothas had flown only 126 hours, in June the total was 407 hours. This trend would continue until a peak average of over 2,000 flying hours per month for the AGS's aircraft was reached in June 1944.

Wg Cdr C H Brandon was relieved by Wg Cdr R I Jones as station commander on 20th June 1942, and a period of routine began with regard to the flying training programme. The organization of the airfield itself was, unbelievably, still lacking any kind of flying control. A control tower, really a control office, as it was of a bungalow type design, was eventually built but was without any trained staff, a situation that would continue for years to come. In addition, the majority of aircrew were Polish, and they were frustrated at having to fly on a training unit. It is unsurprising therefore that there were catastrophic consequences. Flying discipline with the Poles was generally lacking, with many performing unauthorized low level fly-pasts of local towns and 'beat ups' of the airfield. Enquiries and courts martial were continuous at Morpeth.

On 4th August 1942, Morpeth became host to 72 Squadron, equipped with the Spitfire Mk.Vc and Mk.IX, under the command of Sqn Ldr R W Oxpring DFC. With fond memories of the squadron's activities while stationed at Acklington in 1940, the local population gave the squadron members a warm welcome. However, Oxpring later wrote in his autobiography about Morpeth: 'This hutted habitat was depressing.' On 12th August the squadron left for Ayr in preparation for its participation in the North African campaign, not returning to the United Kingdom until its re-formation in 1947 at Odiham in Hampshire with the Vampire jet.

Aircrew were not always responsible for the continuous stream of accidents involving aircraft at Morpeth. On 13th September 1942, a fitter had been working on an engine of Botha Mk.I W5123. The aircraft was not chocked, and, once the fitter started the engine for testing, the aircraft swung in a neat semicircle and collided with a tractor parked nearby. Damage was caused to the tailplane and fuselage and the fitter joined the many ranks of officers and airmen that were on the receiving end of disciplinary action. W5123 was quickly repaired and continued its service with the AGS without incident.

The association with 4 AGS and the Lysander came to an end at the beginning of November. The majority of the unit's Lysanders were moved onto other units, and several continued to serve for at least

155

another year. They had served the AGS well, having achieved a combined flying time of 2,600 hours with only three aircraft actually written off in serious accidents. The Miles Martinet was now employed for target towing duties, becoming the first aircraft specifically designed for that purpose to enter service with the RAF. Based upon the Master trainer, the Martinet first flew on 24th April 1942 and remained in service for many years after the war's end. 4 AGS was allocated 25 aircraft, but through accidents and general attrition over 50 passed through the unit. The school now looked forward to a replacement for the increasingly unpopular Botha.

On 16th November 1942, an accident happened in the middle of the airfield, which could without doubt be blamed upon the still-lacking implementation of flying control. Sgt Moszoro, in Botha Mk.I L6339, was beginning his take off on one of the two short runways, completely unaware that another aircraft was doing the same on the other short runway. Sgt Zalenski, in Botha Mk.I W5139, was actually taking off on the incorrect runway and was equally oblivious of the presence of another aircraft. The two aircraft collided at the intersection of the two runways, which was 250 to 300 yards from the beginning of their respective start points. They continued for some distance in a tangled mess of metal and flame, with onlookers not expecting any of the crew from either plane to survive. Incredibly only LAC Wignall was killed, a gunner under training who was inside Sgt Zalenski's aircraft. Unfortunately, though, worse was to follow.

On 29th March 1943 the station was visited by an air-vice marshal from 29 Group (responsible for the operation of all Air Gunnery Schools in the north of England). With low cloud, the weather was poor over the airfield that day, so normal gunnery sorties would have been abandoned. However, a flying display was insisted upon, and two Bothas, W5137 and W5154, were scheduled to take part in it. The first aircraft, W5137, being flown by Flt Lt Zarski, who, at age 46, was by far the most senior Polish pilot on the AGS, took off and climbed away. He was followed by W5154 with Pilot Officer G R Jackson RNZAF at the controls. The lack of discipline within the airfield's circuit, especially during the poor weather conditions, resulted in the two aircraft colliding at 1,200ft as they prepared to land seemingly at the same time. One aircraft dived straight into the ground at a high angle, while the other entered a more shallow descent enabling one airman to bail out. Sadly, his chute did not deploy correctly and he fell to his death. Nine officers and airmen died that day, including five Dutch trainee air gunners, one of whom was only seventeen.

One of the WAAF Flight Mechanics who arrived on station on 6th April 1943, to be employed by 4 AGS. A first for Morpeth and the RAF.

The Hawker Henleys, Tiger Moths and Martinets of 1614 Anti-Aircraft Co-Operation Flight arrived in early April 1943. The Flight was detached from Cark in Lancashire and probably worked with 15 LAAPC at Whitby until their return to Lancashire in June.

WAAFs were not an uncommon sight on RAF airfields, although they were usually found in trades unrelated to the aircraft themselves, for example in the roles of clerks, cooks, drivers, etc. On 6th April 1943, two airwomen flight mechanics arrived on station to be employed by 4 AGS, the first airwomen in the fitter trade to do so. Later, in June, trade training was organized at Morpeth for WAAF ex-balloon operators to be trained as flight mechanics.

It was not unusual for a gunnery school to have an instructional airframe on site for use by the trainees on the ground. This was usually a time expired airframe or sometimes a 'mock up' of an aircraft fitted with a turret and live guns. 4 AGS was incredibly lucky to be the proud owner of an Avro Manchester Mk.I, the ill-fated predecessor of the Lancaster. By the beginning of 1943, this was a particularly rare aircraft because so many were either lost on operations or wrecked in flying accidents. Manchester Mk.I L7419 had seen a lot of flying, including 14 operations. This was quite an achievement, considering the average was approximately six. First delivered to 207 Squadron in July 1941, the veteran bomber was passed to 50 and then 408 Squadron until its flying career ended with 1654 CU (Conversion Unit) at Wigsley in Nottinghamshire. In early June 1943, the Manchester was delivered to Morpeth by a crew from 1654 CU, still adorned with its unit code, UG-B2, and a painting of 'Dopey' from *Snow White and the Seven Dwarfs*. The aircraft proved invaluable for giving the trainees the experience of being inside a large bomber, which internally was very similar to the Lancaster. Many of the new gunners would end up serving on such an aircraft. Immediately after its arrival, the Manchester had its engines and outer wing panels removed; many on the station suggested that it was to deter the Polish airmen from flying it over Germany on a bombing raid!

Otterburn Camp, and its large range, was situated approximately 20 miles away, making Morpeth convenient for housing several Auster AOP Mk.IIIs belonging to 652 Squadron for a few weeks. 'A' Flight was detached to Morpeth from their home airfield at Methven, near Perth during June. The flight took part in several practice artillery shoots, acting as air observation platforms and artillery spotters.

The replacements for the rapidly depleting Bothas began to arrive on 13th June 1943, a new aircraft for the AGS but no stranger to the RAF.

The Avro Anson, affectionately nicknamed 'Faithful Annie', first entered service in 1936 and, remarkably, remained until 1968. Usually crewed by three, the aircraft was smaller than the Botha, but despite this it was far superior in all respects. Nearly 11,000 aircraft were built in Britain and Canada, and it remained in production continuously for 17 years. One hundred and thirty aircraft were being built per month at Avro's Yeadon factory in the peak period of 1943/44. The aircraft delivered to 4 AGS were the Mk.Is, that were converted from general reconnaissance versions to armament trainers. Over 300 aircraft were fitted with a Bristol dorsal turret containing a single 0.303 inch Browning machine gun, although some aircraft had a pair fitted.

Three more Bothas would be lost, two of them proving fatal, before this troublesome aircraft was grounded and eventually removed from the 4 AGS inventory. On 9th June, Botha Mk.I L6441 crashed after an engine failure on final approach to the airfield. The pilot, Pilot Officer Zaleski, and his crew were killed as their aircraft came down in the

Delivered in June 1943, the AGS received an Avro Manchester Mk.I similar to this 207 Squadron machine. The retired bomber was used for familiarity training for student air gunners.

grounds of Gateshead Mental Hospital at Stannington. Following this tragedy, Botha Mk.I W5156 crashed on the main runway on 22nd June. Pilot Officer Reszk aborted his landing; then stalled to the ground after the controls of the Botha jammed. The three-man crew was killed, and a few weeks later the entire Botha fleet was removed from the flying programme. The final, less serious, accident occurred on 17th July 1943, when both engines failed on Botha Mk.I W5044. The aircraft managed to make a forced landing on the airfield but collided with one of its Anson replacements en route. Fifteen Bothas were lost during 4 AGS' thirteen months of service, many resulting in fatalities. The bulk of the aircraft were flown out of Morpeth during August. The last Botha to be scrapped was at Abbotsinch, Renfrewshire, which today is Glasgow Airport, in November 1943. It is ironic that the very last Botha to leave Morpeth had to force land before reaching Abbotsinch and the pilot, Flying Officer Ilott, was commended for not damaging the aircraft.

An impressive milestone was reached in July 1943, when 4 AGS produced the 2,000th trained air gunner. The throughput of airmen now included Free French and Norwegian trainees. The Chief Instructor (CI) and Senior Gunnery Officer (SGO) of the AGS were now able to offer the new air gunners the option to fire gun cameras as part of the six week gunnery course. This cine film capability gave the instructor the chance to watch the air gunner's performance on the

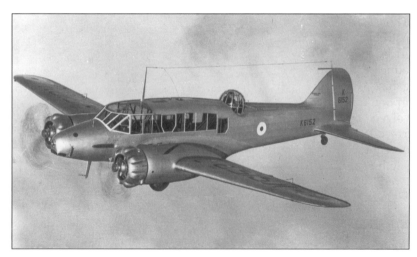

The Avro Anson began to arrive at Morpeth from June 1943, making the AGS more efficient and reducing the accident rate.

ground as well as in the air. For cine gun exercises an attacking force was needed and the CI and SGO visited both Acklington and Boulmer to arrange for fighter co-operation. Both grabbed the opportunity to fly against another moving target, especially one that was not firing live ammunition at them. Cine gun exercises began in September 1943 and averaged over 10,000ft of film shot every month. This peaked at over 28,000ft in June 1944.

Like most units throughout the RAF, 4 AGS used aircraft that were impressed from the civil register not long after the outbreak of the war. One, a De Havilland DH.94 Moth Minor, was first flown in 1937. Originally registered as G-AFPH, the Moth had been in RAF service since January 1940. In September, the pretty little two-seat low wing monoplane left for the Technical Training Command Communication Flight stationed at White Waltham in Buckinghamshire. The aircraft was restored in April 1947 and ended up in Singapore with the registration VR-SDI. Its replacement, although an RAF aircraft, was even older. On 11th September, Avro Tutor Mk.I K3256 arrived from No.1 Flying Instructors' School at Church Lawford in Warwickshire. This particular aircraft first entered service in July 1933 and 4 AGS was to be its thirteenth unit. When Morpeth's new station commander, Gp Capt A H Fear, arrived on 27th September, he took quite a shine to the pre-war biplane and virtually made the aircraft his own. The Tutor left Morpeth on 25th April 1944; eleven years of continuous service had taken its toll, and the aircraft was struck off charge a few weeks later.

Thousands of workers throughout the country were involved in the construction of aircraft, the majority making components. To help increase morale and show the workers that their efforts did actually produce an aircraft at the end of the day, aircraft manufacturers would organize displays by the relevant aircraft. The North East Aircraft Corporation Ltd of Gateshead and Northern Coachbuilders Ltd were involved in making components for the Fairey Swordfish and Barracuda. The Ministry of Aircraft Production arranged a visit to Morpeth for 132 members of staff and employees from both companies on 25th September 1943. Appropriately a Swordfish and a Barracuda, crewed by personnel from the Fleet Air Arm, gave a flying display.

Flying continued unabated until December when a host of repairs was carried out on the airfield. The runways and perimeter track had suffered, having been continuously used by the AGS aircraft. The training programme did continue through the winter, although the average hourly flying time was halved owing to the weather and the work being carried out on the airfield.

February 1944 was recorded as the worst month for accidents since the airfield opened; so it seemed quite fitting that, after 22 months of continuous flying, a flying control officer was finally posted to Morpeth. Although aircraft from Morpeth would continue to be involved in accidents, none was lost through collisions on or around the airfield itself.

During the same month, a unique experiment was carried out at Morpeth. When constructed, the airfield was equipped with 17 'Extra Over' Blister hangars produced by Messrs C. Miskin & Sons, these particular hangars being referred to as 'Miskins'. The Blister hangars were 69 ft wide and 45 ft long and could accommodate a single Botha or, at a squeeze, a pair of Ansons. It had been decided that several of these hangars were in the wrong position on the airfield and that they should be moved. The experiment was to move the Blisters without dismantling them, a task that had never been attempted before. It is not known exactly how it was done, but a single Blister was moved successfully over half a mile to a more appropriate site. The Air Ministry recorded a film about this unique event, and in March two more Blisters were moved across the airfield. By the end of April, a total of nine hangars were moved, but, later in the year, Mother Nature decided that she could do a better job. On 4th November 1944, a 70-80 mph gale lifted a pair of Blisters onto their backs, totally wrecking them.

A single Fairey Swordfish made a rare appearance at Morpeth on the 25th September 1943.

Rescue teams from the airfield were called out in the middle of the night on 3rd March 1944. A Lancaster from 1666 Heavy Conversion Unit, based at Wombleton in Yorkshire, had gone missing in the Cheviot Hills. Although Morpeth was 36 miles away by road, it was one of the nearest airfields capable of mounting a rescue in the area and its airmen would continue this task until the war's end. The wreckage of the Bristol Hercules-engined Lancaster Mk.II DS650 was found one and half miles east of Catcleugh Reservoir on the edge of the A68. Unfortunately, there were no survivors from Pilot Officer R G Calder's RCAF seven man crew, four of whom were Canadians.

Morpeth's status rose slightly on 21st April, when it became the parent station of Usworth, which had been temporarily placed under Care and Maintenance. The resident 62 OTU moved to Woolsington while repair work was carried out at Usworth.

Visits from Bomber Command aircraft were rare, but in the early hours of 10th June 1944, Lancaster Mk.III LM597 from 463 Squadron, based at Waddington, landed at Morpeth. The aircraft had taken part in an attack on the railway junction at Étampe and was diverted north on its return to Lincolnshire. Pilot Officer Totenham and his crew

Marshal of the RAF, Sir John M. Salmond GCB, CMG, CVO, DSO, DCL, LLD, takes the salute during the ATC parade at Morpeth on the 5th July 1944. The Marshal's Beech Expeditor sits inside one of the airfield's T.1 hangars in the background and on the right-hand side is an 'Extra Over' Blister.

stayed overnight, giving a few of the trainees the opportunity to investigate the Lancaster. LM597 was lost on operations against flying bomb sites in the Prouville area on 24th/25th June. The officer commanding 463 Squadron, Wg Cdr D R Donaldson, was at the controls and, like four other crew members, managed to evade capture. Three others became POWs.

The Women's Auxiliary Air Force (WAAF) was formed on 28th June 1939, and its fifth anniversary was to be celebrated in style at Morpeth. It was originally intended for a large event to be held in Newcastle, but on 28th June 1944 a large WAAF birthday parade was held on the airfield. A week later, on 5th July, the airfield was visited by the Marshal of the RAF, Sir John M. Salmond GCB, CMG, CVO, DSO, DCL, LLD, and another large parade was organized. As well as officers and airmen from the unit, air cadets from 404 (ATC) Squadron, Morpeth also took part.

The airfield began to host Italian POWs from 19th July 1944, although the Italians were described as co-operators and were quite willing to be put to work on the airfield. Many of the Italian POWs remained in Britain after the end of the war, the majority never wanting to fight in the first place.

In comparison to the Botha, the Ansons of 4 AGS were considerably more reliable and the accident rate was therefore much lower. Up until October 1944, the unit had only lost two Ansons in serious accidents; so it was a tragedy when Anson Mk.I W2632 was lost on 6th October. The Anson collided with a similar aircraft of 62 OTU in the circuit over Ouston, with the loss of both crews; W2632 came down at Higham Dykes, a few miles north of Ouston. Two days later, 4 AGS lost its last aircraft, Martinet Mk.I MS850, when its engine cut and a safe belly landing was made in a field near Warksworth.

One of 4 AGS's old instructors was Flt Lt F T Roberts, a very experienced pilot who was posted to 1426 (Enemy Aircraft) Flight at Collyweston, Northamptonshire on 22nd August 1944. The flight operated captured Luftwaffe aircraft in RAF markings, demonstrating them throughout the country for aircrew and ground crew alike to see a German aircraft close up. Roberts, complete with a Spitfire escort, returned to Morpeth on 23rd November, flying Junkers Ju 88A-5 EE205. This type of aircraft was no stranger to the locals, and Roberts flew an impressive display over the airfield the following day.

Despite its early troubles with the Botha, 4 AGS was a success story as far as output of trained gunners was concerned. In Morpeth's case, the statistics are worth mentioning: between May 1942 and November

Captured Junkers Ju 88A-4 'EE205' of the Enemy Aircraft Flight visited Morpeth on 23rd November 1944.

1944, the AGS trained over 4000 gunners on 69 courses. They expended over 12 million rounds in the air and on the ground, flying for 37,771 hours on five different types of aircraft, and the cine film section processed 253,262 ft of film between September 1943 and the unit's closure.

4 AGS was disbanded on 9th December 1944 and course number 70 was transferred to 3 AGS at Castle Kennedy in Wigtownshire, where the 73 air gunners finished their training. Two of Morpeth's Ansons were also sent to Castle Kennedy, while the majority were transferred to 9 (O)AOS at Penhros in Caernarvonshire. The same fate awaited the Martinets: the majority were placed into storage and later scrapped, while a few others were transferred to various gunnery schools.

Morpeth now entered its own period of Care and Maintenance under the control of Woolsington and it looked like the airfield had served its purpose with the end of war approaching. However, on 23rd April 1945, a new unit, within 12 Group, was formed at Morpeth in the shape of 80 (French) OTU. The unit was to train French single-seat fighter pilots for service with one of the four French Spitfire squadrons flying with the 2nd Tactical Air Force (TAF) in Germany. These units were

329 'Cicogne', 340 'Ile de France', 341 'Alsace' and 345 'Berry' Squadrons. The OTU was equipped with 24 Spitfire Mk.IXs, 14 Master Mk.IIs, four Martinet Mk.Is and a single Dominie Mk.II. All of the Spitfires supplied to the OTU had seen service with a front line squadron. For example, 441 Squadron, based at Digby, gave up virtually all of its Spitfires for service with the OTU. The unit's stay at Morpeth was short, and there is no record of how many courses passed through the airfield, although its brief time did pass without any incident involving an aircraft. In July 1945, the OTU moved the short distance to Ouston, bringing to an end flying at Morpeth.

One final military role for Morpeth came with the arrival of 261 Maintenance Unit (MU) in September 1945. The unit was formed at Longbenton near Newcastle and was already using Morpeth as a satellite on its formation in June. The MU was responsible for the collection and disposal of a variety of now surplus ground equipment and, apart from a few RAF personnel, was staffed by civilians. The MU had four sub-sites, namely Eshott, Holme-on-Spalding Moor, Riccall and Wombleton. 261 MU was disbanded on 31st May 1948 bringing with it the closure of Morpeth's RAF history.

The airfield was retained by the Home Office throughout the 1960s and served as a storage area for RAF 'Green Goddess' fire engines in the event of a fire brigade strike. Loosely speaking, military aviation

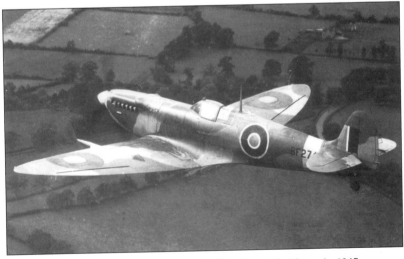

80 (French) OTU operated the Spitfire Mk.IX during its brief stay in 1945.

A single 'Extra Over' Blister survives on the old airfield today as well as several blast shelters, of which one can be seen in the foreground. (Author)

returned to the airfield in the mid 1960s after a suspected radiation leak from the Calder Hall power station in Cumbria. Several wartime barrage balloons were flown above the airfield with equipment that could detect radiation. Despite this display being a very public event, the local authorities gave a typical cold war response by denying their very existence.

The majority of buildings on the site were demolished by the early 1950s, although many bases still exist as well as a lone single Extra Over Blister. Large sections of runway, perimeter track and a bigger than normal dispersal area still survive. The airfield was unusually equipped with a pair of gun butts, although it is possible one was used for the harmonization of aircraft guns while the other would have been used for small arms. Both survive; one is easily accessible via a local bridleway, while the other is visible in open land on the south side of the airfield. The domestic accommodation, which was once located in the woods on the north side of the airfield, is now the site of a collection of more salubrious buildings.

While the concrete still remains visible from the air, Morpeth will continue its less demanding role as a Visual Reference Point (VRP) for Newcastle Airport and tentatively retain a link with aviation.

9
OUSTON

Aircraft have long since left Ouston, but it remains virtually complete and is now under the control of the British Army with the name Albemarle Barracks, a name associated with a Second World War aircraft, despite the fact that the type was never stationed at Ouston. The airfield was built for fighters and was second only to Acklington as being one of the busiest airfields in the region.

After initial confusion as to the exact location of the new airfield, work began just after the beginning of the Second World War. Located north of the hamlet at Harlow Hill, it gained its official name from another hamlet, Ouston, to the north-west. Construction was of a mixed pre-war standard, while accommodation and technical buildings were of a permanent design. Other aspects, especially concerning the airfield, were more limited. The technical site was, and still is, approached from the B6318, which follows the course of Hadrian's Wall. The accommodation is the traditional pre-war 'H' Block design, which, because of central heating and running water, was always popular with officers and airmen alike. A large station headquarters and elaborate heavily protected control rooms were also constructed, indicating a potentially important role for the airfield once opened. Comfortable officers', sergeants', and airmen's messes made Ouston a popular posting for wartime airmen.

The airfield itself was built with three runways, the longest being of 1,400 yards with two shorter runways of approximately 1,200 yards each. Unusually for the period, the runways were built so that they almost intersected at the same point. This design in the early years of the war was usually frowned upon, because, in the event of an enemy bombing raid, a well-placed stick of bombs could close all three runways simultaneously. The runways were linked by an encompassing perimeter track with only a few fighter-sized dispersals attached to it. A single large 'J' Type hangar stood in front of the technical site with a Type 5845 control tower, both indicators of a late expansion period airfield. At least eight Blister hangars were built later on in the war, but generally the airfield was not significantly changed until long after the war's end.

Despite the design of the airfield, the chance of an enemy air attack was still seen as quite high; so Ouston gained its own decoy airfield at Berwick Hill, only a few miles north of Ponteland, which could have served to protect Woolsington as well.

Before the airfield was completed, light aircraft from 13 Group Communications Flight made use of the levelled grass in late 1940. Using Woolsington as a Relief Landing Ground, the flight flew an interesting collection of aircraft, including several civilian types that had been impressed into service on the outbreak of the war. By December 1940, the flight had a Percival Vega Gull and Proctor, a Miles Whitney Straight, a de Havilland Hornet Moth and more traditional military types including two Miles Magisters and three Gloster Gladiators. The flight remained at Ouston until 15th July 1943, and

The Percival Vega Gull was a very pretty pre-war aeroplane. One was used by 13 Group Communications Flight at Ouston in late 1940.

Intended as a primary trainer, the Miles Magister was also used as a light communications aircraft.

was a busy unit that eventually gained a very impressive collection of aircraft including Spitfires and Hurricanes.

Another unit that made use of the airfield before it opened was the Calibration Flight of No.3 Radio Servicing Section (RSS), based at Hallington Hall, eight miles to the north-west. The flight only operated a single Hornet Moth and later a Blenheim; so little disruption could have been caused by their activities.

The airfield officially opened on 10th March 1941 and was immediately given the title of Fighter Sector Headquarters under 13 Group, taking over from Usworth. Weeks after opening, the communication flight's Gladiators were taken over for the Station Flight, all serving long after the type was removed from front line service.

55 OTU, based at Usworth and flying the Hawker Hurricane, used Ouston as a satellite airfield from 11th April 1941 until 24th April 1942. The airfield's first casualty occurred, courtesy of the OTU, on 15th April. Hurricane Mk.I L1926 swung on landing and tipped onto its nose, sufficiently damaging the aircraft not to warrant repair. The following day, a carbon copy incident occurred with Hurricane Mk.I N2433 after a tyre burst on landing.

Ouston received its first operational squadron on 29th April. 317

170

'Wilenski' Squadron, under the command of Sqn Ldr A N Cole, was one of several new Polish fighter units. Formed at Acklington the previous February, it was from there that it arrived with its Hurricane Mk.Is. The Polish became quickly frustrated by the boring work of convoy patrols and were constantly complaining about the lack of German aircraft to attack in the area. Before they had the chance to gain a victory, the Luftwaffe managed to press home an attack against Ouston in the early hours of 7th May 1941.

Twenty eight enemy aircraft attacked Tyneside and a variety of targets throughout Northumberland, including Ouston. Several incendiary bombs were dropped across the airfield, causing limited damage that was quickly repaired the following day. However, one victim of the attack was Hornet Moth W9382, which belonged to 3 RSS. The pre-war biplane was destroyed by a single incendiary, becoming the one and only loss caused by enemy action at the airfield.

Despite the increasing risk of air attacks, the airfield still housed detachments of various units. In May, No.7 Anti-Aircraft Co-Operation Flight (AACF) visited with a diverse collection of aircraft, mainly made up of Lysanders. 13 Group AACF with Blenheims and Lysanders followed them in the summer. Both flights stayed for only a few weeks.

Gloster Gladiator Mk.I K6132 belonged to Ouston's Station Flight in April 1941 before being passed on to 13 Gp CF later in the year. K6132 was only the fourth production aircraft to be built and managed to survive until April 1946.

317 Squadron's thirst for action was eventually quenched on 2nd June when Pilot Officer Niemec and Sgt Baranowski encountered a Ju 88A off the east coast. In rapidly fading light, the German bomber was shot down four miles north-east of Tynemouth, killing two of the crew instantly, the two survivors becoming POWs. 317 Squadron left Ouston on 26th June for Colerne in Wiltshire and was replaced the same day by the Spitfires of 122 Squadron.

Formed at Turnhouse, Midlothian the previous month, the squadron had worked itself up to operational status very quickly with its new Spitfire Mk.Is. Another new Spitfire squadron joined it on 30th June. 131 Squadron re-formed at Ouston, also with the Spitfire Mk.I, although the squadron never managed to become operational during its time at Ouston. Despite being called the 'County of Kent' Squadron, the unit was made up mainly of Belgian pilots, the majority of whom would eventually form 350 (Belgian) Squadron later in the year.

131 Squadron left for Catterick in North Yorkshire on 9th July, their space filled by the Hurricane Mk.Is of 232 Squadron, which had up until now spent their entire existence at various airfields in Scotland. The squadron's weary Hurricane Mk.Is were replaced by the more heavily armed Mk.IIb in August. The Mk.Is were fitted with eight 0.303-inch Browning machine guns, the Mk.IIb was fitted with an impressive twelve.

On 31st August, 122 Squadron also departed for Catterick, having spent a frustrating few months at Ouston without firing a shot against an enemy aircraft. Two days later, the Luftwaffe once again targeted the airfield. A force of 25 bombers caused considerable damage throughout the area, the bulk of which fell upon Newcastle. However, a single aircraft managed to drop an HE bomb in the centre of the airfield. The resulting explosion caused a crater 20 feet across and six feet deep to appear, and damage included a fractured water main and several blown-out windows. Luckily, there were no casualties amongst the personnel or aircraft but this incident once again highlighted how vulnerable Ouston was to air attack.

A detachment of Boulton Paul Defiants of 'A' Flight from 410 Squadron stayed at Ouston in October 1941. The Canadian night-fighter unit was employed to defend Newcastle, but unfortunately no contact with the enemy occurred during their brief stay. The same month, 232 Squadron was made non-operational in preparation for deployment overseas. The squadron left Ouston on 11th November, en route to Singapore and a very brief fight against the invading Japanese in protection of the island. After arriving on 17th January 1942, the

410 Squadron brought the Boulton Paul Defiant to Ouston but unfortunately made no contact with the enemy.

squadron was sent into combat immediately, but, up against over-whelming odds, was put out of action in just over a week.

Another small unit made Ouston its home from 19th December 1941. Formed at Kaldadarnes in Iceland, 1423 Flight was formed from 98 Squadron, which served for nearly a year with Coastal Command on the volcanic island. Despite being a bomber squadron, the flight's main equipment was the Hurricane, ten of which were on strength by July 1941. One of the unit's high points was providing an escort for HMS *Prince of Wales*, which was carrying Winston Churchill to the United States of America. It is presumed that the flight's main role at Ouston was communication duties for 13 Group Headquarters, a task that it carried out until its eventual disbandment in October 1943.

Spitfires returned to the airfield in January 1942, this time the Mk.Va, operated by 81 Squadron from Turnhouse. Between January and May 1942, the squadron used Ouston for four detachments, all of which were spent on fruitless North Sea patrols. Only one incident involving an 81 Squadron Spitfire occurred on 7th February, when an aircraft overturned after landing on the main runway. On their final visit, the squadron had re-equipped with the Spitfire Mk.Vb, leaving for the last time on 14th May en route to a new home at Hornchurch in Essex.

The majority of newly formed squadrons in the Second World War were either allocated the role of fighter or bomber. However, there were, of course, other specialist jobs that warranted the formation of a large organized unit. At the start of the war, air-sea rescue duties were carried out by small flights or detachments from larger units, which usually operated autonomously from an airfield near the coast. From late 1941, the squadron numbers 275 to 284 were allocated for the use of air-sea rescue units, and, on 15th March 1942, 281 Squadron was formed at Ouston so as to provide cover for 13 Group. With no specialist aircraft available, the squadron's first type was the Defiant, which were converted so that they could drop a dinghy to a stranded crew at sea. Trials involving the Defiant dropping a dinghy had been completed only the previous month and had involved converting a pair of light-series bomb racks. The aircraft now had the ability to carry a pair of cylindrical M-Type dinghies under each wing. The aircraft's rear turret was kept in place, giving it the ability to defend itself when operating over more hostile waters.

The first Defiant was delivered to the squadron on 3rd April, the unit eventually receiving just nine aircraft in total. Four of these were lost or written off in accidents, only one of which was fatal. In January 1943, the squadron's capabilities were improved by the arrival of the Supermarine Walrus Mk.I and Mk.II. The Walrus had a distinct advantage over the Defiant, having the ability to both land on and take off from water. The option was briefly available for both aircraft to work side by side; the Defiant was relatively quick and could arrive at the scene ahead of the Walrus. The Defiant would drop a dinghy and then the Walrus would arrive to pick up the downed airmen. There was little opportunity to put this method into practice, as the Defiant was coming to the end of its air-sea rescue career. The Anson Mk.I was the squadron's new acquisition in March 1943, an aircraft capable of carrying far more rescue equipment over a greater distance, with the added bonus of good reliability.

281 Squadron moved the short distance to Woolsington on 14th June 1943. Less than five months later, the unit was disbanded into 282 Squadron, to continue its operations around the Scottish coast.

A squadron more associated with the Hurricane arrived to replace 81 Squadron on 15th May 1942. Now re-equipped with the Spitfire Mk.Vb, 242 Squadron had achieved great success during the Battle of Britain, especially under the leadership of Sqn Ldr D R S Bader. After moving to the Far East, the squadron was effectively destroyed and overrun by the Japanese. The squadron then re-formed at Turnhouse, using Ouston to acclimatize to their new aircraft before returning to

Drem, East Lothian on 1st June. Two days later, the squadron claimed a Junkers Ju 88 off the Scottish coast.

Another squadron that had fought bravely against the Japanese in Singapore was 243 Squadron, which was re-formed at Ouston on 1st June 1942. Originally equipped with the woefully inadequate Brewster Buffalo, the squadron was now operating the Spitfire Mk.Vb. Only twelve days after re-forming, the squadron was declared operational and began flying coastal patrols and scrambles in defence of the North-East. Despite the squadron's enthusiasm and a regular detachment at West Hartlepool, no enemy aircraft were encountered. The squadron moved to Turnhouse on 2nd September, only to become non-operational three months later and to return to overseas operations in North Africa.

In early August, the airfield was used by a detachment of 226 Squadron from Swanton Morley in Norfolk operating the Douglas Boston Mk.III. The unit was not as yet operational on their new American built twin-engined bombers, using the relatively clear skies of the North-East to take part in local exercises, practise tactics and use the local bombing ranges. Twelve aircraft from the squadron were due to arrive at Ouston on 2nd August; however, poor weather delayed their arrival until 4th August. Before the day was out, three aircraft had

A trio of Supermarine Spitfire Mk.Vbs of 243 Squadron flying from Ouston in the summer of 1942.

crashed, one of which was fatal. Boston Mk.III AL679 was the first casualty, crashing on approach when one of the engines cut. Unfortunately, one of the crew was severely injured and died later in the day. Boston Mk.III AL275 had both engines cut and had to belly land near Great Whittington, while another made a spectacular forced landing on the airfield. The remaining aircraft took part in an Army co-operation exercise called 'Dryshod' without any further loss to the squadron. This was the only occasion that a squadron from Bomber Command used the airfield in any capacity.

The American-built North American Mustang was one of the greatest fighters of the Second World War, but arguably it did not achieve this status without the power of a British engine. However, it was one of the RAF's Army Co-Operation Units which took the original version of the aircraft into action for the first time on 10th May 1942. Several Royal Auxiliary Air Force units operated in the co-operation role. One of these, 613 (City of Manchester) arrived at Ouston on 28th August. Equipped solely with the Mustang Mk.I, the squadron would take until December to become operational on the American fighter. The Mk.I was primarily used in a low-level tactical reconnaissance role, as its American 12 cylinder Allison engine was not a good performer at higher altitudes.

613 Squadron flew the North American Mustang Mk.I, the equivalent of the P-51A.

The squadron's first operations were flown during detachments from Odiham, Hampshire and Gatwick in Surrey. It was on one of the unit's early forays into Northern France that the squadron lost its first aircraft on 7th December 1942. Despite the fact that the squadron's main hunting ground was Northern Europe, 613 Squadron remained at Ouston until 1st March 1943, moving to Wing in Buckinghamshire.

With space at a premium at Acklington, 1490 Target Towing Flight moved into Ouston on 4th September 1942. Used to provide air gunnery refresher training to all units within 13 Group, the flight was made up of Lysanders, Masters a single Martinet and an aging Hawker Henley. By April 1943, the flight had moved to Ayr, Ayrshire, disbanding into 14 Armament Practice Camp in October.

No stranger to the North-East, 72 Squadron made an appearance at Ouston on 26th September. Recently re-equipped with the Spitfire Mk.Vb, the unit used the airfield to prepare for operations overseas, leaving for North Africa on 8th November. The squadron would not return to the United Kingdom until 1947, when at Odiham it re-formed with the Vampire jet.

One of the longest users of the Boulton Paul Defiant was 289 Squadron, which provided co-operation duties with anti-aircraft

289 Squadron operated the Supermarine Walrus Mk.I and Mk.II from Ouston from March 1942 to June 1943.

batteries in the north-east of England. Flying the Mk.I and Mk.III, the squadron made a brief appearance at Ouston in late 1942 from its home base at Turnhouse. The unit's aircraft would continue to visit the airfield until the end of the war, although by then the Defiants had been replaced with the Martinet, Spitfire and Vengeance.

The Royal Navy arrived at Ouston on 3rd January 1943 in the form of 804 Squadron flying nine examples of the Hawker Sea Hurricane Mk.IIc. The naval version of the Mk.IIc was equipped with an arrester hook and different radio equipment; otherwise, it was very similar to its RAF counterpart. The unit, under the command of Lt Cdr A J Sewell DSC, RNVR, had just a short stay at Ouston, leaving for Twatt in the Orkneys on the 3rd February.

Despite the Hawker Typhoon being a fairly common aircraft in the region, the airfield hosted only one unit of the type. 198 Squadron had re-formed at Digby in Lincolnshire in December 1942 and arrived at Ouston on 23rd January, although it was not yet operational. It was equipped with the Typhoon Mk.Ia and Ib, but eventually the latter took over as the main type for the squadron. The squadron's stay was brief at Ouston; the unit moved to Acklington on 9th February and gained operational status, although it did not see action until it moved to Manston in Kent.

Fifteen new air observation post (AOP) squadrons were formed between 1941 and 1945, generally equipped with light aircraft. Their tasks included artillery spotting and liaison duties. The squadron's aircraft would rely on slow speed and manoeuvrability to evade enemy aircraft, often operating at extremely low levels. The most common aircraft operated by the AOP squadrons was the Auster, a two-seater developed from the highly successful pre-war civilian aircraft. 657 Squadron was formed at Ouston on 31st January 1943 and was equipped with the Auster Mk.I and Mk.III. While at Ouston, the squadron took part in several exercises gaining valuable experience working with the many Army units which trained in the area. Declared operational by mid April, the squadron flew south to Westley in Suffolk on 1st May, and then, by the end of August, saw action for the first time in North Africa.

Posted north to Acklington in March 1943, the Belgian pilots of 350 Squadron were becoming frustrated by the continuous boredom of convoy patrols and the lack of enemy aircraft. A move to Ouston on 8th June with their Spitfire Mk.Vbs did not improve the situation. Sadly, the only casualties inflicted during their stay at Ouston were upon themselves after a tragic mid-air collision near the airfield on 11th July.

Spitfire Mk.Vb BM399, piloted by Flying Officer R Van de Poll, and EN860 with Sgt Grawl at the controls were completely unaware of each other as they approached the runway to land. Both pilots were killed instantly as their crippled Spitfires plunged into the ground on the edge of the airfield. 350 Squadron returned to Acklington on 20th July, becoming Ouston's last operational squadron. The airfield was now destined to see out the war as a training station.

Industrial pollution and the hazard of a balloon barrage around Usworth caused 62 Operational Training Unit (OTU) to look elsewhere for a more appropriate training area. A flight of Avro Anson Mk.Is arrived at Ouston on 21st June 1943, followed by the headquarters and main party on 15th July. The unit's task was to improve the standard of training given to radio operators/observers in the relatively advanced art of using airborne radar. The Anson was an ideal aircraft for this; all of the unit's aircraft were fitted with Airborne Interception (AI) Mk.IV radar. The aircraft so fitted were easy to identify, as they had a large 'arrowhead' aerial protruding from the nose. By September, the aircraft on strength had increased to over 50 Ansons, and operations from Ouston were now becoming rather cramped. Woolsington was taken on as a satellite airfield on 22nd November in an attempt to relieve the congestion, although the risk of aerial collisions was still high.

Durham University Air Squadron flew a single Tiger Moth out of Ouston during 1944.

Durham University Air Squadron (UAS) arrived in its entirety from Woolsington on 23rd March 1944, an event that could easily have been missed, as at that time, like many other similar UASs, the Durham squadron had only a single de Havilland Tiger Moth on charge. This was briefly increased by the addition of a single Airspeed Oxford later in the year. However, the Oxford was quickly transferred to Thornaby's Station Flight. By the end of the war, the UAS returned to Woolsington but would again return to Ouston in a more substantial form.

The arrival of 1508 Beam Approach Training Flight (BATF) on 26th June 1944 swelled the OTU even further. Within weeks, the flight's Airspeed Oxfords were disbanded into a new 'C' Flight within the OTU, tasked with GEE training. GEE was the first radio navigational aid introduced into Bomber Command, and, by 1944, highly trained operators were in demand and would remain so until the war's end.

Considering how high the OTU's workload was, accidents were thankfully quite rare. Anson sorties alone would have been in the thousands; despite this only three such aircraft were lost in flying accidents, with only one resulting in fatalities. A combination of a disciplined flying programme, coupled with experienced instructors and reliable, well-maintained aircraft must have contributed to the light loss rate.

With many Ansons still on strength, the OTU increased in size yet again. The larger Vickers Wellington Mk.XVII and Mk.XVIII were now available as radar trainers, and 29 examples arrived at Ouston in March 1945. These marks of Wellington were converted from earlier versions to provide 'classroom' training specifically for the radar operators of de Havilland Mosquito night fighters. As if the airfield wasn't cramped enough, a further 23 Hawker Hurricane Mk.IICs and IVs also arrived in the same month to provide moving targets for the trainee radar operators. This influx of aircraft was certainly a good indication of the output of the aircraft industry at that time; training units like 62 OTU could now employ aircraft that only 12 months previously would have been needed on front-line squadrons.

The Royal Navy returned, albeit briefly, on detachment between 19th and 23rd April. 770 Squadron was formed as a Fleet Requirements Unit specializing in aerial gunnery and had operated a vast array of aircraft. On this occasion, the unit brought a flight of Hurricane IIcs from their home base at Drem, East Lothian.

On 3rd May, the OTU lost its one and only Hurricane in a flying accident. Mk.IIc LF644 suffered an engine failure and the pilot performed a successful belly landing near Eshott Farm. Four days later, the war in Europe came to an end, and all flying by the OTU ceased on 14th May 1945. With no immediate need for night-fighter crews, the unit was officially disbanded on 6th June 1945.

80 (French) OTU from Morpeth became the airfield's first post-war resident in July, their arrival marking a return of the Spitfire. The unit was eventually disbanded into the Armée de l'Air in March 1946.

The rasping engine note of the North American Harvard T.2b underscored the training theme, with the arrival from Calverly, Cheshire of 22 Service Flying Training School (SFTS) on 31st May 1946. The School remained at Ouston for almost two years before moving south to Syerston in Nottinghamshire.

After leaving Usworth in January 1941, 607 (County of Durham) Squadron Auxiliary Air Force had seen non-stop action throughout the war, mainly in the latter stages against the Japanese in the Far East. Disbanded at Mingaladon in Burma on 19th August 1945, the squadron was re-formed at Ouston on 10th May 1946. Initially equipped with the Spitfire FR.14, followed by the powerful F.22, the squadron then entered the jet age with the arrival of the de Havilland Vampire FB.5, in

A pair of Harvard T.2s of 22 Service Flying Training School at Ouston in 1946. (G Fentrell)

March 1951. Despite the diminutive size of the new aircraft, their arrival resulted in a major expansion of the airfield. The main runway was extended, quick reaction areas were added at both ends and a large concrete apron was built near to the 'J' Type hangar. All of these were typical modifications of a post-war jet fighter station.

The Vampires of 607 Squadron were to be the only jet aircraft stationed at Ouston. The demise of all of the RAF's Auxiliary flying squadrons came in early 1957, 607 Squadron disbanding on 10th March. Throughout the late 1950s and 1960s, the airfield was used by a variety of small units, including the elaborately titled 2 Civilian Fighter Control C-operation Unit, 11 Air Experience Flight (AEF) and 11 Group Communications Flight. The latter supported 11 (Fighter) Group Headquarters, that briefly moved into the airfield between January and September 1961.

The brightly coloured training aircraft of 6 Flying Training School, stationed at Acklington, used the airfield for circuits and bumps from 1961 to 1968. Also, the old Durham UAS was re-formed as the Northumbrian Universities Air Squadron at Ouston on the 1st August 1963, eventually moving to Leeming in September 1974, where it remains today.

607 Squadron Vampire FB.5s in the snow at Ouston in February 1955. (via P H T Green)

Delivered by road to Ouston in September 1955, Spitfire Mk.XIVe TE462 never served at Ouston or in 607 Squadron whose markings the aircraft displayed. The aircraft left Ouston in 1970 and today takes pride of place in the Royal Scottish Museum of Flight at East Fortune. (A Ferguson)

The airfield's old satellite at Woolsington had become Newcastle Airport in the mid-1950s, but in 1967 the airport's operations were transferred to Ouston while its runway was being extended. With this role complete, the only aircraft at Ouston were the Chipmunks of the UAS and the Cadet and Sedburgh gliders of 641 (Volunteer) Gliding School.

The Gliding School became the last RAF unit to occupy Ouston. It departed for Dishforth in North Yorkshire on 31st Dec 1974.

Although, even today, often referred to as RAF Ouston, the Army took over the airfield in 1975, renaming it Albemarle Barracks. This retention by the Ministry of Defence has resulted in the airfield remaining complete in almost every way; even the control tower still stands. All the runways and perimeter track are intact, with only the dispersals having been removed. The site is very secure and is now the home of 39 Regiment Royal Artillery.

10

USWORTH

It was Friday 29th January 1983 when Sunderland Airport received its final significant visitor with the arrival of Avro Vulcan B2 XL319, now taking pride of place at the North East Aircraft Museum (NEAM). Sadly the airfield was closed within months of the cold-war bomber's arrival. The local council decreed that the airport was no longer viable and the land was sold for development. Today the site is the home of the Nissan car factory, but, thankfully, the NEAM still exists, retaining a permanent connection with the airfield's aeronautical past.

Avro Vulcan B.2 XL319 has taken pride of place at the North East Aircraft Museum since its spectacular arrival on 29th January 1983. (Author)

Originally known as Hylton, a small landing ground was cleared on West Town Moor for the use of 'B' Flight of 36 Squadron. Their main role was the protection of the North-East against Zeppelin attacks. 'A' Flight took over in August 1917, and, by the end of the First World War, the small airfield was known as Usworth. With the threat of an enemy air attack removed, the landing ground was abandoned in June 1919.

The future for a new airfield at Usworth would be decided indirectly by the formation of the Auxiliary Air Force (AAF) on 9th October 1924. The AAF was the vision of Lord Trenchard, 'The Father of the RAF', whose idea was for civilians to serve in flying squadrons in the RAF in their spare time. By the beginning of the Second World War, there were 20 flying squadrons and a variety of smaller units including 47 balloon squadrons. During the Battle of Britain, 14 of the 62 squadrons involved were AAF, and they accounted for over 30 per cent of enemy kills. In 1947, the AAF became the Royal Auxiliary Air Force (RAuxAF), as granted by King George VI, but ten years later all of the flying squadrons were disbanded. The RAuxAF still exists today; it received its own badge in 1984 from the Queen.

The AAF squadrons initially used the squadron numbers 600 to 616, and, on 17th March 1930, 607 (County of Durham) Squadron was formed on the old First World War airfield at Usworth, under the command of Sqn Ldr W L Runciman. The squadron was formed only on paper, as the airfield was not ready to accommodate airmen, let alone aircraft. Usworth was divided into two camps: north and south. The north camp was built mainly for domestic use, with accommodation and messing facilities for both officers and airmen. The south camp was made up of technical buildings, and a 'D' Type 'Lamella' hangar was constructed on the north-west edge of the airfield. The German company Junkers designed the Lamella in 1930; its name came from the German word *Lamellendach*, meaning 'segmented roof'. The Horsley Bridge and Engineering Company acquired the British rights to it, and the example at Usworth was only the second to be built in the country.

By September 1932, the all-grass airfield was ready for use, but 607 Squadron's main equipment would not arrive for a few more months. Formed as a light-bomber squadron, the unit received its first Westland Wapitis in early 1933. These big, single-engined biplanes served the squadron well until 23rd September 1936, when the unit was redesignated as a fighter squadron. Their new aircraft was the Hawker Demon, a two-seat fighter variant of the Hawker Hart bomber.

The part-time 607 Squadron was joined on 26th February 1937 by a regular unit. 103 Squadron arrived from Andover in Hampshire, flying the Hawker Hind light-bomber. The squadron had been re-formed only the year before. In July 1938, the squadron's Hinds were replaced by the Fairey Battle light bomber, and, by September, 103 Squadron flew south to Abingdon in Berkshire, going on to become one of the first RAF units in France at the outbreak of the Second World War.

In July 1937, 1 Group Practice Flight was formed at Usworth, flying the Avro Tutor trainer. Little is known about their activities, although they did remain on the airfield until at least June 1938. The Demons of 607 Squadron had become obsolete very quickly and their replacement, although still a biplane, was a huge technological leap towards a more effective fighter. The squadron started to receive the Gloster Gladiator in December 1938 and would retain it for many months after the start of the Second World War. Compared to its predecessors, the Gladiator was reasonably fast, at over 250 mph, carried four Browning machine guns, and its enclosed cockpit not only provided comfort for the pilot but also good visibility.

Another new unit was formed at Usworth on 1st May 1939. G Flight No.1 Anti-Aircraft Co-Operation Flight was one of 25 flights formed to work with many Heavy and Light Anti-Aircraft Practice Camps scattered around the country. G Flight was mainly equipped with the

No. 1 Group Practice Flight flew the Avro Tutor at Usworth. This particular aircraft is the only airworthy example in the world. (Author)

Hawker Henley, although they did receive a Westland Wallace as well. The flight stayed at Usworth only until 15th May, moving to Cleave in Cornwall to work with No.12 LAAPC at Penhale.

The airfield underwent a major development programme in August 1939, which included the construction of two concrete runways, perimeter track and numerous dispersals and protective pens. Buildings were constructed on both north and south camps, and by the beginning of the Second World War the airfield was becoming very difficult for 607 Squadron to operate from. A run of seven years of continuous use came to an end when 607 Squadron flew north to Acklington on 10th September 1939. They would, however, return. The airfield was temporarily closed while work on the runways continued.

Usworth re-opened as a Sector Fighter Station within 13 Group in March 1940, elevating its status within Fighter Command. It was planned that 607 Squadron would return to Usworth immediately. They were in the thick of the action in France, however, so 64 Squadron would become the airfield's first wartime resident, on 1st May 1940. The squadron had re-equipped only the previous month with the Supermarine Spitfire, and spirits were very high. This was to be the only time Spitfires would be seen at Usworth, as, by 15th May, the squadron had flown south to Kenley in Surrey as the Battle of Britain beckoned.

A Hawker Henley target tug, similar to those operated by 'G' Flight 1 Anti-Aircraft Co-Operation Unit at Usworth in May 1939.

After leaving Usworth for Acklington, 607 Squadron was sent overseas to France as one of two Gladiator squadrons to take part in the air component of the British Expeditionary Force (BEF). Re-equipped with the Hawker Hurricane in May 1940, the squadron fought hard against the overwhelming German opposition, claiming 72 enemy aircraft destroyed. After returning from France, the remnants of the squadron assembled at Croydon in Surrey but were deemed unfit to form part of Fighter Command's front-line. On 4th June, a bedraggled 607 Squadron, under the command of Sqn Ldr J A Vick, returned to Usworth to begin re-equipping again with new Hurricanes.

The chief designer of the Hawker Aircraft Company, Sydney Camm began working on the design of a monoplane fighter named the Hurricane back in January 1934. While the Hurricane was still on the drawing board, Camm heard that Rolls Royce was developing a new 12 cylinder V engine called the Merlin. The design was immediately altered to accommodate the new power plant, and the first aircraft took

607 Squadron flew the Hawker Hurricane from Usworth through the early months of the Battle of Britain.

to the air on 6th November 1935. Despite early problems with the Merlin engine, the fighter was a tremendous performer, reaching a maximum speed of 315 mph and capable of climbing to 15,000 ft in just over five minutes. The Hawker Company was so confident about its new product that plans were immediately put into place for mass production of the aircraft. The Hurricane instantly became a record breaker for the RAF by becoming the first aircraft to shatter the 300 mph barrier; it was the first monoplane fighter and the first to carry eight machine guns. In June 1936, the Air Ministry placed an order for 600 aircraft, the first entering RAF service in December 1937. Incredibly, the Hurricane remained in production until late 1944 and over 14,000 aircraft were built. The Hurricane never received the accolades and glamour that were bestowed upon the Spitfire. But it was by far the most prolific destroyer of enemy aircraft. During the first year of the Second World War, the Hurricane could claim well over half of all German aircraft shot down.

It was the Hurricane Mk.I that was being delivered to 607 Squadron in the summer of 1940. The Mk.I differed from the ground breaking prototype with a slightly more powerful engine, redesigned exhaust pipes and a sliding canopy. By the end of July, the squadron was back to full strength and hungry for the fight, but despite increased enemy activity over the North-East none of the encounters bore fruit.

The gentler engine note of a de Havilland Hornet Moth was occasionally heard at Usworth from 1st July 1940. No.3 Radio Maintenance Unit (RMU) was formed to control local radar units and was also tasked with the repair of radar tracking equipment. Hornet Moth W9386 was named the Calibration Flight but it seems to have spent more time at Woolsington than at Usworth. On 21st September, the RMU was renamed 3 Radio Servicing Section, and by 13th October the ground element had moved to Hallington Hall and the lone Hornet Moth moved to Ouston.

With the Battle of Britain raging in the south, the senior staff of the Luftwaffe felt confident that the time was right to start sending larger forces to attack airfields in the north-east of England. Completely oblivious to the fact that at least four squadrons were resting from the fight in the south, the Luftwaffe dispatched 65 Heinkel He IIIs of KG26, escorted by 34 Messerschmitt Bf 110s of ZG76 from Denmark and Norway, against Tyneside on 15th August 1940. The Germans were so confident of meeting no fighter opposition that the Bf 110s left their rear gunners at home to extend the range of the twin-engined fighter. This would prove to be a fatal mistake.

RAF fighter pilot's view just before opening fire on a group of He 111s.

Recognizing its importance as a Sector Airfield, the Luftwaffe chose Usworth as the focus of its attack. Acklington-based 72 Squadron confronted the enemy first, followed by 79 Squadron, also based at Acklington. In the meantime, the pilots of 607 Squadron waited for the call to scramble and, along with the ground crew, were quite aware of the effect of an enemy raid against their own airfield. While in France, the squadron's home airfield at Vitry, north-east of Dijon, was attacked by German bombers while they attempted to get in the air. This would, hopefully not be allowed to happen at Usworth, thanks to the support of radar and the controllers.

The call to scramble came at 01:15 hours and twelve Hurricanes, led by Flt Lt W F Blackadder, as Sqn Ldr Vick was on leave, took to the air. The enemy aircraft had now split into two, a northern group attempting to attack Tyneside and a southerly one heading for targets in North Yorkshire. After several false alarms, which involved 607 Squadron traversing Tyneside, the Hurricanes were joined by Catterick-based 41 Squadron, and the southerly force was intercepted south of Sunderland. On encountering the fighters, several of the He 111s jettisoned their bombs in panic, but it was too late for many of them as 607 and 41 Squadron Spitfires tore into the attacking force. Within minutes, Flt Lt Blackadder sent an He 111 into Seaham Harbour, and so did Sgt Burnell-Phillips and Sgt Cunnington. Flying Officer Bowen brought an He 111 down into the sea ten miles off Saltburn and Pilot Officer Welford chased another, 25 miles off Sunderland, eventually bringing the bomber down. 41 Squadron focussed on the fighters and achieved equal success, with three Bf 110s and a single He 111 shot down. The day had been a total success for the defences of the North-East and a total disaster for the Luftwaffe, which would never repeat such a blatant daylight attack again.

607 Squadron had incurred no casualties of their own that day, and, during their stay at Usworth, had only lost one Hurricane in a fatal accident on 26th June 1940, when N2707 stalled and crashed south of Sedgefield. With morale higher than ever, the call came for 607 Squadron to move south to Tangmere in Sussex on 1st September. They would join the Battle of Britain at its busiest and most crucial stage.

43 Squadron was also at Tangmere flying Hurricanes. Ready for a rest, they arrived at Usworth on 8th September. The squadron had suffered heavy losses during the Battle of Britain and needed time to train an influx of new pilots rather than sending them to the slaughter against the Luftwaffe. Experience was being drained from the unit as well. Only the previous day, the squadron had lost its commanding

Armourers re-load a Hawker Hurricane's eight Browning machine guns.

officer, Sqn Ldr C B Hull, and one of its Flight Commanders, Flt Lt R C Reynell.

The squadron received new Hurricanes during their stay at Usworth and the unit began to take shape again as new pilots gained flying experience. Encounters with the enemy were non-existent, but this did not stop at least four of the squadron's aircraft being damaged or written off in flying accidents. One particular accident could be indirectly attributed to the enemy when Pilot Officer C K Gray made a heavy landing in his Hurricane at Usworth on 14th September. Gray had been wounded in the arm and had bailed out over Portsmouth on 26th August; he had only just returned to flying duties. His Hurricane got caught in his leader's slipstream and his inability to correct the aircraft was attributed to the arm injuries he had received. Luckily, Gray and his slightly bent Hurricane lived to fight another day. Not so lucky was Sgt D R Stoodley, who, on the evening of 24th October, was trying to land his Hurricane Mk.I V7303 at Usworth. After six failed landing attempts in a cross-wind, the fighter stalled at 250 ft and crashed into a dispersal pen. Stoodley was killed instantly.

The Luftwaffe never gave up on Usworth as a worthy target, although they never inflicted sufficient damage on the airfield to put it out of action. The airfield was attacked twice in October 1940, once at night on 2nd/3rd October and again with incendiary bombs, on 28th/29th October. The majority of these fell in open countryside. All future attacks were classed as near misses, although the threat remained. High Explosive bombs were dropped near Castletown in September 1941; more fell in April 1942, but the only direct hit occurred in March 1943. Usworth must have been charmed, as this particular bomb landed in the centre of the main runway but failed to explode and was dealt with by the local bomb-disposal team.

Visiting aircraft were not an unusual sight at Usworth, especially the Armstrong Whitworth Whitley, of which several were based in the north of England during this period. 51 Squadron, based at Dishforth in North Yorkshire, was taking part in a raid against a target in Glesenkirchen on 18th November 1940, when Whitley Mk.V T4218 attempted a landing at Usworth instead of its home base. The Whitley overshot the landing and on touchdown swung violently, ending up wrecked in the airfield's ammunition dump. Luckily, all the crew walked away, leaving the Whitley slightly bent and never to fly again. Another visitor was taking refuge in one of Usworth's hangars during a particularly heavy snowstorm on 20th February 1941. The aircraft was Miles Magister V1029, which actually belonged to 258 Squadron, which had been stationed at Acklington. The aircraft was destined never to rejoin its squadron, as the snow was so heavy that the roof of the hangar collapsed, damaging the two-seat trainer beyond repair.

On 12th December 1940, 43 Squadron left Usworth for Drem, East Lothian, and the same day 607 Squadron returned from Tangmere. The squadron had suffered heavy losses during the Battle of Britain and certainly appreciated the distinct lack of enemy activity compared to the skies over the south coast. After a few weeks of rest and another influx of replacement Hurricanes, 607 (County of Durham) Squadron left Usworth for the last time, bound for Macmerry, East Lothian, on 16th January 1941. The squadron would return to the North-East, but not until after the war. It continued as an AAF unit into the jet age until it was disbanded in 1957.

With 607 Squadron's departure the airfield's status was reduced to that of training, although within weeks the sound of Merlins would return. Formed at Aston Down in Gloucestershire out of 5 Operational Training Unit (OTU), 55 OTU was destined to become Usworth's new unit. Once again the main equipment was the Hurricane, and a single flight first arrived at Usworth on 12th February 1941. The main unit

A memorial to 607 (County Durham) Squadron is located outside the NEAM. (Author)

195

arrived on 14th March, making a total strength of 68 Hurricanes, 21 Masters and at least six target tugs, that were initially made up of Fairey Battles. With this number of aircraft, Usworth took on both Ouston and Woolsington as satellite airfields so that they could relieve the pressure from Usworth's busy circuit.

The threat of a German invasion was still at the forefront of the senior planners' minds in early 1941. All OTUs, especially those operating on the eastern or southern coast, were given a withdrawal airfield; in Usworth's case that was Crosby-on-Eden in Cumbria. In the event of an invasion, the unit would have become 555 Squadron, equipped with 18 fully armed Hurricanes, and initial orders would have sent them to Turnhouse, Midlothian. This was later modified so that 555 would respond along with 556 Squadron, based at Tealing, Angus, and all 36 Hurricanes would move to Ouston under the control of 12 Group Fighter Command. Thankfully, the invasion never came, but every training unit in addition to the front line squadrons was prepared and, more importantly, organized to take on the enemy.

An intriguing incident involving a Hurricane from the OTU actually came to light many years after the war's end. On 18th September 1941 two airmen took off from Usworth to practise dog-fighting tactics off Sunderland. In one Hurricane was a Polish pilot and in the other was a Czechoslovakian named Augustin Preucil. During the dogfight the Pole witnessed Preucil's Hurricane diving towards the sea, apparently out of control, and this is how the incident was recorded. However, Preucil, in Hurricane I W9147, never crashed and actually continued across the North Sea, eventually landing in Belgium. Preucil turned out to be a German spy who went on to work for the Gestapo, betraying many of his countrymen. He had been gathering as much intelligence as possible about the RAF during his time in England, but after the war he was arrested in Czechoslovakia and was executed in 1947.

The airfield briefly housed a rather unusual unit between 10th and 12th October 1941. The Glider Exercise Unit arrived on detachment from Ringway in Cheshire with their pre-war Hawker Hector glider tugs towing a pair of General Aircraft Hotspur gliders. The Hotspur was crewed by two pilots in tandem making the glider very suitable for training. It was recognized very early on in the war that the glider had a serious role to play, especially in the eventual invasions of both southern and northern Europe.

Flying instruction on the dual controlled Miles Master was the last stepping-stone for the trainee pilot before being allowed to fly the comparatively powerful Hawker Hurricane. As in all training units, the casualty rate was high, and it would make for very grim reading if all of 55 OTU's losses at Usworth were commented upon. Losses could be attributed to a lack of experience or, on some occasions, unauthorized aerobatics or high-spirited low flying, but an element of mechanical failure cannot be ruled out. In all, 16 Hurricanes were lost in flying accidents on or near the airfield, with many more in the surrounding local area. Even the flying instructors could make mistakes, and that is exactly what occurred over Sunderland on 30th December 1941 when Miles Masters N8076 and T8587 collided over the city, with the loss of two instructors and student pilots.

A vast array of nationalities passed through the OTU. In addition to the usual Commonwealth pilots, airmen from Latvia, Lithuania and Ceylon passed out as fully trained fighter pilots. Despite the high loss rate, which was, as ever, deemed more than acceptable by senior staff, several hundred pilots passed through Usworth before being posted onto a front line squadron. Many fighter pilots who went on to survive the war described their time on an OTU as being as dangerous as combat with the enemy! On 28th April 1942, the unit moved to Annan in Dumfriesshire, bringing an end to a turbulent and often hair-raising period of Usworth's history.

The airfield was now in a temporary state of care and maintenance, with just a few airmen in residence. It was several weeks before a

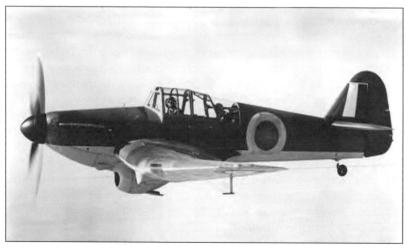

The Miles Master Mk.I was powered by a Rolls Royce Kestrel engine, giving it a completely different appearance from the later marks.

197

62 OTU was formed at Usworth on the 1st June 1942. Its main equipment was the Avro Anson Mk.I.

decision was made to form a new OTU with a very specialist task. Airborne radar systems were advancing at a rapid rate, and more thorough and specialist training was needed for the observers who would operate the equipment on night-fighter squadrons. 62 OTU was formed at Usworth on 1st June 1942 to improve upon training that was previously undertaken by 3 Radio School at Prestwick in Ayrshire. The same day, the school sent 'A' Flight, equipped with ten Avro Ansons, to Usworth, this flight being absorbed by the OTU on 23rd June. The Ansons would feature as the unit's main equipment, all characterized by arrowhead aerials protruding from the nose. The aerials gave away the fact that the aircraft was fitted with Airborne Interception (AI) Mk.IV radar, and by August at least 34 Ansons were in use by 62 OTU. Each aircraft was effectively a flying classroom where an instructor could comfortably view a pupil's progress on an additional cathode ray tube AI indicator. A typical course lasted for six weeks, by which time the average trainee operator was able to guide his pilot to within 300 yards of the target.

62 OTU's accident record up until early 1943 had been faultless, with no incidents of any significance being recorded since its formation. Aerial collisions were a continuous hazard, but, when both aircraft came from the same unit, the dangers of aircrew training would really hit home. It is not known whether or not Ansons I L7908 and DJ686 were training together or if they were simply coming and going from the airfield, but on 19th February 1943 they collided in a tragic accident that claimed eight lives from 62 OTU. Both aircraft came down three miles north-east of the airfield. Emergency crews from Usworth attended the scene as quickly as possible but could do nothing but control the flames on arrival.

Such was the standard of training at Usworth that the USAAF sent a group of AI operators for training at the OTU at the beginning of 1943. These Signal Corps officers were destined to fly in one of several new American Beaufighter squadrons which had been formed to fill an important gap in the USAAF's inventory. Later, a detachment of the 416th Night Fighter Squadron, operating the Beaufighter Mk.VI, arrived at Usworth on 14th May 1943. After gaining valuable experience from the OTU's instructors, the 416th moved to Acklington on 10th June before eventually going into action in North Africa and later Italy.

The Royal Navy descended upon Usworth on 5th March 1943 in the shape of 776 Squadron, whose permanent base was Speke in Lancashire. This unit had been formed at Lee-on-Solent in Hampshire in January 1941 as a Fleet Requirements Unit, resulting in this busy unit operating 17 types of aircraft until its disbandment in October 1945. Throughout 1943, the squadron moved from detachment to detachment, including Usworth. Under the command of Lt Cdr J Goodyear RNVR, 776 Squadron brought a collection of aircraft to the airfield including the Blackburn Roc and Skua, the de Havilland Dominie and the very rare American-built Vought-Sikorsky Chesapeake. The squadron left Usworth on 12th July 1943, although there were several occasions throughout the remainder of the war when naval aircraft visited the airfield.

62 OTU was outgrowing Usworth. Not only had its aircraft strength increased, but accommodation was limited. Industrial pollution was also proving to be a problem, and the airfield's proximity to the dense Sunderland balloon barrage meant that a move was inevitable. The unit did not have to travel far, as Ouston had become available, and, on 21st June 1943, a large part of the OTU departed. By 15th July, the headquarters and remainder of the unit had left, becoming the last major RAF flying unit to use the airfield in wartime.

The airfield's role took a steady downward spiral, with no flying units of any description being allocated for the foreseeable future. Lengthy periods of inactivity continued through 1943 and a state of

Usworth hosted a detachment of the 416th Night Fighter Squadron in the spring of 1943. Their aircraft was the Beaufighter Mk.VI; an example is pictured in North Africa.

care and maintenance under the control of Morpeth continued until November 1943. The airfield was then handed over to 20 Initial Training Wing (ITW) from Bridlington in East Yorkshire, which was responsible for the ground training of wireless operators/air gunners. The intention was to train flight engineers as well, although no record exists of their arrival at Usworth. The average strength of the ITW was approximately 1,100, of which an average of 900 were trainees, the remainder being made up of permanent staff and instructors. This number of personnel put great pressure on the facilities at Usworth, and the ITW did what it could to improve the messing facilities and accommodation on the airfield. The airfield had been busy on the ground, but during its stay at Usworth the ITW had witnessed hardly any visiting aircraft and by April 1944 they had departed.

Once again, Morpeth looked after the welfare of the airfield when aviation returned in April. No. 31 Gliding School (GS) was formed with the task of providing elementary flying training for the local Air Training Corps (ATC) squadrons. The GS flew the Slingsby Cadet and the Slingsby T.4 Falcon III, both evolving from the pre-war German designed Schleicher Falke. 31 GS would become the longest serving

31 Gliding School was Usworth's longest serving unit and one of their aircraft was the Slingsby Falcon Mk.III.

flying unit at Usworth, the school disbanding into 641 GS on 1st September 1955 and then moving to Ouston in 1958.

One of many Aircrew Disposal Units (ADU) arrived at Usworth from Chessington in Surrey on 24th June 1944, with the sole responsibility of finding posts for aircrew that had completed their flying tours. A pair of RAF Regiment squadrons arrived on 10th August, only to depart for overseas on 18th September, followed by the ADU, which moved to Keresley Grange near Coventry on 22nd September. Yet another period of quiet ensued before the airfield was selected as one of many sub-sites for 14 Maintenance Unit. The MU was first formed at Carlisle in September 1938 and it was destined to become one of the longest serving, as it was disbanded only in September 1996. Its role was primarily as an equipment supply depot, and Usworth in particular was used to store aircraft-related items, from instruments to engines. 14 MU took over Usworth on 1st December 1944 and retained the airfield until 30th September 1948.

Post war, the airfield became the home of the newly formed 23 Reserve Flying School (RFS) from 1st February 1949. Operated by the civilian company Airwork Ltd, the RFS's main equipment was the de Havilland Tiger Moth, which was later replaced by the de Havilland Chipmunk. Other aircraft included the Percival Prentice, the Airspeed Oxford and the Avro Anson. Airwork was also responsible for the formation of 2 Basic Air Navigation School (BANS) at Usworth on 18th April 1951, which operated the Anson T.21 in this role until its disbandment on 30th April 1953. A re-organization of training units also resulted in the demise of 23 RFS on 31st July 1953, bringing to an end military flying training at the airfield. A small group of Auster AOP.4, 5 & 6s moved to Usworth from Ouston on 14th February 1954 and remained until 10th March 1957. The final RAF unit to be formed at Usworth was No.2 Civilian Fighter Control Co-Operation Unit, on 8th March 1957. The Anson T.21 was the main equipment again, but, with the airfield's military future in doubt, this small unit departed for Ouston on 15th October 1957.

Once the gliders had left in 1958, the RAF had no further use for the airfield and it was quickly run down. However, Sunderland Corporation was quick to see the potential in Usworth for use as a municipal airport and it was purchased on 3rd July 1962 for the grand sum of £27,000. The airfield was quickly renamed Sunderland Airport and it thrived throughout the 1960s and 70s, with a peak in 1977 of nearly 30,000 aircraft movements and over 7,000 passengers passing through its gates.

The North East Aircraft Museum has been established at Usworth since 1975 and has steadily grown into a diverse and well kept collection of aircraft. (Author)

The hammer fell on Sunderland Airport at exactly 15:00 hours on 31st May 1984. The RAF marked the event by sending a solitary Jet Provost over the airfield, and many of the resident aircraft said farewell by making low passes. The airport manager, Bob Henderson, fired a Very pistol in a final gesture, and within hours the bulldozers had arrived in preparation for the site's new role.

The NEAM was established near to the surviving Lamella hangar in 1975 and has since grown into an interesting and diverse museum with 35 aircraft on display. The Nissan Company made use of the Lamella hangar for many years and until late 2003 used it as a store. Sadly, the rare and only visible surviving link with the airfield's past was knocked down in December 2003.

11
WEST HARTLEPOOL
(GREATHAM)

With a determined 'air-minded' borough council behind it, West Hartlepool gained its own aerodrome and almost managed to expand it into a post-war municipal airport. Often overlooked, this small grass airfield was used for almost 20 years, supporting fledgling airlines as well as providing a very useful military airfield for fighters protecting Teesside during the Second World War.

In 1928, six potential airfield sites were surveyed around Hartlepool with a view to providing the area with a municipal aerodrome. The locations included Seaton, South End, Outon Manor and, the favourite from the beginning, Greatham Cottages, which was situated on land adjoining the West Hartlepool and Greatham road. This particular site was first inspected on 16th April 1931 by Major Mealing, one of the leading characters for bringing aviation to the area.

Financial constraints meant that the site remained dormant for several years, although it was selected and reserved for future consideration as an airfield. In April 1934, the subject was re-opened and, with sufficient funds now available, the owners of the land were approached. No agreement was reached; so on 4th March 1935 a Compulsory Purchase Order was raised and titled 'West Hartlepool (civil aerodrome)'. Further inspections of the site were carried out on 18th March purely to ascertain whether the area had changed, with specific attention being paid to any new obstructions. Officials from the Air Ministry found no new problems and officially endorsed Major Mealing's original survey.

The locals, who lodged 17 objections against it, did not receive the purchase order readily. However, only one was claimed as 'deserving of special notice'. The Hospital of God in Greatham, which was founded in 1272 by Robert Stichell, then Bishop of Durham, owned all but two of the properties in the entire parish. Their case against the order was simply: 'This charity resents the intrusion of the aerodrome upon peace and quiet and the taking of lands from the charity for aerodrome purposes.'

Mr G Ewart Rhodes of the Ministry of Health held the inevitable public enquiry from 28th May to 31st May 1935. After much debate and objection, Mr Rhodes had little hesitation in recommending that the site was the best from all points of view and that the Compulsory Purchase Order should be confirmed. With regard to the charity's objections, he dismissed them as a submission of 'ad misericordiam' (appeal to pity). On 1st June, the local *Northern Echo* newspaper reflected the mood of the locals with an article entitled 'Greatham Fights for its Age-Old Quiet', 'Bitter Feeling if West Hartlepool gets its Aerodrome Site'.

Construction began on the 175-acre site on 19th December 1935, initially on levelling and preparing the aerodrome. The exact location was to the north-east of Greatham village and, at 1,100 yards long and 800 yards wide, the site stretched to Red Barns Farm, also to the north-east. Progress was slow with more attention being paid to sundries like the type of perimeter fence to be bought rather than preparation of the surface.

The entire airfield site was officially 218 acres, and on 10th May 1937 £13,640 was released for its purchase, followed by £600 for legal fees and £2,135 in compensation to the tenants and for the valuer's fees. It was not until 15th November 1937 that Mr Allan Attride, the Director of Home Civil Aviation visited to decide upon the most satisfactory runway layout. The project was now gaining momentum; money began to change hands and another £28,797 was borrowed for completion of all the remaining work on the aerodrome. The airfield specialists of the day, 'En-Tout-Cas', were employed for the main construction work and the town council paid them £7,440 for their work on 8th April 1938.

By May 1938, the airfield was taking shape, although it was still covered with workmen, who, in accordance with aviation regulations, constructed a 10ft square with a red base covered in yellow diagonals and with a white cross in the centre so as to deter any local aviator from landing on the unfinished airfield.

An aviation official visited on 15th August 1938, and the West

Hartlepool council was hoping for a positive report so that flying could begin. The report stated that levelling and drainage had been completed; however, only a 2-acre area in the north-west corner of the airfield was sprouting grass. This meant that a very limited licence was issued, which allowed light aircraft to operate only in dry conditions. Whether or not any aircraft made use of the airfield in this condition is not known.

Giving an indication of a potential use in the near future, a group of RAF Volunteer Reserve Officers visited the airfield on 20th January 1939. They must have been pleased with what they saw because three months later the airfield was taken over by the RAF. On 15th April 1939, a new training unit was formed at West Hartlepool, within 50 Group, which was part of Reserve Command based at Hendon in north London. 32 Elementary and Reserve Flying Training School (E&RFTS) was operated by Portsmouth, Southsea and Isle of Wight Aviation Limited (POIOW), which had its home airfield at Apse Farm, near Shanklin on the Isle of Wight. The E&RFTS were formed to accommodate service pilots from the forthcoming RAF Volunteer Reserve, and civilian firms like POIOW ran the majority. These schools were not officially formed until April 1937 and the scheme enabled men between the ages of 18 and 25 to enroll as airman pilots with the rank of sergeant.

Aircraft flown by individual schools differed throughout the country, with many schools choosing to fly the Hawker Hart, Hind

The first unit to operate from West Hartlepool was 31 E&RFTS, with a variety of training aircraft including the de Havilland Tiger Moth.

or Miles Magister and the de Havilland DH.82A Tiger Moth. The Tiger Moth is undoubtedly one of the world's most famous training aircraft, and it remained in RAF service for over 15 years. Originally a development of the DH.60 Gipsy Moth, the first Tiger took to the air on 26th October 1931. Designed as a fully aerobatic trainer, the little biplane was an instant success with many civilian owners and operators. The Tiger Moth Mk.Is were powered by a 120 hp Gipsy Major engine, but later on the main production version, the Tiger Mk.II, had a 130 hp Gipsy Major fitted. The following year, the first of many were ordered by the RAF. Production reached over 1,000 by the outbreak of the Second World War. The majority of Tigers ordered before the Second World War served on E&RFTSs, equipping 44 out 52 schools by 1939.

32 E&RFTS also flew the Hawker Audax and the Avro Anson; the latter was used for ferrying and liaison duties rather than flight training. With the outbreak of war, all civilian-run training schools were closed, and 32 E&RFTS was officially disbanded on 3rd September 1939.

Responsibility for the airfield was now handed over to Thornaby, a coastal command station located a few miles to the south-west of Middlesbrough, although initially it was little used, from a flying point of view. During October, visits were made to West Hartlepool (now being identified in official records as Greatham) by Thornaby's Barrack Officer and Warden to check on the status of the storehouse and barrack equipment. The same month, Military Transport (MT) vehicles were serviced and driven over to Thornaby.

As well as being a satellite for Thornaby, West Hartlepool also took on the role of a forward operating base for Catterick in North Yorkshire. Coastal patrol and convoy protection duties were the main responsibilities of the fighter aircraft, although, if necessary, they would be used to help with the defence of the North-East. 41 Squadron first arrived at Catterick in October 1939; it was a unit that uniquely remained equipped with the Spitfire for the entire duration of the Second World War. The routine was for a flight of four aircraft to depart from Catterick at first light and to stay at West Hartlepool until scrambled by the local controller.

The first of these daytime detachments began in early 1940, but it was not until April that 41 Squadron saw their first action from West Hartlepool. At midday on the 3rd April a German bomber was reported as attacking shipping four miles off Whitby. Twenty minutes later, despite the weather being poor, a single Spitfire piloted by Flt Lt

N Ryder was scrambled from West Hartlepool. The enemy aircraft was a Heinkel He 111 H-3 of KG26, one of several sent out on an armed reconnaissance mission. By the time Ryder had intercepted the Heinkel, approximately 15 miles north-east of Whitby, the enemy aircraft was already in trouble. After attacking the convoy, defensive fire had hit the port engine and, flying at only 400ft above the sea, the aircraft was in no condition to perform evasive manoeuvres. Ryder overshot the enemy bomber, allowing it to open fire with its front gun and hit the Spitfire several times. A single six second burst of the Spitfire's eight Browning machine guns put the starboard engine out of action, giving the Heinkel no option but to ditch into the sea.

Before the Heinkel ditched, it passed over a Scarborough-based drifter called the *Silver Line*; thinking they were under attack, a Lewis gunner on board fired into the German plane, wounding the observer in the head. Ryder circled overhead, watching his quarry ditch into the sea and the eventual rescue of the five-man crew by the *Silver Line*. After setting a course for home, the Heinkel's original attack on the Spitfire began to take effect. Ryder's oil temperature gauge went off the scale and then noxious fumes began entering the cockpit. It was becoming obvious that the Spitfire would not make landfall. Spotting the trawler *Alaska* below, Ryder lined up for a ditching near to it. Just before the forced landing, the engine gave up, sending the Spitfire into the sea much harder than Ryder had planned. He was knocked unconscious, only waking up when both he and his aircraft were under

Spitfires wait for the 'scramble' – a typical scene representing 41 and 54 Squadrons' time at West Hartlepool.

the waves. After a terrifying struggle, Ryder made it to the surface, only to discover that his Mae West would not inflate. Thankfully, the *Alaska* made it in time and returned the bedraggled pilot to Hartlepool.

This combat was particularly significant; Ryder's Spitfire N3114 was the first British fighter to be shot down in the defence of England during the Second World War.

41 Squadron would continue to make use of West Hartlepool during its five tours of Catterick. 54 Squadron, also flying Spitfires, passed through Catterick, taking its turn to operate detachments from West Hartlepool. On 3rd September, the squadron had just arrived from Hornchurch as one of several squadrons that were resting from the Battle of Britain.

Flt Lt Alan Deere, a natural pilot who went on to claim 22 enemy aircraft destroyed, was on duty at West Hartlepool on 7th September 1940. Compared to what he had experienced at Rochford and Hornchurch, he described the duty at Greatham as very boring, spending the entire day with only a phone for company, which rarely rang. On that particular day, Deere and his wingman, Pilot Officer W Krepski, were scrambled to intercept a Junkers Ju 88 near Whitby. Before they could get anywhere near the enemy bomber, the German climbed into the clouds and headed east, further out to sea. Deere realized that it was pointless going in after him, but his Polish wingman, who had not seen a German aircraft since arriving in England, had different ideas. Ignoring Deere's orders, Krepski flew into the clouds and was never seen again. Deere doubts whether the young Polish pilot managed to get the Junkers, but Luftwaffe records for that day do show the loss of a Junkers Ju 88 of II/KG54.

Detachments from Catterick continued throughout 1941, although no encounters with the enemy were ever recorded. 6 Operational Training Unit (OTU), based at Thornaby, began to make use of the small grass, airfield from 6th September 1941 to early 1943. Several of their Lockheed Hudsons, used West Hartlepool for circuits and bumps, relieving congestion at Thornaby.

Formed at Catterick on 16th January 1942, 332 (Norwegian) Squadron maintained a detachment at West Hartlepool for the next six months. Equipped with the Spitfire Mk.Va and Mk.Vb, the squadron made its first attack against an enemy plane while operating from West Hartlepool. Two of the squadron's original pilots, Sgt Soren Kjell Liby and Sgt Gunnar Piltingsrud were scrambled on an interception patrol off Whitby on 29th April. They came across a Junkers Ju 88, which they both attacked, causing damage, but not downing the enemy aircraft. The Ju 88 returned fire, damaging Spitfire Mk.Vb AB269, piloted by Liby. The aircraft's armoured glass panel was shattering sending splinters into the pilot's eyes. Liby returned to West Hartlepool, recovered from his injuries and returned to flying within a month. 332 Squadron still exists today as part of the modern Norwegian Air Force, which is now operating the ultra modern F-16MLU Fighting Falcon.

The airfield accommodated its one and only permanently based unit on 17th April 1942, namely 'N' Flight No.1 Anti Aircraft Co-Operation Unit. This elaborately named unit was formed at Thornaby on 13th January 1942 to work with 15 Light Anti-Aircraft Practice Camp (LAAPC) located near Whitby. As its title suggests, 'N' Flight flew sorties over a coastal range, towing various targets for trainee anti-aircraft operators to fire at.

The flight operated six Hawker Henley target tugs plus an obligatory Tiger Moth. The Henley was designed under the direction of Sydney Camm as a light day-bomber, using the wings and tail unit of the Hurricane as part of the design. By the time the aircraft first took to the skies, the specification was abandoned and all remaining Henleys were produced as specialist target tugs. Virtually all of the 200 built served with air gunnery schools and anti-aircraft co-operation units.

332 Squadron's convoy protection duties were taken over by 403 (Wolf) Squadron RCAF from June 1942 to 22nd January 1943. The

6 OTU, based at Thornaby, used West Hartlepool as a satellite airfield. The unit's Lockheed Hudson operated in the local area until it moved to Silloth in early 1943.

211

Several Spitfires based at West Hartlepool were involved in action against the enemy. These Heinkel He 111s receive a blast of fire from an RAF fighter.

Canadian squadron saw no enemy action with their Spitfire Mk.Vbs, bringing an end to the detachments by Catterick-based squadrons.

Ouston-based 243 Squadron, also with the Spitfire Mk.Vb, operated a small detachment from West Hartlepool in the late summer of 1942. As in the case of their Canadian colleagues, no success against the enemy was recorded.

On 4th November 1942, 'N' Flight was renamed 1613 TT (Target Towing) Flt and was now under the command of Flt Lt Benson. Poor weather was a continuous problem while the Flight operated from West Hartlepool. Many sorties were abandoned as a result of natural weather as well as the industrial fog generated by neighbouring Teesside. Christmas Eve 1942 saw the only accident involving a Henley of the TT Flight. Pilot Officer Warnock was on approach to land in Henley L3259, when, in a momentary loss of concentration, he raised the flaps rather than lowering the undercarriage. The immediate loss of lift resulted in a very heavy landing that caused sufficient damage to write off the aircraft.

Bad weather continued to disrupt the flying programme in January

1943. With this in mind, Flt Lt Benson visited the Station Commander of Catfoss with a view to moving the flight to Lisset, near the Yorkshire coast. After this visit, the weather ironically improved and the flight was able to achieve a 100% sortie rate through the remainder of January. On 4th February a movement order was received for the flight to move to Driffield, also in Yorkshire, although the area suffered from the same poor weather as West Hartlepool. Benson appealed against the move, but this was ignored and by 13th February the flight had departed for Driffield.

2782 Squadron RAF Regiment carried out airfield defence for West Hartlepool during most of 1942. Another RAF Regiment unit, No. 4054 Anti-Aircraft Flight, under the command of Flying Officer W C Cummings, joined them from Thornaby on 18th November 1942. The main equipment of this unit was the standard Swedish designed 40mm Bofors gun, capable of firing between 60 and 90 rounds per minute. The flight also brought with them a Bedford OYD 'Armadillo', which was basically a mobile pillbox. This remarkable vehicle had the wooden pillbox perched on its rear. The skin of the pillbox had a cavity built-in and this was filled with gravel for protection. A whole host of weaponry was fitted to these vehicles; they included Lewis light machine guns, grenades, rifles and even a 'COW' gun. Local RAF Regiment Flights tended to fit whatever weapons were to hand. In West Hartlepool's case, the Armadillos were fitted with a combination

'N' Flight AACU, later renamed 1613 TT Flight, was West Hartlepool's only permanent flying unit. Its main equipment was the Hawker Henley.

of Browning Mk.II machine guns, Hispano 20mm cannons, and, on one occasion, an unusual fitment of quadruple Vickers water-cooled machine guns.

The flight used its Bofors guns several times in anger, in particular during the heavy raids throughout County Durham on 12th and 14th December 1942. During their stay at West Hartlepool, 4054 Flight caused no casualties to the enemy; however, one airman did manage to accidentally shoot himself in the leg. Flying Officer Cummings and 55 of his men left by rail on 25th July 1943 for Langham in Norfolk, bringing to an end any serious RAF occupation of the airfield.

The airfield was devoid of any aviation until the formation of No.26 Gliding School during October 1943. The school was well-equipped with Slingsby gliders; models included the Cadet Mk.I, II and III, King Kite and Falcon II. By May 1944, the school had gone, a departure that had not gone unnoticed by the local council.

At the end of the Second World War, authorities and councils throughout the United Kingdom made proposals and plans to convert their local military airfields into regional airports. Very few plans actually came to fruition, the land being retained by the Air Ministry, returned to agriculture or swamped by industry. Discussions about West Hartlepool's post-war future began in June 1944, eleven months before the conflict in Europe would end.

The first official meeting was held on 5th June 1945; by then the RAF had expressed no intention of keeping or using the airfield. Members at the meeting included several serving RAF officers, including a Wg Cdr Hargreaves, who appeared as the main exponent for encouraging civil aviation in the area. The first of several council meetings was held on 1st August 1945 to discuss the proposition of Greatham becoming a major airport. Extensions to the runways and expansion of the airfield's facilities were on the agenda as well as the ambitious suggestion of a marine airport nearby at Greatham Creek, close to the Tees Shipyard, although at least one individual at the meeting suggested that the age of the passenger flying boat may already be over. A great deal of time, effort and expense was put into plans and surveys for a new road and rail system as well as an elaborate system of four new runways, the main one being 2,000 yards long. Only one, albeit significant, problem was raised against the proposal of an airport, namely, the weather and local pollution problems.

During November 1945, gliding returned briefly to West Hartlepool; this time a civilian club made use of another quiet period in West Hartlepool's history. In March 1946, the County Borough of West

Hartlepool received a proposal by a fledgling airline that wished to use the airfield for private, charter and club flying. Mr A C L Barrett of The Northern Air Charter Company, which was sponsored by the Percival Aircraft Company, was willing to take on the operation of the airfield.

Northern Air Charter began flying from the airfield, now unofficially known as Greatham Airport, in May 1946. The company also successfully applied to lease all the facilities available on 24th July. They included lease of the landing rights, petrol pumps and buildings. These buildings were described as the Air Traffic Control Head Quarters, General Room, Watch Office and Main Headquarters Building.

It is not known exactly what kind of aircraft Northern Air Charter flew, but the company was reasonably busy. Between 6th May 1946 and 22nd March 1947, 276 landings took place at Greatham, bringing in revenue of £307.10 to the council.

Greatham Airport became part of a feasibility study by the Ministry of Civil Aviation in late 1947. The study, by a Mrs Alison Murn, was entitled 'The Feasibility of Air Development of the North East Region'; it is not known how seriously Greatham Airport's contribution was taken in this.

Steady expansion continued with the purchase of three second-hand Blister hangars by the Council of West Hartlepool. Hangars were to be

Aerial view of West Hartlepool/Greatham in the late 1940s. (via A Ferguson)

BKS operated from West Hartlepool from 1953 to 1956, and one of its aircraft was Douglas C-47B G-ANAF, which still survives today, now operated by Air Atlantique Ltd. (Author)

built on the airfield in late 1939, but the start of the war disrupted this. The hangars were purchased from Messers Thornes of Bexley Heath at a cost of £2,250 plus £560 for erection in February 1948. With a 91ft span and 45ft long, the three hangars were joined together to make one building providing cover for several aircraft at once.

The success or demise of Northern Air Charter is not known; however, on 7th February 1952 another new airline was formed called BKS. The initials stood for the founder members, James Barnby, Thomas Keegan and Cyril Stevens. The company grew quickly after purchasing its first Douglas DC-3 from the struggling airline 'Crewsair'. One of its first scheduled routes was from Greatham Airport to Northolt in north-west London on 18th May 1953. This route continued until 1956, when aviation came to an end at Greatham. Now called BKS Air Transport Ltd, the company went from strength to strength until it was taken over by British European Airways, eventually becoming one of the four components that made up British Airways.

In those last three years of its life, Greatham came as close to becoming a full-blown airport as it ever would. Those of the opposers who suggested using the airfield for industry got their wish, because the airfield has now disappeared under the massive Corus steel works, leaving not a trace of its aeronautical past.

12
WOOLSINGTON

Now celebrating its 70th continuous year of flying, the humble all-grass airfield at Woolsington has since been developed into a thriving international airport. Newcastle Airport boasts an annual passenger throughput of over five million, which, it has been predicted, will more than double by 2016. Recent multi-million pound investment has produced a new terminal extension and it is stated that 1,000 jobs will be created for every one million new passengers attracted to the airport.

In the early 1930s, Newcastle Corporation was searching the local area for a suitable site for a new municipal airport. Existing airfields

North Eastern Airways Ltd flew out of Woolsington in the 1930s. This aircraft is a de Havilland DH.89A Rapide.

were viewed, including the old Royal Flying Corps airfield at Cramlington, north of Newcastle. The First World War site had been re-opened in July 1925 and was operated by the newly-formed Newcastle Aero Club; and the club objected to the Corporation turning their airfield into an airport.

The search ended in late 1934 when a suitable site was found between the villages of Prestwick and Woolsington. The Corporation had the foresight to purchase the land that stretched as far as the main road which runs through the village of Dinnington to the north-east, shrewdly covering any option for expansion in the future.

Despite the earlier rebuke, the Corporation approached the Newcastle Aero Club for advice and assistance on the construction and, later, running of the new airport. A pleasant terminal building was built plus a pair of hangars and a variety of administrative buildings. Four runways were eventually marked out on the grass; the shortest was 1,050 yards and the longest 1,350 yards. (During wartime, a Bellman and four Blister hangars were also added.) The land was quickly graded and levelled, and the fledgling airport was officially opened on 26th July 1935. With overall control of the site remaining the responsibility of the Corporation, the Aero Club was asked to manage the airport and provide all necessary services. The new manager was a Mr J D Irving, who was the chairman of the Aero Club, and he would remain in this position until the post-war years. The Aero Club's previous airfield at Cramlington was virtually abandoned and all flying from it had ceased by the beginning of the Second World War.

In early 1939, with the clouds of war looming, the airfield received a group of RAF Volunteer Reserve Officers. The group was impressed with the way the Aero Club was operating the airfield, choosing it as one of 32 Elementary and Reserve Flying Training Schools (E&RFTS) within 50 Group. 43 E&RFTS was formed at Woolsington on 1st June 1936 and was operated entirely by Newcastle Aero Club. The training schools were created in response to a distinct shortage of pilots. Aircraft used by the E&RFTS included the Hawker Hind and Audax, the Miles Master and the Tiger Moth, the favourite training aircraft of every training school in the country. 43 E&RFTS's existence was short-lived, because with the outbreak of war on 3rd September, all operation by civilian-run schools came to an abrupt end.

When 13 Group moved their headquarters north to Kenton Bar, near Newcastle, on 24th July 1939, it was not long before a supporting Communication Flight (CF) was formed. 13 Group CF started operating from Woolsington on 1st August 1939 with a few Miles

Magisters and a Gloster Gladiator. By the beginning of 1940, the flight was moved to Ouston, although it continued to use Woolsington as a Relief Landing Ground (RLG) until its eventual departure to Inverness in 1943. On moving to Ouston, the flight began to expand its fleet of aircraft, many of which were civilian aircraft impressed into RAF service. It would not have been unusual to see a Percival Vega Gull, Proctor or Q-6 Petrel use the airfield.

When 72 Squadron arrived at Acklington on 2nd March 1940, it was decided that they should operate a 'Night Flight' from Woolsington for the added protection of Tyneside. The squadron was operating the

13 Group CF flew a variety of ex-civilian aircraft, including the Miles Whitney Straight.

Another civilian type operated by 13 Group was the Miles Mentor.

Spitfire Mk.I at the time, an aircraft completely unsuited to night operations; so the expectation of seeing the enemy let alone shooting him down was low. On the night of 26th/27th June, over 100 enemy aircraft crossed the Scottish and north-east coast, indiscriminately attacking targets of opportunity with high explosive and incendiary bombs. At 23:57 hours, three Spitfires were scrambled from Woolsington in the hope that they might come across one of the fleets of enemy raiders. While in the Blyth area, Flying Officer R A Thompson in Spitfire Mk.I L1078 spotted a cone of searchlights with an enemy aircraft seemingly caught in the powerful beam. Thompson closed in on the aircraft, which was making no effort to shake off the searchlight. Thompson identified the aircraft as a Junkers Ju 88, and, at 7,000ft, attacked the twin-engined bomber east of Beacon Point, north of Newbiggin. After two bursts of his eight Browning machine guns, Thompson saw smoke pouring from both engines, followed by a large explosion. Diving to avoid the debris, Thompson did not see the final demise of his target; but witnesses at Acklington and several people in the Lynemouth area confirmed that a bomber had been destroyed and had been seen crashing into the sea near Cambois. That night, the Luftwaffe did not record a loss of a Ju 88; however, they did lose an He 111 in the same area. This made no difference to Flying Officer Thompson and 72 Squadron; they had achieved one of only a handful of night kills by the Spitfire. L1078 had a short flying career, as it was wrecked at Acklington on 6th August and never flew again. When 72 Squadron joined the Battle of Britain, Flying Officer Thompson was shot down over Hythe, Kent on 1st September by a Messerschmitt Bf 109. Seriously wounded, he managed to bail out and many months later re-joined his squadron.

In July 1940, No.3 Radio Maintenance Unit was formed at Usworth to control local radar units, testing their effectiveness with airborne equipment. The unit's Calibration Flight was based at Woolsington and operated de Havilland DH.87 Hornet Moth W9382 and Bristol Blenheim Mk.I L1525, the latter having seen active service with 601 Squadron at Biggin Hill and Tangmere.

No permanent war role for the airfield had presented itself until the formation of No. 83 Maintenance Unit (MU) on 25th July 1940. The MU was under the control of 43 Group, which had assumed total control of all salvage work from the beginning of the war. The MU's main role was repair and recovery of aircraft and any associated ground equipment, although its main occupation was clearing up the multitude of crashed aircraft that occurred in the area, with little time for actual repair. The unit's area of responsibility was huge, stretching through Northumberland and Cumbria. Woolsington quickly became a dumping ground for the remains of hundreds of different aircraft, and, where possible, all useful components were stripped from redundant carcasses for use on other aircraft. Many aircraft crashed in very inaccessible areas, making their recovery demanding work, not to mention dangerous, with the often volatile combination of fuel and unexploded ammunition.

The very first University Air Squadrons (UAS) were formed in 1925. However, the bulk of modern day UASs first appeared in the early years of the Second World War. The wartime UAS was usually

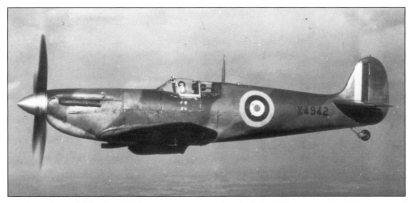

72 Squadron with the Spitfire Mk.I operated a 'Night Flight' at Woolsington and achieved success over the north-east coast on 26th/27th June 1940.

Not a particularly common type in the area, a single Bristol Blenheim Mk.I was flown by 3 Radio MU at Woolsington during 1940.

provided with only one aircraft, and this was held on charge by the station at which the squadron was located. Durham University Air Squadron was formed at Woolsington on 1st February 1941, with a single de Havilland Tiger Moth. The UAS also served Newcastle and Sunderland Universities before it was moved to Ouston on 25th March 1944. Renamed Northumbrian Universities Air Squadron in August 1963, the squadron is as active as ever and now resides at Leeming in North Yorkshire.

When 55 OTU arrived at Usworth on 14th March 1941, both Ouston and Woolsington became satellite airfields for the use of the unit's Hurricanes and Masters. Woolsington was used to a lesser extent, but, until the unit's departure to Annan in Dumfriesshire in April 1942, several incidents took place on or near the airfield involving 55 OTU. The first was on 2nd September 1941, when Hurricane Mk.I V7009 suffered an engine failure immediately after take off. The pilot managed to force land the powerless Hurricane into a field 0.5 miles south-west of the airfield. A similar incident occurred on 17th October 1941, when Master Mk.I T8623's engine failed while on approach and the Master was belly landed a mile short of the runway.

Woolsington was mentioned as one of a group of northern airfields

55 OTU operating the Hawker Hurricane used Woolsington as a satellite airfield from April 1941 to April 1942.

that would be affected by the re-formation of No.33 (Army Co-operation) Wing at Fulford Road, York, on 15th August 1941. Several army co-operation squadrons were under the control of the wing and the very nature of these units meant that they did not take up residence at an airfield for very long, and so if any of them passed through Woolsington, it was a brief unrecorded visit.

Having just replaced its tired Boulton Paul Defiants, 281 Squadron arrived from Ouston on 14th June 1943 equipped with the Supermarine Walrus and the Avro Anson. The squadron was formed at Ouston in March 1942, specifically for air-sea rescue duties and equipped initially with Defiants. These were replaced by the Anson in April 1943, but the arrival of the Walrus the previous February considerably expanded the squadron's rescue capability. Affectionately known as the 'Shagbat', the Walrus was designed by R J Mitchell and entered production in 1936. Designed primarily as a catapult-launched reconnaissance aircraft, the Walrus was later used for communication work and eventually was associated more with air-sea rescue. Being an amphibian, the Walrus could land on the sea rather than simply dropping a dingy to the stranded crew. On many occasions, the

A Supermarine Walrus or 'Shagbat' rescues a downed airman, just one of 3,723 RAF airmen rescued around the British Isles during the Second World War.

223

aircraft would land on a rough sea and end up taxiing back to the coast because it was either overloaded or conditions were too difficult to take off. 281 Squadron sent at least one detachment to Drem, East Lothian during its stay at Woolsington, and on 6th October 1943, the squadron moved in its entirety to the Scottish airfield.

The same month No. 27 Gliding School (GS) was formed at Woolsington. Block numbers were issued to eleven areas of the

The Slingsby Cadet Mk.II was one of the aircraft operated by 27 Gliding School, which was formed at Woolsington in October 1943.

Avro Ansons served at Woolsington with 62 OTU as radar trainers and with 281 Squadron in the air-sea rescue role.

country specifically for identifying the location of the schools, originally known as Elementary Gliding Schools. For example, the North-East was allocated numbers 21 to 40, although only eleven of these numbers were taken up. 27 GS was equipped with Slingsby Cadets Mk.I, II and TX.3 and the Sedburgh TX.1. 27 GS eventually moved to Ouston in June 1948.

Another air-sea rescue unit arrived on 6th October 1943, although this time on detachment. 278 Squadron brought their Anson Mk.Is from Coltishall, only to leave for Acklington on 10th December. Woolsington was the first of seven detachments throughout northern England and Scotland. The unit returned to Bradwell Bay in Essex on 21st April 1944.

62 OTU had been at Ouston since July 1943, and, with an ever-increasing workload, adopted neighbouring Woolsington as its satellite airfield on 22nd November. The main task of the OTU was to train radar operators for night fighter operations, using the Anson equipped with the early AI Mk.IV radar. With over 50 Ansons on strength, many of them operated from Woolsington on a regular basis so as to relieve congestion at Ouston. In March 1945, the OTU began to receive 23 Vickers Wellington Mk.XVII and XVIII radar trainers, of which a few made fleeting appearances at Woolsington. Flying training was terminated on 14th May, and on 6th June 1945 the OTU was disbanded and Woolsington ceased to be a satellite airfield.

In peacetime, 83 MU was the only unit still in residence, with plenty of work still to do clearing wreckage and equipment. The end of the war seemed to have little effect on the flying accident rate in the RAF, although a reorganisation in 1946 brought 83 MU's existence to an end on 30th April 1946. On the same day, 63 MU moved in from Carluke in Lanarkshire to continue its predecessor's work. As in the case of many other RAF airfields, an MU was to be the last military presence on Woolsington; 63 MU departed for Montrose on 24th March 1947.

Despite still being an all-grass airfield with limited facilities, civilian aviation began to grow steadily in the post-war years. The Lancashire Aircraft Corporation was the first serious company to make the airfield one of its bases for servicing. Hunting Clan began operating their Dakotas in 1953, opening a series of international routes. Formed in 1945 as Hunting-Clan Air Transport, the airline began, like so many others, using ex-RAF aircraft and continued to operate from Wool-sington until 1957.

The first concrete runway was laid in 1954, making the newly-named Newcastle Airport very attractive to the airline industry. Larger

The cockpit of an Avro Anson. 'Faithful Annie' was a popular aircraft with both aircrew and ground crew.

aircraft, such as the Vickers Viscount, could now use the airport, and, in early 1957, BKS arrived, taking over the Hunting Clan facilities. The airline made history on 1st April by opening a new scheduled service to Dublin, of which over 2,000 seats had been sold even before the first flight. BKS became the first British airline to operate scheduled services to Ireland since the end of the war. The airport routes continued to grow, as did the airport itself, with a new terminal being constructed in 1967.

Bearing so little resemblance to its wartime past, one wonders how many of the millions who pass through its gates each year realize how much history the airfield contains.

13
CIVILIANS AT WAR

For the older generations of the North-East, the threat of attack from above first presented itself during the First World War. Zeppelins roamed relatively freely over the country, and both Tyneside and Teesside were bombed. At the time, despite the fact that relatively few casualties were caused, the very presence of these giant airships was as effective as the bombing itself.

By the beginning of the Second World War, aerial bombardment from the skies had reached a new level. Technology had advanced dramatically, aircraft could now fly further and more efficiently, and carry a bomb load that had the capacity to cause death and damage to everything below on a grand scale.

Since the Prime Minster Neville Chamberlain's infamous conference with Adolf Hitler in Munich in September 1938, the country was preparing itself for war. Early in 1939, once again with air attacks in mind, the government ordered the distribution of over 38 million gas masks throughout the country. In Middlesbrough alone, over 100,000 respirators were distributed in a mere five days.

The threat of a gas attack was foremost in the minds of the local authorities, especially those who remembered the horrific effects of gas during the First World War. It was certainly anticipated that it would be dropped by aircraft onto the civilian population. However, people began to resent carrying gas masks around very soon after the beginning of the war. To gain admission to virtually all places of entertainment, you were required to carry your gas mask. One cinema manager in Newcastle would often find the building littered with improvised containers meant to represent gas mask boxes!

The ARP (Air Raid Precautions) was first established in late 1935 after receiving Cabinet approval as part of the contingency planning for a potential war. By the end of 1938, over 1.4 million people had joined the ARP; 90% of them were part-timers, and approximately 20% were women. Each individual ARP warden was allocated a sector and would be required to know not only every individual who lived in it, but also where they slept and where they would shelter in the event of a bombing raid. Every fire hydrant and stirrup pump's location was also known to them as well as any fire hazards within their sector.

Initially, the ARP's work was preventative, and mainly involved making sure everyone was evacuated and keeping a close eye out for breaches of the blackout rules.

The ARP was eventually embraced by one organization simply called Civil Defence. This was not only responsible for all ARP wardens but also controlled first aid and stretcher parties, rescue and demolition parties, along with fire guards and decontamination squads. As the threat of gas attack subsided, the latter were also employed to assist the rescue parties.

The ubiquitous 'Anderson' air raid shelter can trace its roots back to late 1938, when the Home Secretary, John Anderson, announced the beginning of a colossal distribution scheme. The shelter was actually designed by Dr David Sanderson but has always been incorrectly linked to the Home Secretary, who also announced that anyone earning less than £250 per year would a receive a shelter free of charge. Despite being very uncomfortable, cold and damp, Anderson shelters certainly saved many lives, and by the war's end approximately 2.25 million had been erected. For many, in particular people without gardens or the space to build an Anderson shelter, one alternative was the Morrison shelter. The Morrison was an indoor shelter that looked like a large cage. Approximately the size of a dining-room table (its usual use during daylight hours), it was first introduced in early 1941. Another option was the communal air raid shelter; for example, communal shelters in Middlesbrough provided protection for over 100,000 people, and the bulk of these were in place before the outbreak of war. Many were purpose built, while others utilized underground constructions already in place. In Newcastle, the Victoria Tunnel provided protection for approximately 1,000 people and the Ouseburn Culvert was a safe haven for at least 500 more.

On 1st September 1939, the first of 44,000 Newcastle children were evacuated to a variety of new homes throughout Northumberland, Yorkshire and Cumbria. The country as a whole had been expecting mass bombing raids; they did not come, and over a third of the children evacuated had returned to their Newcastle homes by the end of October. This was the general pattern throughout the country, with many families preferring to take their chances in the comfort of their own home. By the summer of 1940, many regretted this decision.

After the initial flurry of activity generated by the declaration of war on 3rd September 1939, the country became slightly complacent, and the period was labelled the 'Phoney War'. In the North-East, hundreds of large silver barrage balloons over the industrial targets in Tyneside

The delivery of Anderson air raid shelters began in February 1939. (Newcastle Evening Chronicle and Journal Ltd)

and Teesside became a familiar sight for most of the war and for many were the only indication that we were actually involved. Heavy anti-aircraft guns were positioned all around; at first 28 batteries were placed in the Tyneside area and a further 19 around Teesside. Both these figures increased as the war progressed, and many more light anti-aircraft batteries provided local protection for individual factories and strategically important buildings. Searchlight sites were also prolific. Newcastle and the immediate area had 36 searchlight sites, all manned by the Royal Artillery, who were attached to the Northumberland Fusiliers.

At sea the German forces were very active and quick to recognize the importance of the east coast convoys, which traversed the country on an almost daily basis. The first local victims of U-boats and aircraft-laid mines were the many cargo ships and steamers that operated off the north-east coast. Enemy aircraft were on the increase, but at this stage were operating in singles or very small groups on reconnaissance missions. This did not mean that they were not armed, and many took the opportunity when it arose to attack shipping, with limited success. By now even the smallest trawler would have at least a machine gun on board for its own protection.

The first time the anti-aircraft guns on Tyneside opened up in anger was on the morning of 11th January 1940. A small group of enemy bombers crossed the coast near South Shields, and the local batteries managed to scare the aircraft away. No bombs were dropped, although many people took cover when the shrapnel from the anti-aircraft shells began to fall in the streets.

The first air raid on an industrial target in Britain took place on 24th/25th May 1940. The target was the Cargo Fleet Ironworks and Dorman Long's Steelworks, both located in Grangetown on the eastern edge of Middlesbrough. At least seven high explosive bombs plus a variety of smaller ones were dropped across the two works, causing minimal damage to both factories. Eight workers were injured in the attack, becoming the first civilian casualties of the Second World War.

By the end of May 1940, Chamberlain had resigned, and Winston Churchill became Prime Minister. The British Army was on the back foot in France, and a total of 338,000 men were evacuated via Dunkirk. Britain now stood alone, poised and prepared for the inevitable invasion. Apprehensive of what was about to come, the entire population was stirred up by one of Churchill's famous speeches on 4th June 1940, which contained the all-important last line: 'We shall never surrender.'

232

The first full-time civil defence worker to be killed by enemy action was in West Hartlepool on the night of 19th/20th June. The first of 43 raids on the Hartlepool area and district caused considerable damage to houses and a school in West Hartlepool. Two people were killed, including ARP warden, John Punton. Despite this serious raid on the North-East, what was later viewed as the beginning of the German air campaign against Britain began on 21st/22nd June. Several enemy aircraft indiscriminately attacked Whitley Bay, South Shields and Tynemouth, where three policemen were killed in the bombing. This would set the tone for air attacks against the North-East and would continue until the middle of 1943.

The Luftwaffe's earlier reconnaissance flights over the Newcastle area would now pay dividends for the attacking bombers. Targets singled out for special attention in Tyneside included the Docks, Swan Hunter's, Newburn Steelworks, the oil tank complex at Jarrow and the Tyne bridges. So confident of their own ability, the Luftwaffe launched a major raid against Newcastle in broad daylight on 2nd July. One particular bomber approached from the west of the city, shooting down a barrage balloon on its bombing run, and then dropped its lethal cargo on the Spillers factory and the Hawthorn Leslie engineering works and narrowly missed the Tyne High Level Bridge, all of these being primary targets for the German raiders. Thirteen people were killed and over 120 were injured.

The Battle of Britain officially began on 10th July 1940, and naturally all focus was given to the defence of the south-eastern corner of the country. However, part of Britain's industrial strength stemmed from the North-East and the Luftwaffe continued to attack targets relatively unchallenged by defensive fighters.

Newcastle was attacked again on 28th/29th July, when a line of 25 HE bombs was dropped across the city; unbelievably, no air raid warning was sounded. Many civilians showed bravery of the highest order, especially during the bombing raids. One of the first women to be killed by enemy action was Mary Mackay, tragically losing her life while trying to warn others when several bombs fell on the Heaton Secondary Girls' School. Nearly all of the bombs fell on residential areas but, in spite of the lack of warning, only three people were killed and another three injured.

The testimony to the effectiveness of the Anderson shelter was shown when a single HE bomb was dropped into the garden of a South Shields home on 9th August. The stray bomb landed no less than 10ft from the shelter and, incredibly, all four occupants survived uninjured.

School children go through an evacuation rehearsal in August 1939. (Newcastle Evening Chronicle and Journal Ltd)

The main attack was aimed at Laing's shipyard in Sunderland, but this was purely by accident, as the enemy bomber, a Heinkel He 111 was dumping its bombs trying to escape a group of RAF fighters. Four people were killed and 78 were injured, the Heinkel getting no further than Whitburn, where it was shot down into the sea.

15th August was to become a great day for the RAF and a general turning point in the Battle of Britain. It was also a lucky day for the civilian population of the North-East that so many RAF squadrons were resting from the main battle in the south of England. Many people on the ground had no idea how important the fight above was, only learning later how successful the defending fighters had been in repelling the biggest attack on the North-East since the start of the war. The majority of bombs that were dropped fell across County Durham, causing minimal damage. Thirty people still lost their lives, but if the combined force of 65 He 111s had been able to attack unhindered, the death toll would have been considerably higher. The village of Dawdon, south of Seaham, suffered more than most when it was blasted by nearly 30 HE bombs. Eight houses were demolished and many more were seriously damaged. Sadly, eleven people were killed and over forty injured.

The Luftwaffe never attempted a daylight raid again on this scale for the remainder of the war. This did not deter them from increasing the night raids on the area, each raid involving more and more aircraft and every attack becoming more accurate. Over 250 enemy aircraft bombed targets of opportunity throughout the night of 29th/30th August. Even

One of the Luftwaffe's best medium bombers was the Junkers Ju 88, which was a common sight over the North-East.

hospitals were attacked including Moor Park Hospital in North Shields. A single incendiary bomb (IB) crashed through the roof of the diphtheria ward and began to burn the hospital's wooden floor. Able Seaman Furse, who was recovering from diphtheria, was still in the ward keeping a fellow patient company who could not be moved. Furse managed to pick the burning bomb up in a bundle of bedclothes and throw it outside, where it burnt itself out. Furse's brave act saved the hospital, which was constructed of wood. Many more bombs fell in the grounds of the hospital, but the local Home Guard and staff quickly extinguished them.

It took only a single German bomber to reduce several streets to near rubble on the evening of 13th October 1940. Four HE bombs were dropped in the Marsh Road area of Middlesbrough, one of them destroying a cast iron communal shelter at the junction of Marsh Road and Farrer Street. Twenty-one people were killed and 15 houses were demolished, with 37 more demolished at a later date; over 100 were badly damaged and 300 more suffered from the effects. The narrow streets and back-to-back houses helped to contain the blast of the bombs, resulting in so much damage.

As if the civilian population had not enough to deal with, the Luftwaffe began using a new weapon during their raids on the North-East. First used against land targets in September 1940, the land mine or parachute mine was a devastating weapon which could cause structural damage on a grand scale. Effectively a modified sea mine, the land version came in two sizes: a 500kg version and the more commonly used 1,000kg, which measured 8ft 8in long. These large cylinders had a small parachute attached, which controlled the descent rate. Once on the ground, a clockwork fuse was activated, sometimes giving anyone unlucky enough to be in the vicinity no chance to take cover. A pair of mines was dropped on Tynemouth in the early hours of 24th October, one on the bowling green in the park and another near Kennersdene Farm. Both caused considerable damage, leaving craters measuring 35ft across and 15ft deep.

By the winter of 1940/41, most of the country's civilian population was involved in a variety of morale boosting activities, which included the collection of salvage and fund-raising campaigns. Much of the salvage was of no use, but the psychological effect on the individual donating the pot, pan or garden railing to be turned into a fighter or battleship was invaluable. While everybody was seen to be making a sacrifice, morale would remain high.

The 'Dig for Victory' campaign encouraged individuals and local

A typical 'Dig for Victory' poster encouraging everyone to grow their own food.

councils to turn any spare land into allotments; virtually every park in the region fell under the plough. At the beginning of the war, at least 100,000 farm workers left the land to join the armed forces. The introduction of the Women's Land Army helped correct this deficiency, and by 1944 over 80,000 women had volunteered.

The announcement of compulsory fire-watching training by Miss Ellen Wilkinson, Parliamentary Secretary to the Ministry of Home Security in Britain, on 20th January 1941, certainly helped reduce the damage caused by a heavy raid on the mining district of Northumberland. The raid, which took place on, 15th/16th February focussed on Blyth, Tynemouth, Newsham and Bedlington. Damage was extensive, and hundreds of IBs were dropped, but thanks to the vigilance of the volunteer fire-watchers, the majority of them were extinguished before a serious fire broke out. During this attack, a barrage balloon over South Shields managed to bring down an He 111; the bomber crashed into Bent's Park in the town. Unknown to the auxiliary firemen who attended the crash, the German bomber still had a large mine on board. The mine exploded 25 minutes later, killing three firemen and a policeman. Four of the bomber's crew died in the crash, a fifth, believed to be the pilot, managed to bail out, only to be electrocuted after he fell onto a live trolley bus cable.

The first of many heavy raids throughout 1941 began on 9th/10th April. Over 100 enemy aircraft bombed dockyards and industrial targets in the Newcastle, Tynemouth and South Shields areas. More than 150 tonnes of HE bombs and thousands of IBs were dropped, causing many casualties and considerable damage. It was another night of selfless bravery, and many men where decorated for their efforts. In the Hendon area of Sunderland, several IBs fell on a railway line, setting light to a pile of wooden pit props. Parked on the line at the time were 300 railway wagons filled with live ammunition. Railway workers nearby managed to move 274 of them, saving the area from certain destruction. Robert Hume and John Steele were presented with the second highest civilian gallantry award, the George Medal. Four others received the British Empire Medal (BEM).

Despite German radio reports boasting of a 'heavy attack on Sunderland', it was Heaton, a suburb of Newcastle, which suffered the most on the night of 25th/26th April. Forty seven people were killed in Heaton, sadly 35 of them in a single location in Guildford Place. The power of a single parachute mine caused total devastation, with many of the bodies taking up to five days to be recovered, but for Tyneside the worst was to come.

Tragedy struck North Shields on the 3rd/4th May 1941 when the Wilkinson's Lemonade factory was struck by single bomb; 105 civilians in the air raid shelter below the factory were killed.

The local inhabitants were by now used to the routine of taking to the air-raid shelter as soon as the warning sirens sounded and the community spirit was strong. One particular communal air-raid shelter in North Shields was very popular with locals, as it was seen to be not only secure but also warm and comfortable. The shelter was located in the basement of the Wilkinson's Lemonade factory at the corner of King Street and George Street. It was never overcrowded, purely because of one reservation shared by many in the area. The factory contained a lot of very heavy equipment, and, despite the shelter being reinforced, the risk of the machinery crashing through the floor if hit by a bomb was high. On the night of 3rd/4th May 1941, this is exactly what happened when a single German bomb scored a direct hit onto the factory. Debris, machinery and bottling equipment crashed through the factory floor into the shelter below, crushing and trapping many of the occupants. Of the 192 people who took shelter that evening, 105 were killed, making this Tyneside's worst incident of the entire war.

Living near to an active airfield held the risk not only of having your home hit by an aircraft but also that it could be bombed during an enemy air raid. One particular family decided it would be safer to move away from the airfield at Thornaby in North Yorkshire to the comparative safety of Stockton-on-Tees, not far from the ICI works at Billingham. During a raid on the works on the night of 11th/12th May, several wayward bombs fell into St Peter's Road in Stockton. The family who had moved only the week before were killed in the raid.

It seems surprising that anyone would knowingly move closer to the Billingham plant; it was certainly a higher priority target than Thornaby, and it was expected that the Luftwaffe would bomb the plant as soon as the war began. It was one of the most important chemical producers in the country, providing the raw materials for the production of explosives, hydrogen gas and synthetic spirits. As the war progressed, the company workshops were employed in the production of aircraft engine parts and later a variety of armaments including anti-tank weapons and mortars. The plant was bombed on at least 11 different raids and, despite over 100 HE bombs falling on or around the building, damage was never serious and at no point did the enemy manage to disrupt production.

In recognition of the importance of the work carried out in the shipyards and armament factories, King George VI and Queen Elizabeth visited both Tyneside and Teesside. The Royal party's tour included Smith's Dock in North Shields on 18th June 1941, accompanied by the Mayor of Tynemouth, Councillor Anderson. The following day the King and Queen visited the Billingham plant and inspected bomb damage around the Middlesbrough area. This was followed by an inspection of the local Civil Defence workers in Albert Park, an event witnessed by thousands of Middlesbrough residents who turned out to see the Royal couple.

A raid that lasted one hour and involved only 25 enemy bombers caused considerable damage to Newcastle on the night of 1st/2nd September 1941. Over 100 houses were demolished, killing 49 people and making approximately 1,000 homeless. Almost all RAF airfields in the area were attacked but only Ouston and Brunton, the latter still under construction, were actually hit. The remainder were also bombed; however, it was the surrounding villages that received the worst damage. North Hylton, near Usworth, was hit, also Milfield village, and both Ovington and Stamfordham suffered more damage than the intended target of Ouston.

North Shields took the brunt of a particularly heavy raid on the night of 30th September/1st October. The borough of Tynemouth had at least 38 HEs dropped on it, causing 61 deaths and widespread damage. The following night was the turn of South Shields, which was attacked by 50 bombers; once again the damage and destruction was high, although on this occasion the casualties were lower.

A lack of discipline during a blackout was blamed for the village of Alnmouth on the Northumberland coast being singled out by a German bomber on 8th/9th November 1941. From the beginning of the war it was quickly realized that the majority of bombing raids would take place at night; so it was essential that all lights were either extinguished or shrouded so as not to be visible from above. It was a criminal offence to allow light to escape from a building, and by the end of the Second World War nearly one million people had been prosecuted for breaching the blackout rules. Most people were fined, but one man was sentenced to one month's hard labour in February 1940. Two HE bombs fell upon Argyle Street in Alnmouth, demolishing three houses and leaving seven people dead. The bombing was blamed on a pair of buses parked at the terminus in Argyle Street; apparently their headlights were reflected on the water of the River Aln. However, the bus owner denied this, claiming that there was only one bus and that the blame should fall upon a group billeted in some military huts in the town who opened a door with the internal light still on. Whoever was to blame, this opportunistic attack would never have happened if the blackout rules had been observed.

Tyneside was bombed again on 29th/30th December 1941, making it the last raid of the year; the North-East would not be seriously attacked again for another four months. Attacks by lone raiders and small groups of aircraft continued unabated, and if well executed could cause as many casualties and damage as a larger raid. In what was later claimed by the enemy to be a raid on Sunderland, it only took four HE bombs to kill 28 people and leave over 50 injured on 15th/16th April 1942. The bombs actually fell in the Newport area of Middlesbrough, causing considerable damage which resulted in 39 houses becoming uninhabitable. Over 1,700 were damaged and 1,156 people were made homeless.

Two concentrated attacks on the ICI plant at Billingham were carried over two nights, the first on 6th/7th July. Seventeen fires were started around the plant; the worst one of all was when an oil tank received a direct hit. However, despite the death of a fireman, all the fires were quickly brought under control, with little or no effect on the output of the plant. The following night a German attack set the plant on fire again, and on this occasion output was reduced by the damage caused.

Targets in County Durham were beginning to receive more attention from the enemy; Middlesbrough, West Hartlepool and the Billingham plant were attacked again on 25th/26th July. However, it was the area around the ICI plant that was suffering more, and Middlesbrough in

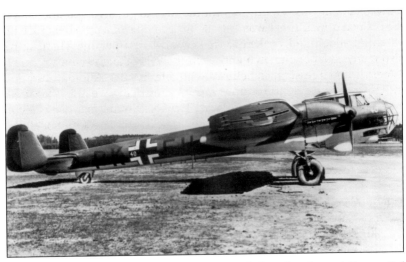

A single Dornier Do 217 clinically bombed Middlesbrough railway station on 3rd August 1942.

particular suffered one of its worst raids of the war so far. It was recorded that on this night more than 38 tons of bombs were dropped on the city, killing 16 people and destroying 68 houses and 76 business premises. Only two industrial targets suffered any significant damage, including the ICI plant. This was the last time the plant was singled out for an attack, and if the Luftwaffe had continued they would have definitely brought production to a grinding halt, as, despite morale boosting claims to the contrary, the continuous raids were affecting the plant's output.

A single Dornier Do 217 swooped low over Middlesbrough on 3rd August 1942, singling out the railway station for an attack. Four bombs were dropped; two of them struck the station, a third demolished Kirkup's warehouse in Station Street and the fourth destroyed several houses in Crown Street. The railway station's roof was ripped open by the blast and a Middlesbrough to Newcastle train waiting at the platform was seriously damaged. Eight people were killed and 58 others were injured, but, despite the serious nature of this bombing raid, the railway was re-opened within 24 hours.

There were several incidents throughout the war when our defences caused damage and even death to our own population. Due to the density of barrage balloons in the area, it was not uncommon for the odd one to break loose. The balloon, completely out of control, dragging its cables through streets and over houses, could cause a lot of damage, and it was not unusual for the RAF to get involved and shoot the balloon down. There was at least one example of a man being killed when a balloon had broken loose and exploded nearby. There were also many cases of our own anti-aircraft shells falling on the streets of Tyneside and Teesside, sometimes with fatal results. Another instance involved the recently introduced Z-gun, a terrifying weapon that fired a barrage of unguided 3-inch rockets. The object of the exercise was for the rockets to explode over a wide area up to 19,000ft, hopefully destroying a few enemy bombers in the process. No damage on the enemy was ever recorded, but on 6th/7th September 1942 several rockets caused damage to houses in East Bolden, Heworth, Jarrow and South Hylton! During a raid throughout the North-East on 11th/12th March 1943, our own anti-aircraft guns and rocket batteries caused more casualties to our population than the bombing itself!

Claims of success were often exaggerated on both sides throughout the war and one such example was on 11th/12th December 1942, when the German propaganda machine stated that 'waves of bombers' bombed Sunderland. The objects dropped over Sunderland that

The Queen visits the John Readhead & Sons shipyard in South Shields in April 1943. (IWM)

evening were flares, and a total of only ten bombers was involved. The raid spread from Seaham to West Hartlepool.

A large raid on Sunderland on 15th/16th May 1943 caused the most casualties and damage suffered in the town for the entire war. During the attack, that only lasted an hour, one particular parachute mine produced a crater 99ft across and 40ft deep. IBs rained down, causing many fires, especially in the dock area. Casualties included T W Greenwell & Company in the South Dock, British Ropes and the King's Theatre; the Avenue Paint Works was completely destroyed. Seaham, especially the harbour area, was also heavily bombed, the raid eventually claiming 75 lives and injuring over 100. During the raid a large quantity of propaganda leaflets was dropped with the message *'Here is the reason why the British Government says nothing about shipping losses.'* A list of over 400 ships allegedly sunk was supplied with the leaflet. Four of the ships on the list were actually in the Tyne at the time of the bombing raid!

The North-East had been suffering continuous bombing for nearly two years, and the wail of the air raid sirens was almost a daily occurrence. What was to be the last major air raid on the North-East came on the night of 23rd/24th May 1943. The worst of the bombing fell upon Sunderland and South Shields, with scattered bombing throughout the county. Damage was severe and casualties were high. Many were killed in three public air raid shelters that were hit in North Bridge Street, Monkwearmouth and Hendon, all in the Sunderland area. In South Shields alone, 28 people were killed as parachute mines, HEs and IBs demolished over 40 buildings. The raid claimed 83 people killed and over 200 injured, marking the end of the Luftwaffe's bombing campaign against the north-east of England.

A period of relative normality fell upon the North-East with the threat of aerial bombing now gone and morale of the civilian population as high as it was at the beginning of the war. All focus was now on the invasion of Europe and the production of warships, tanks and armaments in the region's factories. Contracts were now being commissioned for equipment specifically for the invasion. Swan Hunter received orders for 18 LCTs (Landing Craft Tank) and William Gray's on Teesside produced two of the many huge concrete sections that went on to form the Mulberry Harbour off the Normandy coast.

When the invasion of Europe took place on 6th June 1944, the nation could now taste victory, the national press and General Eisenhower claiming that the war would be over by Christmas. Life on the Home Front did become slightly easier when in September 1944 the blackout

London evacuees at Newcastle station in July 1944. (Newcastle Evening Chronicle and Journal Ltd)

restrictions began to ease, with the exception of several areas along the coast. The same month saw fire-watching duties being reduced as well as the reduction of the Home Guard. A final parade of the region's Home Guard was held on 3rd December 1944 in both Newcastle and Middlesbrough.

The country had been experiencing a new German weapon since the first one fell on British soil in June 1944. The V-1, more commonly known as the doodlebug, was launched from sites in northern France. However, after the invasion a new method was developed to launch the lethal pilotless flying bombs. A special unit of converted Heinkel He 111s were modified to carry a single V-1 underneath and launch it off the English coast. The rocket's range of approximately 150 miles had meant that it was the south of England that suffered the most V-1 attacks, but with this new method of delivery more northerly targets could be attacked. Luckily, the area suffered only one such attack, in the early hours of 24th December 1944. The V-1 came down on Tudhoe cricket field, destroying the pavilion, injuring eleven people and causing damage to hundreds of houses in the vicinity.

Many civilians in the North-East had been killed as result of enemy action and the area as a whole had contributed greatly to the war effort. The war in Europe finally came to an end on 8th May 1945. The day was called Victory-in-Europe (VE) Day and was treated as a holiday. The war in the Far East continued for many more weeks, and the war did not officially end until Japan surrendered on 14th August 1945. Numerous events were organized throughout the area, including a victory parade in Newcastle that was attended by more than 100,000 people.

APPENDIX

A breakdown of all RAF, FAA and USAAF Units and their main aircraft types that were stationed at north-eastern airfields during the Second World War.

Acklington

7 ATS Overstrands and Seals. **607 Sqn** Gladiator I. **Fighter Flight** Gladiator I. **111 Sqn** Hurricane I. **152 Sqn** Gladiator I, Spitfire I. **43 Sqn** Spitfire I. **72 Sqn** Spitfire I. **79 Sqn** Hurricane I. **32 Sqn** Hurricane I. **610 Sqn** Spitfire I. **258 Sqn** Hurricane I. **315 Sqn** Hurricane I. **317 Sqn** Hurricane I. **141 Sqn** Defiant I, Beaufighter IF. **406 Sqn** Blenheim IF and IVF, Beaufighter IIF. **74 Sqn** Spitfire Vb. **13 Gp TTF** became **1490 TT Flt** Lysander II and III, Henley TT, Master III. **1460 Flt** Havoc I and II, Boston II, III. **167 Sqn** Spitfire VB. **219 Sqn** Beaufighter IF. **1 Sqn** Typhoon Ib. **410 Sqn** Defiant I, Mosquito II, Beaufighter IIF. **409 Sqn** Beaufighter VIF. **416th NF Sqn** Beaufighter VI. **198 Sqn** Typhoon Ib. **6 AA Practice Camp-Target Flight** became **1630 (AA Co-Operation) Flight** Lysander II and III, Martinet I. **350 Sqn** Spitfire Vc. **349 Sqn** Spitfire VA. **316 Sqn** Spitfire IX. **24 (Base). 147 Airfield HQ. 130 Sqn** Spitfire Vb. **4 ADF** Dominie I, Oxford I, Mustang I, Defiant I. **25 Sqn** Mosquito VI, Wellington III. **322 Sqn** Spitfire Vc. **409 Sqn** Mosquito XIII. **56 Sqn** Typhoon Ib. **266 Sqn** Typhoon Ib. **164 Sqn** Typhoon Ib. **222 Sqn** Spitfire LF IXb. **322 Sqn** Spitfire Vc. **3 TEU** Typhoon Ib. **59 OTU** Typhoon Ib, Master II, Martinet I. **19 Sqn** Mustang IV.

Boulmer

57 OTU Spitfire I, II, V and IX, Master I, II and III. **59 OTU** Hurricane I, IIb and X, Master I and III, Typhoon Ia and Ib. **9 Group Battle School**.

Brunton

59 OTU Hurricane I, IIb and X, Master I and III, Typhoon Ia and Ib. **559 Sqn** Hurricane I and II. **FLS** (see Milfield). **56 OTU** Typhoon Ib, Tempest V, Master II, Martinet.

Eshott

57 OTU. Spitfire I, IIa, IIb, V, Vb and Vc, Master I and III, Battle TT, Lysander III. **288 Sqn** Oxford I and II, Vengeance II, Spitfire IX and XVI. **289 Sqn** Spitfire XVI, Vengeance II. **291 Sqn** Martinet I, Hurricane IIc, Vengeance II. **261 MU**.

Middleton St George

78 Sqn Whitley V, Halifax II. **76 Sqn** Halifax I and II. **1516 BAT Flight** Oxford I. **76 CF** Halifax I and II. **78 CF** Halifax I and II. **420 Sqn** Wellington III. **419 Sqn** Halifax II, Lancaster X. **6 AACF** Lysander II and III, Master I. **1535 BAT Flight (RCAF)** Oxford I. **428 Sqn** Wellington III and X, Halifax II and V, Lancaster X. **64 (RCAF) Base**. **13 OTU** Mosquito II, TIII, IV and VI.

Milfield

59 OTU Hurricane I, IIb and X, Master I and III, Typhoon Ia and Ib. **No. 1 Specialized Low Attack Instructors' School** Hurricane IIc, IId and IV, Typhoon Ib, Master III. **184 Sqn** Hurricane IId and IV. **Fighter Leader School** Typhoon Ib, Hurricane I and IV, Spitfire I, II, Vb and Vc, Master II and III. **Day Fighter Development Wing** Spitfire, Typhoon, Martinet, Proctor. **56 OTU** Typhoon Ib, Tempest V, Spitfire IX. **183 Sqn** Typhoon Ib.

Morpeth

4 AGS Botha I, Lysander TT.I, Master II, Martinet TT.I, Anson I. **652 Sqn** Auster III **1614 AACF** Henley, Martinet I. **72 Sqn** Spitfire VB, VC and IX. **80 (French) OTU** Spitfire IX, Master II. **261 MU**.

Ouston

13 Gp CF Magister I, Mentor I, Vega Gull, Gladiator I **3 RSS** Blenheim IV, Hornet Moth. **55 OTU** Hurricane I, IIa, IIb and X. **72 Wg Calibration Flt** Hornet Moth, Blenheim IV. **317 Sqn** Hurricane I. **7 AACF** Lysander II, Oxford I. **122 Sqn** Spitfire I. **131 Sqn** Spitfire I. **13 Gp AACF** Blenheim IV, Lysander II. **232 Sqn** Hurricane I and IIB. **410 Sqn** Defiant I. **1423 Flight** Hurricane I. **226 Sqn** Boston III. **81 Sqn** Spitfire VA and VB. **281 Sqn** Defiant I, Walrus I and II. **242 Sqn** Spitfire

Vb and Vc. **243 Sqn** Spitfire Vb. **613 Sqn** Mustang I. **1490 Flight** Lysander II, III and IIIa, Master II, Martinet TT.I., Henley TT.I. **72 Sqn** Spitfire Vb and Vc. **289 Sqn** Defiant I and III. **198 Sqn** Typhoon Ia and Ib. **804 Sqn** Sea Hurricane IIc. **657 Sqn** Auster IV. **62 OTU** Anson I, Wellington XVII and XVIII, Hurricane IIc and V. **350 Sqn** Spitfire Vb. **Durham UAS** Tiger Moth. **770 Sqn** Hurricane IIc.

Usworth

607 Sqn Wapiti IIA, Demon, Gladiator I. **103 Sqn** Hind. **1 Gp Practice Flight** Tutor I. **'G' Flight 1 AACF** Henley I. **607 Sqn** Hurricane IIa and IIb. **3 RSS** Hornet Moth. **3 Radio MU** Hornet Moth. **43 Sqn** Hurricane I. **55 OTU** Hurricane I, Ia and IIb, Master I, II and III, Martinet TT I and Dominie I. **Glider Exercise Unit** Hector, Hotspur. **3 Radio School 'A' Flight**. **62 OTU** Anson I. **416th NF Sqn** Beaufighter VI. **31 GS** Cadet, Falcon III. **14 MU**.

West Hartlepool (Greatham)

32 E&RFTS Tiger Moth II, Anson I, Hind. **41 Sqn** Spitfire I. **54 Sqn** Spitfire I. **6 OTU** Hudson I. **'N' Flight No.1 AACU** (became **1613 Flight**) Henley I, Tiger Moth II. **2782 Sqn RAF Regiment**. **4054 AA Flt RAF Regiment**. **332 Sqn** Spitfire Vb. **403 (Wolf) Sqn** Spitfire Vb. **26 GS** Cadet I, II and TX.3, King Kite, Falcon II.

Woolsington

43 E&RFTS Hind, Tiger Moth II, Magister I, Audax. **13 Gp CF** Magister I, Mentor I, Vega Gull, Gladiator I, Whitney Straight, Proctor I, Hornet Moth. **72 Sqn** Spitfire I. **3 Radio MU** Hornet Moth. **83 MU Durham UAS** Tiger Moth II. **55 OTU** Hurricane I, IIa and IIb. **33 Wing. 281 Sqn** Anson I, Walrus I and II. **27 GS** Cadet I, II and TX.3, Sedburgh TX.1. **278 Sqn** Anson I. **62 OTU** Anson I. **62 MU**.

Bibliography

Avro Lancaster, Holmes, Airlife
Bomber Squadrons of the RAF, Moyes, MacDonald
Britain's Military Airfields 1939-45, Smith, PSL
Fields of Deception, Dobinson, English Heritage
Fighter Command Losses 1939-41, Franks, Midland
Fighter Squadrons of the RAF, Rawlings, MacDonald
Losses of the US 8th & 9th Air Forces, Bishop & Hey, Bishop
Luftwaffe Night Fighter Combat Claims, Foreman, Matthews &,
    Parry, Red Kite
Luftwaffe Losses over Northumberland & Durham, Norman, Pen & Sword
Luftwaffe over the North, Norman, Pen & Sword
Northumberland Aviation Diary, Walton, Norav
PRO Air 16/332 (Acklington)
PRO Air 16/800 (FLS, Milfield)
PRO Air 28/17 (Acklington)
PRO Air 28/624 (Ouston)
PRO Air 28/824 to 837 (Thornaby)
PRO Air 28/870 (Usworth)
PRO Air 28/871 (Usworth)
PRO Air 29/590 (4 AGS, Morpeth)
PRO Air 29/683 (56 & 57 OTU)
PRO Air 29/684 (59 OTU)
PRO Air 29/685 (62 OTU Usworth & Ouston)
PRO Air 29/708 (FLS, Milfield)
PRO Air 29/874 (Middleton St George)
PRO Air 29/876 (Middleton St George)
PRO Air 29/880 (Acklington & West Hartlepool)
PRO Air 29/883 (West Hartlepool)
PRO Air 29/926 (Morpeth)
PRO Air 29/1025 (Woolsington)
PRO Avia 2/1264 (West Hartlepool)
PRO Avia 2/1350 (West Hartlepool)
PRO Avia 2/1674 (West Hartlepool)
PRO Avia 2/2709 (West Hartlepool)
PRO Avia
RAF Flying Training & Support Units, Sturtivant, Hamlin & Halley, Air Britain
RAF Squadrons, Wg Cdr C G Jefford, Airlife
Royal Air Force, Thetford, Putnam
The Bomber Command Handbook, Falconer, Sutton
The Bomber Command War Diaries, Middlebrook & Everett, Midland
The British Bomber since 1914, Mason, Putnam
The Squadrons of the FAA, Sturtivant, Air Britain
The Squadrons of the RAF, Halley, Air Britain
Wartime Teesside, Norman, Norman
World Aircraft WW2 Part 1, Sampson Low